The Evolving God

The Evolving God

Charles Darwin on the Naturalness of Religion

J. David Pleins

B L O O M S B U R Y

NEW YORK • LONDON • NEW DELHI • SYDNEY

Bloomsbury Academic

An imprint of Bloomsbury Publishing Inc

1385 Broadway	50 Bedford Square
New York	London
NY 10018	WC1B 3DP
USA	UK

www.bloomsbury.com

Bloomsbury is a registered trade mark of Bloomsbury Publishing Plc

First published 2013
Reprinted 2014

© J. David Pleins, 2013

Library of Congress Cataloging-in-Publication Data
Pleins, J. David.
The evolving God: Charles Darwin on the naturalness of religion/J. David Pleins.
pages cm
Includes bibliographical references and index.
ISBN 978-1-6235-6652-4 (alk. paper) – ISBN 978-1-6235-6247-2 (pbk.: alk. paper)
1. Religion–Philosophy. 2. Darwin, Charles, 1809–1882–Religion. 3. Darwin, Charles, 1809–1882. 4. Religion and science. I. Title.
BL51.P559 2013
200.92–dc23
2012049682

ISBN: HB: 978-1-6235-6652-4
PB: 978-1-6235-6247-2
ePDF: 978-1-6235-6867-2
ePUB: 978-1-6235-6840-5

Typeset by Deanta Global Publishing Services, Chennai, India
Printed and bound in the United States of America

For Teresa

Contents

Permissions   viii

Preface: Charles Darwin and the Evolution of Religion   x

Acknowledgments   xii

1   Unsettling Encounters: First Steps Toward an Evolutionary
View of Religion   1

2   A Disposition to Doubt: Darwin as Skeptical Seeker   31

3   Did Religion Evolve?: The Search for a Theory   45

4   The Golden Rule: An Evolutionary Vision of Religion and
Morality   63

5   A Certain Sympathy: Darwin and the Creed of Science   83

Conclusion: Reflecting on Darwin Today   107

Notes   115

Bibliography   149

Index   163

Permissions

Preface: Charles Darwin and the Evolution of Religion

The story of Charles Darwin's religious doubts is generally well known. What is less well known is that Darwin developed his own ideas about the evolution of religion. This book challenges the standard view that Darwin was a religiously "tormented evolutionist" (to use Desmond and Moore's colorful phrase), as if the most important thing that can be said about Darwin on religion is that he "lost his faith." I argue instead that Darwin is best understood as a seeker on a lifelong quest to explain religion's rise and function.[1] The purpose of this book, then, is to explore Darwin's discovery that religion has a natural history. Religion, like the plant and animal world, evolves. We shall trace Darwin's journey in five steps as we unpack five key themes in this quest. We begin with his global voyage, where his encounter with human religious and cultural diversity transformed his understanding of religion. Next, we will watch as Darwin's doubts about traditional biblical religion take root, affecting his career choice and marriage to Emma Wedgwood. Following on the heels of these doubts, we join Darwin as he pens his secret notebooks in search of a materialist theory of religion. We then explore how Darwin applied his discovery to the realm of ethics by formulating an evolutionary view of the "Golden Rule" in his *Descent of Man*. Finally, we consider Darwin's later reflections on the religion question, as he wrestled with whether his views led to atheism, agnosticism, or a new kind of theism. Though he grew skeptical of traditional Christian dogma, Darwin made eye-opening discoveries concerning the role and function of religion as a natural evolutionary phenomenon. The road to a modern view of religion and theology lies along this revolutionary path tread by Darwin. Our aim in this book is to better understand Darwin's more positive contribution to the study of religion. In the process, we shall gain a better appreciation for Darwin as a profound observer of religious ideas, values, and practices.

Darwin's *Beagle* voyage suggests an apt metaphor for the storm-tossed intellectual journey embarked upon by Darwin as he struggled to come to grips with the natural history of religion. Forsaking the comforts of a promising parson's life in England, Darwin braved the expanding intellectual horizon of his age to establish unparalleled insights into the very nature of religion in this evolving universe. All who travel alongside Darwin will struggle as he did with the mystery of the origin and development of life, the design of the universe, the meaning of what it is to be human, the nature of suffering, the consolations of happiness, and the role of religion in the scheme of things. At the end of their voyage, fellow travelers may not see eye to eye with Darwin's evolutionary view of religion, but all who embark on this journey are forever changed by their encounter with this remarkably humble individual, encyclopedic mind, gifted visionary, and pioneer on the uncharted seas of human knowledge. I hope the reader will be as startled and intrigued by the Darwin they find in these pages as I have been in tangling with this would-be cleric who became an ardent advocate of a new way of seeing human religiosity. It is true that Darwin developed "a growing hostility" toward traditional religion—he once wondered if he might be tarred a "Devil's chaplain"—but whether we are theist or not, his deep struggles with the impenetrable processes of life and his insightful grasp of the essential fact that religion evolves can instruct as to how to think more profoundly about the relation between science and religion today.

Perhaps even the harshest critic of Darwin will in the end have to agree that this marvelous intellect deserves to lie at rest in that great citadel of Anglican belief, Westminster Abbey, near another giant in the quest for truth, Sir Isaac Newton. The Darwin we meet in these pages harbors an insatiable curiosity about the great questions—a curiosity that remained with him to the end of his days. The question of how humans became religious stood at the heart of Darwin's intellectual quest. While the development of Darwin's theory of biological evolution is certainly central, his discovery that religion has evolved is terribly important to grasp, whether we are theists, agnostics, seekers, or atheists. In the course of this book, we will not only gain a more nuanced view of Darwin as a religious thinker but will come to understand better what it means to be human. Our encounter with evolution's architect will enable us to see why it is quite natural for humans to be religious.

Acknowledgments

I wish to express my thanks to Santa Clara University for research and travel grant support in the writing of this book. In particular, thanks to Diane Jonte-Pace and Bill Sundstrom for those timely funding extensions. Thanks also to David DeCosse and the Markkula Center for Applied Ethics for their generous Hackworth Grant which facilitated work on the moral aspects of Darwin's thought. Thanks to our generous donor Al Lane, whose gift has helped open up for me the poetry writing of Darwin's colleague George John Romanes. I want to acknowledge in gratitude those who discussed with me various aspects of this project and braved earlier unwieldy drafts by offering much-appreciated encouragement and helpful criticisms, especially Tom Beaudoin, Glenn Branch, Andrea Burrows, Doug Burton-Christie, Paul Crowley, Al Gelpi, Barbara Gelpi, Ron Hansen, David Pinault, Oliver Putz, Jason Smick, Zach Sprague, and Keith Warner. Thanks also to the many anonymous reviewers of previous drafts of this book who urged me to cut to the chase and focus the argument on Darwin's unique contribution while saving me from a number of errors. Of course, the mistakes that remain are due to my own stubbornness. With regard to the research process, I am particularly thankful to my research assistant Chandra Campbell who first crossed these horizons with me and helped me to appreciate Darwin's humility. Likewise, to Jennifer Grisaitis, Laura Skinner, and Heather Lynch for their assistance during the middle stages of this project. For the final stage, I am indebted to Adam Reiss, a research assistant of uncommon ability and determination. Thanks, as always, to the indefatigable Cynthia Bradley of Orradre Library for tracking down those elusive sources.

This book would not be possible without the permission to quote from archival materials and correspondence held in private collections. I would like to acknowledge here the generous spirit which so many have displayed to pave the way for the final publication of this volume. I owe a deep debt of gratitude to Adam J. Perkins, Curator of Scientific Manuscripts, Cambridge University Library, for assisting me in securing permission to quote materials from the Darwin Archive. By extension this gratitude goes out to the Darwin family and heirs. Words of gratitude also go to Marc P. Anderson for granting permission to use of the transcriptions of Darwin's correspondence as published by Cambridge University Press. Thanks as well to David Kohn of the American Museum of Natural History for his gracious permission to quote from the definitive publication of the Darwin

Notebooks. I am obliged to him as well for confirming an alternate reading in one passage of these notebooks. Each increment helps us to understand Darwin better. I wish to thank Annie Kemkaran-Smith, Curator of Down House, for permission to quote from Darwin's *Beagle Diary* which is owned by English Heritage (Down House). With regard to individual letters, I am grateful to Lisa DeCesare and Judith A. Warnement for facilitating the quotation of materials from the Gray Herbarium of Harvard University. Likewise, thanks to Jennifer Jacobsen for helping to navigate the Harvard University Archives permissions process and for successfully locating the Abbot letter. I am grateful to Virginia A. Hunt for permission to quote this material and to Betsey Farber, great-granddaughter of Francis Ellingwood Abbot, for the family's permission to use this letter. Thanks, too, to Daniel Lewis and Catherine Wehrey of the Huntington Library for facilitating the quotation of letters held there. I want to express my gratitude to Amelie Roper of Christ's College, Cambridge, for permission to quote from several letters that Darwin sent to W. D. Fox. Likewise, thanks to Kiri Ross-Jones for arranging quotation of the Henslow material held by the archives at the Royal Botanic Gardens, Kew. I, too, am grateful to Lord Lyell of Kinnordy House for his gracious permission to quote from the correspondence of Sir Charles Lyell. I wish to acknowledge here, too, the kind permission of the Sulivan family to quote from Darwin's letter to his deeply religious friend of longstanding, Sir Bartholomew James Sulivan, 2nd Lieutenant aboard H. M. S. *Beagle* and later Admiral in the Royal Navy. Likewise, I am grateful to Anne Barrett for permission to quote Huxley letters held in the College Archive of Imperial College London. I am also thankful to Lucy Nuttall of the National Library of Australia for facilitating quotation from Darwin's letter to Whitley. Finally, regarding the Romanes material, I am indebted to Mrs Joan Westmacott, granddaughter of George John Romanes, for her generous permission to publish from the poetry of Romanes. The same thanks go out to her niece Helena Greene. I add here a special thanks to Donald Forsdyke and Martin Sykes for facilitating this connection to the Romanes family. I remain indebted to Dr Alfred Lane of Stanford University School of Medicine and Lucile Packard Children's Hospital for his donation to Santa Clara University that made the acquisition of the Romanes manuscript a reality. I wish, too, to acknowledge the kind letter of Deborah Whiteman, Head of Santa Clara University's Archives and Special Collections, granting permission to quote from the Romanes *Typescript* of his "Memorial Poem."

Most hearty thanks to my editor Haaris Naqvi at Bloomsbury for his spirited support of this project. Thanks as well to Subitha Nair for shepherding this work through the production process.

Finally, I am grateful to my wife Teresa, whose keen eye has saved me from numerous infelicities and made this manuscript much more readable. But I am especially appreciative to her for the constant care and support she has given me as this project unfolded. I dedicate this book to her.

Unsettling Encounters: First Steps Toward an Evolutionary View of Religion

There was nothing terribly remarkable about Charles Darwin's religious upbringing or theological training that would lead us to think that he would one day radically alter our way of looking at religion. While his mother's dissenting Unitarianism and his grandfather Erasmus Darwin's religious skepticism lay in the background, his sisters stoked a kind of familial pietism to counteract any freethinking tendencies. During his medical studies at Edinburgh, his sister Caroline urged him to read the Bible "not only because you think it wrong not to read it, but with the wish of learning there what is necessary to feel & do to go to heaven after you die."[1] Charles reassured her about his Bible reading, though his tactful response to her counsel may not have entirely won her over: "I have tried to follow your advice about the Bible, what part of the Bible do you like best? I like the Gospels. Do you know which of them is generally reckoned the best?"[2] These are hardly the sentiments of a committed student of the Bible.

When Charles soured on a career in medicine, his father decided to make a Church minister out of his son to prevent his becoming "an idle sporting man."[3] The young Darwin "liked the thought of being a country clergyman," so he prepared for his time at Cambridge University by thumbing Pearson's *An Exposition of the Creed,* a work dating from 1659 which expounded creationist literalism.[4] He also read and carefully noted Sumner's *The Evidence of Christianity* (1824) with its certitudes about Jesus's messianic role.[5] He even delayed his fall entry at Cambridge to brush up on his knowledge of classical Greek with a private tutor.[6] With Homer and the Greek Testament firmly under his belt, Darwin thought he was ready to pursue training for a career in the Church. He says of this early phase, "as I did not then in the least doubt the strict & literal truth of every word in the Bible, I soon persuaded myself that our Creed must be fully accepted."[7]

To be sure, the sciences were gaining the upper hand in his mind as his time at Cambridge closed. His passion for beetle collecting was joined by an interest in geology sparked by hikes in Wales with his Cambridge mentor Adam Sedgwick.[8] Nonetheless, when he left England to travel around the world, the religious writings he had with him included a durable Authorized Bible, Milton's *Paradise Lost*, and Turner's *Sacred History of the World*. He also took along some notions about Natural Theology derived from the Rev William Paley—the theological view that evidences for God's creative power and character can be found in nature.[9] During his voyage, he firmly intended to read the Greek New Testament on Sundays and he once invoked the Bible as a proof text in a moral argument against his fellow officers who responded with hearty laughter despite their own orthodox beliefs.[10] He also carefully parsed the Book of Matthew using his German New Testament, if only to improve his language skills.[11]

While we would be wrong to depict Darwin as a rabid fundamentalist, his initial forays into religion and theology were conservative and cautious. Needless to say, Darwin's theological formation and sisters' influences left him thoroughly unprepared to make sense of the religious diversity he would encounter on his voyage. His experiences with Catholicism, primitive tribes, and the English missions would prompt new ways to think about religion. Indeed, one of the long unappreciated aspects of Darwin's view of religion is how soon he came to believe that religion is a material phenomenon with an evolutionary history. In this chapter, we explore the unsettling cultural entanglements that put Darwin on the path toward an evolutionary understanding of religion.

A sort of Christian

When Darwin told some "very pretty señoritas" in Chile that he had visited one of their churches "out of mere curiosity," they were quite "horrified."[12] Darwin had made his way south of Santiago to a little ranch house. He had managed to cross the rough waters of the Maypu river, stumbling down roads "made of bundles of sticks placed close together . . . full of holes" and braving bridges that "oscillated rather fearfully despite the weight of a man leading his horse."[13] Having survived the dangerous journey, he spent the night at a local farm house only to find he had entered the equally treacherous territory of religious belief. The señoritas chided Darwin, "Why do you not become a Christian—for our religion is certain?"[14] Darwin responded as best he could. "I assured them," he says, "I was a sort of Christian."[15] By which he meant that he was one type of Christian. But these women were convinced that Darwin could not possibly be worshipping the same God because Anglican clergy married, unlike Catholic priests.[16] This encounter is just one of many during his voyage when Darwin was forced to reflect on religion as belief and practice. Such a vignette is one in a series of well-known and oft-quoted moments in which Darwin appears to be acknowledging his religious indifference. Indeed, much ink has been spilled assessing Darwin's so-called "loss of faith." At times, the focus is on identifying the precise turning point when Darwin's faith gave way, whether due to the influence of evolutionary skeptics at Edinburgh, qualms about the Bible during his voyage, the death of his daughter Annie, or the negative reaction to the publication of the *Origin of Species*.[17] When, so the question goes, did Darwin lose his faith? As if to amalgamate all these moments, the comprehensive biography by Desmond and Moore, *Darwin: The Life of a Tormented Evolutionist*, presents Darwin's entire life as an unfortunate series of faith fracturing events.[18] More recently, Spencer's *God and Darwin* argues that this "loss of faith" paradigm is key to unlocking Darwin's life trajectory. As useful as this "loss of faith" construct may be, the very image serves to eclipse what may be the more profound insight about Darwin's life, namely that in his mind there was a growing awareness that evolution was not just about physical forms but had religious and moral trajectories. Darwin was stumbling toward the view that religion also moved through stages. His so-called "loss of faith" ran in tandem with the exciting realization that religion had evolved. What many have failed to realize is that Darwin's voyage aboard H. M. S. *Beagle* ignited this intellectual search into religion's origin and development.

After strong winds posed annoying delays, H. M. S. *Beagle*, captained by the 26-year-old Robert FitzRoy, set sail on 27 December 1831. Crossing the Atlantic, they arrived at Bahia (San Salvador) on 28 February 1832. The spring and early summer of 1832 were spent in and around Rio de Janeiro, while the rest of the year took them to Montevideo. An excursion far south in the land of the "savages" of Tierra del Fuego in mid-December of 1832 led to a year and a half mapping survey up and down the Brazilian and Argentinean coasts, including a second trip to Tierra del Fuego in February-March of 1834. During this period, there were also side jaunts to Santa Cruz, Patagonia, and the Falkland Islands. As the ship made its coastal surveys or dropped anchor in various ports, Darwin spent much of his time exploring the landscape, collecting specimens, and observing the region's cultures. Leaving the eastern shores of South America behind, the crew headed through the Straits of Magellan in May, 1834 to Valparaiso in Chile. During the first half of 1835, the *Beagle* explored the Chiloe and Chonos archipelagos. Darwin ventured into the mountainous interior of Chile—the Cordillera—and went on into Peru. His historic trip to the Galápagos Islands took place between 15 September and 20 October 1835, where tortoises and finches caught his eye. The fall was rounded out with travels to Tahiti and New Zealand with their very different tribal inhabitants. It would be nearly a year before their return to England, passing through Sydney, the Keeling Islands, Tasmania,

Mauritius, the Cape of Good Hope, and back to Bahia for one last glimpse of South America. His journey ended on 2 October 1836 with their layover at the docks of Falmouth in southwestern England. Darwin's geological and theological studies hardly prepared him for the world he encountered. Yet it was not only rocks and fossils that captured his attention, religion also became a focus of his observations.

While many authors look to Darwin's voyage diary and subsequent *Journal of Researches* (issued in two editions in 1839 and 1845) to document his naturalist ventures, very little has been done to plumb these writings to explore Darwin's many insights regarding the possibility that religion evolves. The treatment of this theme in the scholarly literature is quite uneven. To take just a few representative examples, William E. Phipps' *Darwin's Religious Odyssey* touches on some of the theological aspects of Darwin's voyage in a chapter on "The Christian Voyager" without tying the threads together as the core of an evolutionary view of religion. Frank Burch Brown's *The Evolution of Darwin's Religious Views*, an admittedly brief monograph, overlooks almost entirely the impact of the voyage on the evolution of Darwin's religious views. A standard biography such as Browne's *Voyaging* draws on Darwin's *Diary* and *Journal of Researches* for documentation of his travels but does not spell out the development of Darwin's religious thinking found in these works, although she tantalizingly notes in passing, "His study of the religious customs of wild tribes . . . and his experience of travelling from country to country . . . played a much larger part in generating a feeling of theological relativity."[19] For the most part, however, Browne focuses on FitzRoy's doubts about the Bible and Darwin's misgivings about a future clerical career.[20] Again, Desmond and Moore's magisterial *Darwin: The Life of a Tormented Evolutionist*, despite the obvious interest in Darwin's religious struggles, does not consider this aspect of Darwin's publication on the voyage.[21] What is consistently overlooked is that everywhere during his voyage Darwin encounters clues about religion as a human phenomenon and religion's probable evolution. He makes it a point to document these facts. As he began to think in cultural and even evolutionary terms about religion, Darwin was freed to critique Christian belief, reexamining major theological beliefs and practices. His *Journal of Researches* (also known as the *Voyage of the Beagle*) and the related trip *Diary* can, however, be read with profit as charting the essential moments that sparked Darwin's realization that religion evolves and that monotheism is best understood as a high-point in the human religious venture.[22] Darwin went so far as to comment on key theological problems, including the problem of evil and the question of "just war." The construct of a "loss of faith," I argue, needs to be replaced with the view that Darwin's religious development goes from insight to insight regarding religion's function and evolutionary character. Let us turn now to consider six key themes that arise in his *Journal of Researches*: primitive religion; Catholicism and heresy; natural disasters and the problem of evil; just war theory; Christian missions; and the sublime.

Hideous yells: Darwin on "primitive" religion

Certainly one of the most bizarre aspects of the *Beagle*'s mission was Capt. Robert FitzRoy's compulsion to return several Fuegians who had been seized on his previous voyage (1826 to 1830). Three hostages were snatched in retaliation for the theft of one of the expedition's boats.[23] The hostages were joined by another child that FitzRoy had purchased in exchange for a pearl button. The four were given curious names. They were the "violently passionate" York Minster (Elleparu), age 30, who was named after a prominent rock outcropping in Tierra del Fuego; the "nice, modest, reserved" young girl Fuegia Basket (Yokcushlu); and the "merry" teenage Jemmy Button (Orundellico), who, though he was "vain" about his clothing, was the "universal favorite" of the crew.[24] The fourth—Boat Memory—died of small pox while in England. During their stay in England, the Fuegians were settled for a time at the boarding school of the Rev William Wilson at Walthamstow, northeast of London, where they were instructed in "English, and the plainer truths of Christianity, as the first object."[25] A London phrenologist confirmed for FitzRoy that at least two of the Fuegian captives—Fuegia Basket and Jemmy Button—had shown "strong feelings for a Supreme Being."[26] Having been civilized and Christianized, FitzRoy aimed to reinstall his captives in Tierra del Fuego in order to enlighten the natives and curtail their thievery. Along with the hostages, FitzRoy was bringing the missionary Richard Matthews.

The return of these hostages allowed Darwin to confront human culture and religiosity in its rawest terms. "I do not think any spectacle can be more interesting, than the first sight of Man in his primitive wildness," Darwin wrote his mentor Henslow.[27] That encounter on 18 December 1832, brought Darwin in contact with figures he dubbed "Devils on the Stage," a nightmare straight out of Carl Maria von Weber's *Der Freischütz*.[28] Details of the tribe's chief caught Darwin's attention: "The old man had a white feather cap; from under which, black long hair hung round his face.—The skin is dirty copper colour. Reaching from ear to ear & including the upper lip, there was a broad red coloured band of paint.—& parallel & above this, there was a white one; so that the eyebrows & eyelids were even thus coloured; the only garment was a large guanaco skin, with the hair outside." Of his experiences that day, he added, "I believe if the world was searched, no lower grade of man could be found." The "wild cry" of the savage Fuegian stirred Darwin's imagination, teaching him much concerning humanity's roots.[29] Of this shrill cry he told his old Shrewsbury schoolmate and Cambridge hiking companion Charles Whitley, "There is in their countenances, an expression, which I believe to those who have not seen it, must be inconcevably wild."[30] Depicting the stark scene he wrote, "Standing on a rock he uttered tones & made gesticulations than which, the crys of domestic animals are far more intelligible." Relating this exotic encounter to his sister Caroline, he observed that "an untamed savage is I really think one of the most extraordinary spectacles in the world—the difference between a domesticated & wild animal is far more strikingly marked in man—in the naked barbarian, with his body coated with paint, whose very gestures, whether they may be peacible or hostile are unintelligible, with difficulty we see a fellow-creature."[31] This firsthand experience of the savage raised all sorts of questions in Darwin's mind about what it means to be human.[32] Many years later, he told Charles Kingsley, "I declare the thought, when I first saw in T. del Fuego a naked painted, shivering hideous savage, that my ancestors must have been somewhat similar beings, was at that time as revolting to me, nay more revolting than my present belief that an incomparably more remote ancestor was a hairy beast."[33] Deeply impressed on his mind was that "first sight" of the "native haunt of a barbarian—of man in his lowest and most savage state."[34] Despite their unintelligible expressions and seeming lack of reasoning power, the genesis question was inevitable: "one's mind hurries back over past centuries, and then asks, could our progenitors have been men like these?"[35] But if there was a connection that binds us all, how, asked Darwin, can we explain the variations among people that appear to go deeper than "the difference between a wild and tame animal"?[36] For Darwin the encounter of the "savage" and the "civilized" raised profound and disturbing questions about human nature and its roots.[37]

What Darwin witnessed in Tierra del Fuego forced him to think about variability within the human species. With faces painted as "devils," acting "distrustful, surprised, and startled," and talking with "hoarse, guttural, and clicking sounds," the Fuegians presented an entirely different side of human nature.[38] Darwin couldn't help but think that the gap between the savage and the civilized was "greater than between a wild and domesticated animal."[39] Jemmy Button's transition to civilization was sufficient enough for the lad to be "thoroughly ashamed of his countrymen" when confronted with the reality of his people's lifestyle only three years after his departure.[40]

Leaving the returnees in the company of the missionary Richard Matthews, the *Beagle*'s crew explored the coast for several weeks. Upon returning, they found that Matthews had been mistreated in the interim, with daily threats to his property and life. Of course, the Fuegian population had no idea why Matthews was present nor why he stood guard over such strange housewares and garments. FitzRoy decided to take Matthews to New Zealand, leaving his Fuegian captives to their fates.[41] "When we returned to the Settlement," Darwin told his sister Caroline, "things were in a ruinous condition, almost every thing had been plundered, & the Fuegians had made such signs to Matthews that the Captain advised him not to stay with them."[42] Darwin trusted that York Minster would get on well with Fuegia as his wife. But Jemmy, said Darwin, looked "disconsolate."[43] Having his property pilfered by his own brother, Jemmy could only say they were "all bad men, no sabe (know) nothing."[44] In Jemmy's judgment, he was surrounded by nothing more than "damned fools."[45] To Darwin, these three Fuegians were but a drop of civilization in a sea of savagery. "I fear," worries Darwin, "it is more than doubtful, whether their visit will have been of any use to them."[46] Perhaps to assuage his own conscience, a few days later, FitzRoy went back alone to check on their situation. He reported things were "going on well" and that not much more had been stolen.

Encounters with other primitive cultures forced Darwin to think about the roots and development of all human cultures. Unlike the barbarism of Tierra del Fuego, the way of life of the Tahitians suggested to Darwin that a more nuanced picture of early man was needed. Their mild countenances "at once banished the idea of a savage."[47] In the Tahitians, Darwin found a higher stage of human cultural development. Their "intelligence," he observed, "shows they are advancing in civilization."[48] Despite touches of "civilization," however, the Tahitian way of life preserved a primitive order of being. They lived in thatched houses which only required a few minutes to build, using "bark for rope, the stems of bamboo for rafters, and the large leaf of the banana for thatch."[49] "With withered leaves," he reported, "they made a soft bed."[50]

One incident, though, drove home the unadorned character of the Tahitian way of thinking. Darwin recounted the story from 1817 about a ship which was bringing a horse to Tahiti. While landing, the "slings broke, and it fell into the water."[51] Since they were avid divers who could swim "like otters," several Tahitians went in to rescue the poor beast. Although they nearly drowned the hapless creature, the horse finally made it to shore. Those on the bank fled in terror before this "man-carrying pig."[52] For Darwin, the Tahitians represented a curious mix of humanity's innocent infancy together with its first sure steps toward civilization. As he explained, "I felt the force of the remark, that man, at least savage man, with his reasoning powers only partly developed, is the child of the tropics."[53]

Likewise, Darwin's encounters with the tribal peoples of New Zealand afforded an alternative and even frightening glimpse into the variety of human cultural experiences. "Come on shore and we will kill and eat you all," bellowed these natives as they hurled stones at Captain Cook's ship off New Zealand's coast.[54] Darwin found that time and colonization had not healed this war-torn landscape. Behind the artificial hills or mounds (the Pas) of the double-stockade fort, the European inhabitants gained a brief respite from the bloody wars that raged beyond their zigzag walls. By Darwin's day, the defenses still had the effect of dampening some of the ardor of the tribal attackers, who would willy-nilly mob the walls only to be shot to death. It remained a dangerous place. "I should think a more warlike race of inhabitants could not be found in any part of the world then the New Zealanders," lamented Darwin.[55] In a land beleaguered by a "love of war," Darwin witnessed for himself the tragedy of warfare between the Maori tribes.[56] Lacking the "charming simplicity which is found in Tahiti," Darwin sized up New Zealand as a sorry locale. "It is not a pleasant place," he grumbled.[57] While Darwin's words reflected the cultural stereotypes of his time, his global reach had begun to teach him not only how to classify rocks, plants, and animals but also to see distinct stages in civilization's development. The voyage around the world gave concrete evidence that human traits once deemed God-given were actually the products of the evolution of human societies.

Other cultural encounters helped solidify Darwin's thinking. Although partially clothed, Darwin thought the "good humored and pleasant" Australian aborigines "appeared far from being such utterly degraded beings as they have usually been represented."[58] With no homes or flocks to tie them down, the aborigines relied on their wits and their keen "sagacity" at tracking to maintain their way of life. To Darwin's way of thinking, these abilities, meager though they may be, at least placed the aborigines "a few degrees higher in the scale of civilization than the Fuegians."[59] Despite the white presence, the aborigines managed to preserve their traditions. However, their encounter with the Europeans had terrible repercussions on several fronts, resulting in the plummeting of the aboriginal population. Darwin attributed this attrition to the extermination of wild animals (the main food source), the introduction of liquor, and disease. Diseases such as measles took their toll on the aborigines. The ravages suffered by the aborigines provided Darwin much food for thought regarding the role that migration and invasion played in population reduction. He understood that disease could affect the aborigines and the Europeans in such starkly contrasting ways that it seemed as if the two groups were like "different animals."[60] Behind it all, he said, stood a "mysterious agency."[61] "Wherever the European has trod," he mourned, "death seems to pursue the aboriginal."[62] Yet this culture had not been expunged from the human record just yet and Darwin gained a valuable experience of the otherness of the human species. "Tempted by tubs of rice and sugar," the *Beagle*'s crew cajoled the aboriginal "White Cockatoo men . . . to hold a 'corrobery."[63] The corrobery was a dancing party in which the aboriginal men painted themselves with white spots and lines. The Cockatoo men and the men of King George's Sound formed two lines and danced in response to each other. Darwin found it "a most rude and barbarous scene," but the native women and children loved it.[64] One dance was the emu dance, with a man extending his bent arm to form the neck of a bird. Another dance reenacted a kangaroo hunt, with one dancer grazing while the other hunted. This meeting of cultures had everyone in "high spirits."[65] Imagine, says Darwin, the "group of nearly naked figures, viewed by the light of the blazing fires, all moving in hideous harmony, formed a perfect display of a festival amongst the lowest barbarians."[66] Compared to Tierra del Fuego, this "savage life" seemed to him on a bit higher level, if only because the locals were "so perfectly at their ease."[67]

Darwin's encounters with the Fuegians, Tahitians, New Zealanders, and Australian aborigines afforded him the opportunity to view the varieties of human experience. Most importantly for our theme, these "primitive" cultures stirred him to think about the roots and stages of human religious and moral life. It would be decades before Darwin published a formal statement about religion and ethics in his *Descent of Man*, but his rich travel experiences had already taken him well beyond the limitations of his Shrewsbury upbringing. Such so-called primitive cultures became a source of "astonishment" for Darwin.[68] In his own mind, he was peeling away the biased lens of western monotheism to gaze directly at those primitive promptings that started the human family on the path to belief in a supreme Deity. When Darwin stumbled onto "several small heaps of stones" at the summit of a mountain in the Sierra de las Animas, the stones signaled for Darwin the "universal passion with mankind" to mark events.[69] That passion also took the form of the making of altars, as in the case of the Indian tree dedicated to Walleechu on the plain near the Rio Negro. The Indians travelling with Darwin would issue "loud shouts" the moment the tree came into view.[70] The offerings to the god were generous, including "cigars, bread, meat, pieces of cloth, etc."[71] Poorer Indians would leave poncho threads, while the wealthy would pour out liquor to the god. To demarcate this sacred shine, the tree was surrounded by the "bleached bones of horses which had been slaughtered as sacrifices."[72] The Gauchos informed Darwin that the tree itself was considered a god, but Darwin suggests the Indians merely regarded it as the god's altar. In these stones and altars, Darwin saw remarkable examples of the ancient human tendency to divinize the natural order, a characteristic of this stage of human development.

The Fuegian religion represented a still more basic layer of religious feeling on Darwin's scale. When York Minster reacted to shipmate Benjamin Bynoe's shooting of young ducklings, he warned, "Oh, Mr. Bynoe, much rain, snow, blow much." Darwin interpreted this statement as an indication that the killings would lead to some sort of supernatural retribution for wasting food.[73] On another occasion, York Minster's brother hurled rocks over a cliff to kill a "wild man" who was snatching his birds. York Minster told Darwin that after the slaying "for a long time afterwards storms raged, and much rain and snow fell."[74] In observing this mentality, Darwin concluded that York Minster "seemed to consider the elements themselves the avenging agents."[75] Fuegian beliefs were primeval and nearly impenetrable. By contrast, he wrote, "in a race a little more advanced in culture, the elements would become personified."[76] The Fuegian religion, if such be its name, was ill-defined in its theological conceptions. FitzRoy, reported Darwin, "could never ascertain that the Fuegians have any distinct belief in a future life."[77] Their burials were done in caves or forests, but Darwin did not observe any attendant rituals. The dead were never talked about. Apart from "the muttering of the old man before he distributed the putrid blubber to his famished party," Darwin could discover no forms of prayer or religious ritual among the Fuegians.[78] Every family had its "wizard" (of uncertain function). But even here the supernatural powers that might lie beyond were unclear. He related that Jemmy Button "believed in dreams, though not . . . in the devil."[79] Darwin found in the Fuegians the most primitive layer of religiosity. This is not to say the *Beagle*'s sailors were necessarily made of superior stuff, for Darwin found them more "superstitious" than the Fuegians, especially the old quartermaster's belief that the heavy winds encountered off Cape Horn were the result of having Fuegians on board the ship![80] It is to say, however, that any such superstitions among the crew were vestiges of primitive ideas that were still alive among the Fuegians.

Other cultures and locales displayed their own unique religious practices. The Chilotans of Chiloe had their own special "superstitious fear."[81] They feared the Cheucau bird. This bird emitted such "strange cries" that the Chilotans ascribed supernatural significance to the bird's utterances. Its cry of "chiduco" was taken as an "omen of good," while its ghoulish "huitreu" was regarded as an "unfavorable sign."[82] The practice prompted Darwin humorously to observe, "The Chilotans have chosen a most comical little creature for their prophet."[83]

Some, however, raised themselves above sheer superstition. The Indians around Lima, for example, left impressive ruins which Darwin felt not only gave a "high idea of the condition and number of the ancient population" but also signaled the "considerable advance made by them in the arts of civilization."[84] Likewise, in Tahiti, Darwin ran across a man who at day's end prayed "as a Christian should do, with a fitting reference, and without the fear of ridicule or any ostentation of piety."[85] Instead, the "elder Tahitian . . . with closed eyes repeated a long prayer in his native tongue."[86] Meals, likewise, were greeted with a prayer of "grace."[87] Their sophisticated piety gained Darwin's praise: "Those travelers who think that a Tahitian prays only when the eyes of the missionary are fixed on him, should have slept with us that night on the mountainside."[88] But Darwin was not entirely sure what to make of these practices. Aware that he was trying to peer inside the soul of another human being, he added in his Diary, "Rigidly to scrutinize how far a man, born under idolatry, understands the full motive & effect of prayer, does not appear to me a very charitable employment."[89]

Darwin encountered the more elaborate side of primitive ritual in New Zealand and the Keeling Islands. The daughter of the "heathen" chief in New Zealand had died.[90] The "hovel" where she succumbed was torched and burned to the ground.[91] The girl's body was placed between two small canoes, set upright, and then surrounded by an enclosure fitted with images of the local deities. The entire structure was painted red to be visible at a distance. Darwin recounted that they affixed her gown to the structure and deposited her shorn hair at its base. As part of the ceremony, the girl's relatives gashed themselves in the arms, face, and the rest of their bodies, leaving themselves covered in clotted blood. The day after the burial, Darwin reported, the women were "still howling and cutting themselves."[92] Repelled by the sight, he wrote that "the old women looked most filthy, disgusting objects."[93] As Darwin and his companions proceeded to explore the vicinity, they came across a rocky limestone area that was used for burials. The natives in his group refused to forge ahead since the place was "held too sacred to be approached."[94] Suddenly, one of the younger men bolted ahead shouting, "Let us all be brave."[95] But no sooner had he done so than the "whole party thought better of it, and pulled up short."[96] The natives left it to the foreigners to inspect the site, showing "perfect indifference" to Darwin's more scientific examination of the burial grounds.[97]

In the Keeling Islands, Darwin witnessed a most elaborate ritual. The Malay women enacted a "curious half superstitious scene."[98] They took a large spoon that had been dressed up as a person and carried it to the grave of a dead man. The spoon-man, supposedly inspired by the light of the full moon, danced about in the women's hands. Despite the "delicious" appearance of the full moon, Darwin found the whole affair "a most foolish spectacle."[99] The crudity of the Malay ceremony contrasted sharply with Darwin's experience of the convicts from India who had been exiled to The Isle of France (Mauritius). He found these Hindu practitioners to be "noble-looking figures," at one and the same time quiet, well-conducted, and clean.[100] Somehow their faithful adherence to their "strange religious rites" elevated these wayward souls in Darwin's mind, so that "it was impossible to look at them with the same eyes as our wretched convicts in New South Wales."[101] Where ritual might contribute to the primitive's degradation, complex religious systems could lift others toward civilization.

From as primal a beginning as our "universal passion" of heaping stones, to more elaborate shrines, sacrifices, and ceremonies, Darwin unearthed the foundations of the human religious sense. This sensibility at its most basic sees in the snow, wind, and rain "avenging agents." The primitive religious sense is preoccupied with "superstitious fear," wizardry, and death. But as religion advances it shapes a nobler posture, imbuing adherents with a dignified appreciation of life and death. Darwin was especially fascinated by this primitive layer, resting as it did just beneath the church ruins that dotted the landscape. Freeing himself from Christian ritual and belief, Darwin discovered the deep well-spring of human religiosity. At the same time, he was now free to undo the chains of Church dogma and assess Christianity as a human cultural phenomenon. Let us turn now to look at Darwin's experience of Catholic Christianity.

Heretic in a Catholic world

At the little village of Las Minas, the residents eyed with suspicion Darwin's habit of washing his face in the morning. One of the inhabitants, a "superior tradesman," pressed Darwin for answers. Why such washings? And why do the men of the *Beagle* wear beards while on board ship? Darwin speculated that these suspicions arose from the man having heard about "ablutions in the Mohamedan religion."[102] "Knowing me to be a heretick," Darwin explained, "he came to the conclusion that all hereticks were Turks."[103] Discounting his Christian leanings, Darwin was treated as a religious renegade in the Catholic landscape of South America.

Despite this heretical taint, Darwin gained a better reception than many of his English predecessors. At Coquimbo, the *mayor-domo* recounted his childhood memory of a visit to the town from an English ship captain. Although the school children had been given a holiday to see this remarkable guest, he told Darwin that not one child dared approach this wicked creature. From his earliest days, his Catholic upbringing instilled in him the "idea of the heresy, contamination, and evil to be derived from contact with such a person."[104] The suspicions of the local inhabitants were not entirely groundless. They told Darwin of the outrages of the "bucaniers" who not only stole the statue of the Virgin Mary but also returned the next year to spirit away Joseph, "saying it was a pity the lady should not have a husband."[105] An old woman in the town expressed her astonishment at sharing a meal with an Englishman such as Darwin. She explained that when she was a child, the very word "Los Ingleses" was a signal to grab one's possessions and head for the hills![106] Darwin also heard from residents about their disdain for a pair of Englishmen who reacted irreverently during an earthquake. Though the jolt was a "smart shock," the two were sleeping out-of-doors and, sensing no great danger, simply stayed put on the ground. The town's people fumed, "Look at those heretics, they do not even get out of their beds."[107] Being English and heretical appears to have been synonymous in the minds of many. The French fared a bit better. During Peru's anarchy several Frenchmen were charged with robbing a church of all its plate. The thieves confessed and the property was recovered, but the authorities thought it a "pity" to jail such good furniture makers and as a result set them free.[108] After their release, needless to say, the plate disappeared for good. This time, however, the enraged locals seized and tortured several Englishmen, arguing that only "heretics would thus 'eat God Almighty.'"[109] The government only stepped in when the blood-thirsty mob sought to shoot them. It is not surprising, then, that the Catholic señoritas who chided Darwin, as recounted at the start of this chapter, saw in their encounter an opportunity to put a heretical Englishman in his place. They pressed Darwin by asking, "Do not your padres, your very bishops, marry?"[110] For life-long Catholics, the whole idea of bishops who married struck them as an "absurdity."[111] "They scarcely knew," adds Darwin, "whether to be most amused or horror-struck at such an enormity."[112]

Darwin's forays into Catholicism followed closely on the heels of the Roman Catholic Relief Act (1829) which only a few years before his voyage had granted Catholics the right to stand as members of Parliament and hold other public offices. Not everyone was pleased with these developments. Darwin's curiosities about Catholicism—as well as his misgivings—follow the contours of the religious divisions of his day. In a Spanish-dominated religious landscape, Darwin's wandering constituted a foray into the realm of alien spiritual sensibilities. Coming from a world that was at best ambivalent about Catholics, if not anti-Catholic, Darwin had a unique chance to see Catholicism on its own cultural and theological terms. He witnessed diverse Catholic practices, both official and popular. In his *Diary*, Darwin recorded visits to several churches in Buenos Aires where he "admired the brilliancy of the decorations for which the city is celebrated."[113] He added, "It is impossible not to respect the fervor which appears to reign during the Catholic service as compared with the Protestant." He was particularly struck by the "equality of all ranks." As he paints the scene, "The Spanish lady with her brilliant shawl kneels by the side of her black servant in the open aisle." Popular Catholicism caught Darwin's attention. On the island of Lemoy, he noted, the locals used gunpowder to make noise to honor saints and celebrate feast days.[114] "Each parish," reported Darwin, "has a public musket" for this "very innocent purpose."[115] Castro, the ancient capital of Chiloe, was so poor that the bell ringer was forced to ring the church bell by guessing the time.[116] Though hundreds lived in the town, no one could afford so much as a watch or a clock. Amid the anarchy of Peru, Darwin told of a "high mass" that was held on the anniversary of their independence, a ceremony during which the President received the sacrament of communion. When it came time for the *Te Deum laudamus*, the great hymn of praise, "instead of each regiment displaying the Peruvian flag, a black one with death's head was unfurled."[117] This crass mixture of religion and politics left Darwin mystified. "Imagine," he wrote, "a government under which such a scene could be ordered, on such an occasion, to be typical of their determination of fighting to the death!"[118]

But it was not only living Catholic practice that commanded Darwin's attention. He was perhaps even more fascinated by the church buildings, particularly those in ruins. The curiosity that led to his theological altercation with the pretty señoritas took Darwin to many an abandoned church building. Among the first such sites he visited was the derelict fort and Cathedral at Rebeira Grande. Formerly the "principal place" of the island, the "little town . . . now presents a melancholy, but very picturesque appearance."[119] Darwin, guided by a "black Padre," made a special point to tour the ancient site. He found that governors and military leaders had burials there, some dating back to the sixteenth century. Bananas were growing in the middle of the old church's quadrangle. All that remained in use was an old hospital with "about a dozen miserable-looking inmates."[120] Catholicism, it appeared, had seen better days. Witnessing Christianity quite literally in ruins, Darwin was now in a better position to conceive of religion in human terms.

Natural disasters and divine vengeance

Among the more impressive ruins was that of the basilica at Colonia del Sacramiento in Uruguay. The fragrant groves of orange and peach trees masked the disorder wrought by warfare in the years before Darwin's travels. As a defensive measure, the church building had been used to store gunpowder. Ironically, during one of the "ten thousand thunderstorms" of the area, lightning struck the structure in 1823 and "two-thirds of the building were blown away to the very foundation."[121] The ruins stood as "a shattered and curious monument of the united powers of lightning and gunpowder."[122] In this ruin converged the folly of war, the weakness of religion, and the unforgiving judgment of Nature.

Nature's power against church buildings was revealed to Darwin right before his eyes on 20 February 1835, when a major earthquake struck Valdivia. The quake had a tremendous impact on Darwin's geological thinking, but there was also a religious side to this story. He happened to be on shore at the time and was lying down to rest in the woods. "It came on suddenly," he later recounted, "and lasted two minutes, but the time appeared much longer."[123] As the crew of the *Beagle* surveyed the damage, the collapse of the Cathedral at Concepcion gave Darwin pause. The northeast end was "a grand pile of ruins."[124] The side walls, though heavily damaged, were still standing, but the buttresses were "cut clean off, as if by a chisel, and hurled to the ground."[125] As the city went up in flames and hunger set in, the thieves went to work, as "with one hand they beat their breasts and cried "Misericordia!" and then with the other filched what they could from the ruins."[126] But it was through geologist's eyes—not theological lenses—that Darwin sought to come to grips with this wrenching event. He tried to calculate the devastation that would take place if such "subterranean forces" were unleashed beneath England. "What would become," he wondered, "of the lofty houses, thickly packed cities, great manufactories, the beautiful public and private edifices?"[127] Imagining the worst, namely a quake in the "dead of night," Darwin reacted in horror: "how terrific would be the carnage!"[128] In this doomsday scenario, England would be bankrupted as government authority failed, violence broke out, famine raged, and disease and death stalked the land in the quake's aftermath. Reflecting on these grim scenes, Darwin expressed his unease at a quake of this magnitude: "A bad earthquake at once destroys our oldest associations: the earth, the very emblem of solidity, has moved beneath our feet like a thin crust over fluid; one second of time has created in the mind a strange idea of insecurity, which hours of reflection would not have produced."[129]

As he talked to the locals, Darwin heard many explain the quake in occult terms. He reported that the "the lower orders in Talcahuano" believed the recent quake had been caused by "some old Indian women, who two years ago, being offended, stopped the volcano of Antuco."[130] On the face of it, Darwin thought this was a "silly belief."[131] Yet even in their ignorance, he credited them with having enough sense to link the suppression of volcanic action with subterranean tremors. But there were limits to their knowledge, so they were forced "to apply witchcraft to the point where their perception of cause and effect failed."[132] In Darwin's mind, geological explanation had already displaced such crude religious notions. The line in the sand between science and spiritual explanations had become clearer to Darwin. As he says, "Witchcraft" begins where "knowledge stops."[133] Darwin sidestepped religious explanations to observe rather clinically the ruins of the cathedral at Concepcion. The rupture left some of the walls in a "grand pile of ruins," while other portions remained intact.[134] He noted that Greek temples had suffered similar fates.[135] For Darwin, there was no longer any need to invoke the Bible's avenging God or Zeus's lightning bolts to explain Nature's processes. As he reflected later in his autobiographical recollections, "I had gradually come ... to see that the Old Testament, from its manifestly false history of the world, with the Tower of Babel, the rain-bow as a sign, &c., &c., & from its attributing to God the feelings of a revengeful tyrant was no more to be trusted than the sacred books of the Hindoos, or the beliefs of any barbarian."[136] No doubt this earthquake helped to crystalize Darwin's thinking. As he assessed the Concepcion earthquake, he spoke in passing of that "famous Lisbon shock," the quake of 1755, the event which generated Voltaire's caustic critique in *Candide* against those religionists who smugly proclaimed that the catastrophe on All Saint's Day was an act of Divine wrath.[137] For Darwin, quakes were not religious events but acts of Nature. Though a scientific observer, he was not detached from the scene. Witnessing the cost of the quake in human terms, he admitted having "mixed feelings" over the whole situation and certainly had "compassion" for the victims.[138] Yet he could not help but reflect on Nature's powers unleashed against rock, town, and cathedral. "It is a bitter and humiliating thing," he philosophized, "to see works, which have cost men so much time and labour, overthrown in one minute."[139]

Darwin observed firsthand the power at Nature's command that down through the ages wrought startling changes the world over. Uplift of a few feet might represent merely a wrinkle when viewed from a mountain top, but Darwin now saw that incremental ruptures, so terrible to humans, led eventually to massive changes on the grandest of scales. Nature's laws were at work, not witchcraft. When, in the 1845 edition of the *Voyage of the Beagle*, we hear Darwin speak of the successive uplifts of land over the millennia as "successive small uprisings" due to an "insensibly slow rise" of land, he is using geological phrases that contained veiled hints of his still secret species theory.[140] In asking his readers to inspect church ruins, Darwin promoted a scientific alternative to the religious superstitions and natural theology of his day. His insistence on searching for the causal explanations behind the action of volcanoes and quakes led him to ask questions that locals considered "impious."[141] This shift in method—his willingness to ask theologically uncomfortable questions—provided Darwin an opening to untangle with the knottiest theological issue of all: the problem of evil.

The problem of evil

One of Darwin's favorite theological puzzles that first appears in the *Journal of Researches* was the existence of a particular wasp that paralyzes their prey in order to insert larvae that then feed off these stunned but still-living and presumably still-conscious hosts.[142] This hideous yet elegant contrivance, so emblematic of the necessity of the suffering that drives the onward rush of life in nature, captivated Darwin's attention and raised challenging theological objections. He marveled over the fact that these wasps "seem wonderfully to know how to sting to that degree as to leave them paralysed but alive."[143] The perfection of the arrangement, whose complexity might delight a creationist, had its sinister side: "the larvae feed on the horrid mass of the powerless, half-killed victims."[144] In one confrontation he witnessed, a spider managed to momentarily escape an attacking wasp, only to be hunted down while it hid, much as "a hound did after a fox."[145] He left it to his readers to sort out the theological implications, but inasmuch as this very example returns in other contexts, there is no question that Darwin regarded this arrangement as not only indicative of the cruel side of nature but also a direct challenge to the idea of divine design.[146] Suffering fueled the machinery of nature. If there was a God behind this ordering, then this Deity was a cruel task-master indeed.

From his global vantage point, Darwin was led to entertain new ideas about the Bible, science, and religious philosophy. He even began to wonder if there was a God at all. In his trip *Diary*, he was more candid as he wrestled with the creationist explanation for the workings of the world.[147] While "lying on a sunny bank," he found himself "reflecting on the strange character of the Animals of this country [New South Wales] as compared to the rest of the World."[148] His mentors at Cambridge, such as the geologist Adam Sedgwick and the philosopher of science William Whewell, may have tried to instill in Darwin the virtues of natural theology and a belief in the God of Genesis, but his riverside reverie took an unusual twist. New South Wales was so totally different in its flora and fauna that Darwin couldn't help but wonder what sort of Creator stood back of the world order. "An unbeliever in everything beyond his own reason," Darwin speculated, "might exclaim 'Surely two distinct Creators must have been [at] work."[149] He added that "their object however has been the same & certainly the end in each case is complete."[150] He then turned once again to the question of evil, so closely intertwined in his mind with thoughts of the Creator, as he observed a fly and an "unwary Ant" fall into the "conical pitfall of a Lion-Ant."[151] The Lion-Ant hiding at the base of the pit awaited its unsuspecting prey. The heedless ant fell into the trap and battled fiercely against the Lion-Ant as the sand walls caved in around it, sealing its doom. Somehow, however, after a desperate struggle, the hapless creature managed to escape the clutches of the clever Lion-Ant. The marvel of so simple a mechanism elicited an ecstatic theological outburst from Darwin: "Now what would the Disbeliever say to this? Would any two workmen ever hit on so beautiful, so simple & yet so artificial contrivance?"[152] The obvious answer was, "It cannot be thought so."[153] The delicate arrangements of Nature, despite the apparent cruelties, demanded the affirmation that "the one hand has surely worked throughout the universe."[154] Straining to put the scientific and theological strands together, Darwin suggested: "A Geologist perhaps would suggest, that the periods of creation have been distinct & remote the one from the other; that the Creator rested in his labor."[155] He carried these thoughts no farther, but the Lion-Ant episode was adapted in the first edition of the *Journal of Researches* with the word "sceptic" appearing in place of "Disbelievers" and the word "Hand" capitalized indicating that the question had to do with God. When it came to the second edition of the book, however, he relegated the passage to a footnote, shorn of all its theological freight. By the second edition, Darwin had decided against making God the author of nature's evil. Evil may secondarily result from divinely designed laws of nature, but he was less inclined to hold God directly responsible for nature's cruelties. The problem of evil had by then taken a new turn in his thinking.

Christians killing every Indian

Nature was not the only source of evil in the world. Religion in South America had its dark side. Darwin's travels gave him a firsthand look at war, revolution, government brutality, slavery, and rampant poverty. Sadly, religion was in the thick of things, fostering great social evils. Freed by his travels to ask difficult theological questions, Darwin felt compelled to document Christian practice in South America especially as it related to the wars of genocide that raged around him.[156] In many ways, the *Journal of Researches* was a study of the religious and moral blindness of the human species.

Christian wars were everywhere. In particular, General Juan Manuel de Rosas of Argentina led his "banditti-like army"—a "dour looking" mix of blacks, Indians, and Spaniards—in a war of extermination against the Indians in his territory.[157] Dour though they may have been, they were also fearsome. With grudging admiration Darwin asked, "what other troops in the world are so independent?"[158] He depicted their fierce determination thus: "With the sun for their guide, mare's flesh for food, their saddle-cloths for beds,—as long as there is a little water, these men would penetrate to the end of the world."[159] Grudging admiration for their tenacity gave way to horror over the carnage dealt out by Rosas's military machine. The ghastly truth was that his warring left far too many people dead or enslaved to justify any high-minded talk of the war's righteousness. "Who would believe in this age that such atrocities could be committed in a Christian civilized country?" asked a horrified Darwin.[160] In shock, he searched for the words to express his profound dismay: "This warfare is too bloody to last."[161] The land had been scarred by too many generals, too many skirmishes, too many threats of revolution for anyone to hope for a positive outcome.[162] In fact, as Darwin reported after leaving South America, the war of extermination failed.[163] Nonetheless he observed, "I never saw anything like the enthusiasm for Rosas, and for the success of the 'most just of all wars against barbarians.'"[164] In his *Journal of Researches*, Darwin suggested that this righteous sentiment held some justification because "till lately, neither man, woman nor horse, was safe from the attacks of the Indians."[165] But in his *Diary*, Darwin painted a more startling assessment of all this talk of just war. There he presented in all its gory detail the bloody brutality of battlefield conflict. As Indian warriors fled in terror, abandoning even wives and children, "The soldiers pursue & sabre every man. Like wild animals however they fight to the last instant. One Indian nearly cut off with his teeth the thumb of a soldier, allowing his own eye to be nearly pushed out of its socket. Another who was wounded, pretended death with a knife under his cloak, ready to strike the first who approached."[166] In one incident an Indian begged his pursuer, "Companèro (friend) do not kill me," as he secretly reached for the ball-like weapons hidden on his person to whirl them at the soldier.[167] The soldier told Darwin, "I however struck him with my sabre to ground, then got off my horse & cut his throat."[168] Darwin's verdict was grim: "This is a dark picture."[169]

Darwin had entered a world of failed revolutions, ruined forts, fallen fighters, and religious folly. In Lima, for example, there was so much "anarchy" that the President resorted to dismantling his own fort and selling the guns because he couldn't trust any officer to oversee matters. That distrust was no doubt well-founded, for, as Darwin explained, the President had himself seized power "by rebelling while in charge of this same fortress."[170] Needless to say, the man's career was short-lived. "He paid the penalty in the usual manner," Darwin explained, "by being conquered, taken prisoner, and shot."[171] Elsewhere, at Valdivia, the ruined fort became for Darwin "a monument of the fallen greatness of Spain."[172] It was a fall that engulfed the region in unspeakable blood-letting.

The native inhabitants bore the brunt of Christian Europe's expansionist ways. Darwin sought to come to terms with the Indian's situation. Passing through Corunda, he and his companions were troubled by the many "ransacked" and "deserted" houses.[173] Then a still more gruesome sight came into view. Suspended from a tree was the skeleton of an Indian with "dried skin hanging on the bones."[174] Darwin was taken aback but his guides displayed great delight at the "spectacle."[175] Such were the horrifying results of General Rosas's wish for "exterminating" the Indians.[176] Yet Rosas did have his Indian allies.[177] These collaborators fought alongside Rosas's troops, while the Indian women loaded and unloaded the horses and made the tents. "The duty of women," Darwin observed, was to be "like the wives of all savages, useful slaves."[178] Women on the opposing side faced even worse prospects. After one battle in which an unsuspecting Indian travelling party was spotted by the soldiers, the entire cohort of roughly one hundred men, women, and children were slaughtered by a force of two hundred soldiers. Every male was put to the sword. But what shocked Darwin most of all was the fact that every female who looked over the age of twenty was also executed—"massacred in cold blood!"[179] When taken to task for such "inhuman" brutality, one soldier merely quipped, "Why, what can be done? They breed so!"[180] This is not to say that all Indian women succumbed without a struggle. At one battle in the Sierra Ventana a few years earlier, Indian women who escaped to the top of a cliff hurled "great stones" at their pursuers below and managed to save themselves.[181] One escape, in particular, appears to have gained Darwin's admiration. During a skirmish, an old Indian chief scooped up his son and attempted to flee. Grabbing his saddleless horse, the chief held onto the horse's head and by putting one of his legs on the horse's back was able to race away while hanging astride the far side of the horse. Dodging bullets in this manner, the chief and his boy dashed toward freedom. "What a fine picture one can form in one's mind," Darwin told his readers, "the naked, bronze-like figure of the old man with his little boy, riding like a Mazeppa on the white horse, thus leaving far behind him the host of his pursuers!"[182]

Such triumphs were short-lived, however, as the war of extermination took its toll on the Indian population. Those who managed to survive to live among the Europeans did so with a greatly diminished spirit. Darwin noted that the Indians of Cucao of western Chiloe were "discontented" though "humble" because of the harsh rule they were under.[183] Darwin found it too "painful" to watch this scene, observing how his escort treated such Indians more as "slaves" than as "free men."[184] Giving vent to their frustrations, the Indians told Darwin, "And it is only because we are poor Indians, and know nothing; but it was not so when we had a King."[185] Some, though, who had known a measure of victory over the Spaniards did retain an independent streak. Darwin saw in their curtness of manner the hardness that results from enduring so much conflict.[186]

A "just war" to the victor was a catastrophe to the victims. Darwin was shocked by this Christian moral blindness. Ever since Augustine, Christian theologians had been trying to define the conditions that make for a "just" war. Darwin's travels brought him face-to-face with the disturbing character of the Christian conquest of the Americas. Those conquests raised troubling questions about the long-held Christian belief in the possibility of war's justness. Did noble ends justify the cruel means? If the European conquests had ushered in an age of peace, perhaps someone might argue that the glorious result validated all the mayhem. However, the truth of the matter was that these conquests held no such esteem in Darwin's eyes. Reaching Caylen—a place appropriately enough dubbed "el fin del Christianidad" ('the end of Christendom')—Darwin stopped at a house at the northern end of Laylec.[187] Having reached the "extreme point of South American Christendom," he did not stumble upon a theological pot of gold at the end of religion's rainbow. Rather, he found instead "a miserable hovel."[188] These "extreme Christians," inhabiting a castaway region, were "very poor."[189] In their terrible plight, they "begged for some tobacco."[190] The poverty of the conquered Indians was so desperate that they were forced to hike for "three days and a half on foot, and had as many to return, for the sake of recovering the value of a small axe and a few fish."[191] If abject poverty was one measure of the so-called justness of war, then the situation at "el fin de Christianidad" suggested these conquests were the height of human cruelty. In fact, Darwin found the European conquests in the name of God to be everywhere an abject failure. At one abandoned campsite, Darwin saw further signs of the extent of the genocide committed by these so-called Christian warriors. "The fire, bed, and situation showed the dexterity of an Indian," Darwin observed, "but he could scarcely have been an Indian, for the race is in this part extinct, owing to the Catholic desire of making at one blow Christians and Slaves."[192] Troubled by the fact that the Christian conquerors were driving the native population from the face of the earth, Darwin laid the blame squarely on misplaced religious and military fervor.

To be sure, Christianity was not always to blame. In New Zealand, the Christian missionaries vainly sought to restrain the warlike ways of the southern tribes. Darwin found, however, that the tribal chief just could not bear to let good gunpowder go to waste. Concerning Shongi, the chief who once visited England, it was said that "the love of war was the one and lasting spring of every action."[193] The sole purpose of Shongi's visit to England was to trade for enough arms to settle a score with a tribe that had "oppressed" his tribe in the past. When the rival chiefs met one another by accident in Sydney, they were "civil" enough, says Darwin, but they used the occasion to pledge to destroy each other once they returned to New Zealand.[194] In the end, Shongi's people defeated their enemy and killed the rival chief. Despite "harbouring such deep feelings of hatred," Darwin related that Shongi was reputed to have been "a good-natured person."[195] Darwin saw in the New Zealander's warrior ways evidence that they were of a "lower order" than the more "civilized" Tahitians.[196] But both savage and Christian were lowered by warfare. Indeed, to Darwin's way of thinking the Catholic wars against the Indians were especially egregious, giving the lie to any talk of progress whether in politics, national defense, or religion. The results told the whole story as far as Darwin was concerned: "The children of the Indians are saved, to be sold or given away as a kind of slave."[197] A Catholic society built on massacres and slavery was hollow at its core, bereft of moral and religious sense. It mattered not whether one was "primitive" or "advanced," "pagan" or "religious." As Darwin bluntly characterized the foul state of affairs: "The Christians killing every Indian, & the Indians doing the same by the Christians."[198]

March of improvement

Darwin's global view gave him a keen insight into the havoc wreaked by Catholic imperial ventures. But he held out one bastion of hope for religion: the English Christian missions. Christianity was—to use Nick Spencer's phrase—"one of Britain's finest exports."[199] Darwin's travels offered an opportunity to see the impact of the missionaries on far-flung lands. Assessing their labors pro and con, he found a glimmer of Gospel light in a sea of religious gloom.

The Catholic conquests presented one form of missionizing. As far as Darwin could tell, Catholic efforts at conversion were no more successful than their conquests. He carried a letter of introduction to the friar at the Mission of Cudico. Having taken a long ride out of Valdivia into dense forest, he pressed on to the treeless Llanos where he hoped to give his tired horse a much-deserved rest. The padre at the Mission offered Darwin an insight into the Indian conversions. The Indians around Valdivia were the conquered "reducidos y cristianos," whereas those to the north remained "wild" and unconquered.[200] As Darwin relates, "The padre said that the Christian Indians did not much like coming to mass" but he reported they "otherwise . . . showed respect for religion."[201] The main problem was getting the Indians to follow Christian marriage practices. "The wild Indians," Darwin explained, "take as many wives as they can support."[202] Some chiefs (*Caqique*) had more than ten wives, each wife having a separate fire in their dwelling and all participating in the weaving of ponchos for the husband's profit. In his diary, Darwin also noted the problem with alcohol, calling it "the besetting sin with all."[203] Drinking for days on end left many of the Indians "very dangerous & fierce."[204]

Unlike the Catholic failures, Darwin's experiences in Tahiti caused him to consider the more positive impact of the English missionaries. In fact, as Janet Browne points out, Darwin's first published article was not on science but a joint piece with FitzRoy on the moral state of Tahiti (and New Zealand) in light of the missions.[205] The article—in reality a long letter to the *South African Christian Recorder*—drew on extracts from the journals of Darwin and FitzRoy to confirm the positive effects of the missions with regard to moral improvement, hygiene, farming, Bible literacy, and the ending of tribal warfare. He documented this success story in his writing on the voyage. In Tahiti, the missionaries had effectively stamped out the native's use of the ava plant with its "powerful intoxicating effects."[206] Darwin discovered the plant had "an acrid and unpleasant taste."[207] "Thanks to the missionaries," he reported, "this plant now thrives only in these deep ravines, innocuous to everyone."[208] But their success against intoxicating plants was nearly undermined by the plague of alcohol. However, the English missionaries managed to stamp out alcohol too. Two years before Darwin's arrival, they urged the people to establish a Temperance Society to keep their land from "going to ruin."[209] "From good sense or shame," explained Darwin, "all the chiefs and the queen were at last persuaded to join."[210] Through a campaign of searches and fines—"even the houses of the missionaries were not exempted"—the effort had a tremendous impact.[211] So much so that when Darwin unknowingly pulled out a flask to take a drink, the locals, who felt obligated to share the gift, "put their fingers before their mouths, and uttered the word 'Missionary.'"[212] Darwin admired the fact that the "free will of the people" led to the banishment of alcohol the very year the decision was made to introduce spirits into the island of St Helena. Tahiti presented a missionary success story unlike anything Darwin found in South America. "When one reflects on the effect of intemperance on the aborigines of the two Americas," he wrote, "I think it will be acknowledged that every well-wisher of Tahiti owes no common debt of gratitude to the missionaries."[213]

Prior to seeing Tahiti firsthand, Darwin had an admitted bias against the missions. He had read the travel narratives of Frederick Beechey and Otto von Kotzebue, authors who led Darwin to assume that "the Tahitians had become a gloomy race, and lived in fear of the missionaries."[214] But his personal experience suggested that tales of gloom and doom presented a "decidedly incorrect" view.[215] "It would be difficult in Europe," confessed a chastened Darwin, "to pick out of a crowd half so many merry and happy faces."[216] He found Tahiti's "morality and religion of the inhabitants" to be "highly creditable."[217] The credit for these developments, said Darwin, rested squarely on the shoulders of the tireless missionaries. He castigated their critics, pointing out that the detractors obviously didn't know the dire situation that existed twenty years before out of which the missionaries had rescued the natives. To decry the fact that "Gospel perfection" had not resulted was not a valid criticism, since, argued Darwin, the missionaries could not be blamed for what "the Apostles themselves failed to do."[218] The evidence of the missionaries' positive impact was plain for all to see. They abolished human sacrifice along with the idolatrous priesthood and a "system of profligacy unparalleled in any other part of the world."[219] Gone were infanticide and bloody wars. Dishonesty, intemperance, and licentiousness were in decline. Darwin pressed home the point, saying that it was "base ingratitude" for a voyager to downplay these cultural advances. A shipwrecked sailor, he insisted, would wish "the lesson of the missionary may have extended thus far."[220] He turned the tables on the critics, suggesting that because they were "disappointed in not finding the field of licentiousness quite so open as formerly, they will not give credit to a morality which they do not wish to practise, or to a religion which they undervalue, if not despise."[221] Inasmuch as the "character of this class of men have been so frequently attacked," Darwin felt compelled to offer in his Diary a defense by name of the missionaries' qualities and deeds.[222] These missionaries—George Pritchard, Charles Wilson, and Henry Nott—were presented as well-educated individuals.[223] Likewise, their daughters were said by Darwin to have been "properly educated."[224] He was dismayed that the critics had impugned the good character of these women. On the other hand, he was impressed that ordinary looking English gentlemen could parlay in the Tahitian language as if they were natives. While he was struck by the obvious moral impact of the missions, he was less enthusiastic about the worship life of the Tahitian believers. He participated in a Christian worship service to which he gave mixed reviews. Captain FitzRoy took them to a "divine service" which was conducted in both Tahitian and English. Led by the head missionary, Pritchard, the chapel—"a large airy framework of wood"—was filled with "tidy, clean people."[225] While Darwin admitted that the parishioners were less attentive than he might have expected, they were "quite equal to that in a county church in England."[226] Despite the fact that the sermon in Tahitian was a bit "monotonous," filled as it was with "*tata ta, mata mai*," Darwin found the music "very pleasing."[227] Obviously there was room for improvement on that score, but of the moral worth of the missions he had no doubt.

Darwin had similar praise for the missionary work in New Zealand. The missionaries' residences at Pahia painted a pretty picture: The white-washed cottages sported front yards planted with English flowers—roses, honeysuckle, jasmine, and briar hedges—"quite pleasing to behold."[228] Likewise, the missionary residence at Waimate looked as if it had been "placed there . . . by an enchanter's wand."[229] The abundant crops grown by the locals under the careful tutelage of the missionaries suggested to Darwin that "the lesson of the missionary is the enchanter's wand."[230] Having seen the successes of the English missionaries in Tahiti and New Zealand, he exuded a "triumphant feeling," foreseeing what Englishmen could affect as they raised "high hopes" for the "future progress" of New Zealand.[231] These missionaries were quite literally redeeming the population from slavery to become productive farmers in their own right. There was a humble hopefulness in these missionaries. Far from finding them to be guilty of "austerity," as their critics charged, Darwin reported that their sons were avid cricket players. That lively fortitude spilled over into the servant women who bore a "clean, tidy, and healthy appearance, like that of the dairy-maids in England."[232] Hygiene was one of the by-products of the missionary campaign, getting the locals to buy soap on market days.[233] The native women formed a stark contrast to the "women of the filthy hovels in Kororadika."[234] Despite all the positive change, the wives of the missionaries could not stamp out tattoos. "We really must just have a few lines on our lips," protested the local women, "else when we grow old, our lips will shrivel, and we shall be so very ugly."[235] The missionaries' opposition to tattooing did not obliterate this "badge of distinction between the chief and the slave."[236] Even the missionaries had to admit to Darwin that a plain native face "looked mean, and not like that of a New Zealand gentleman."[237]

Basking in this missionary progress, Darwin prepared for the fifth and last Christmas Day of his voyage, a joyous celebration in the "land of cannibalism, murder, and atrocious crimes!"[238] Children gathered round as Darwin drank his tea. Attending a "divine service" in the chapel at Pahia, Darwin experienced an intercultural blending of worship as some portions were read in English while others were intoned in the native language. As there had been no recent acts of cannibalism, Darwin was able to reflect on the continued positive impact of Christianity on the moral condition of the locals. Under the influence of the missionaries, Darwin predicted, "It is probable that the moral state of the people will rapidly improve."[239] Mr. Bushby, one of the missionaries, gave Darwin "proof of the sincerity of some, at least, of those who profess Christianity," saying that he overheard the men one night by the campfire reading the Bible, with no small difficulty, and then kneeling to pray on behalf of the missionaries and their families.[240] Not all things English, of course, led to the native's moral improvement. When one of the chiefs became "notorious" for having hanged one of his wives and a male slave for adultery, the missionary's condemnation was met with the retort that this is what happened in England as well, no doubt referring to the cruel justice of Henry VIII. Nonetheless, Darwin found in the missionaries an indomitable spirit of progress, a "march of improvement" that would attend the further spread of Christian morality. Sixty years after the journey of Captain Cook and his crew—whom the natives had threatened to devour— Darwin saw a New Zealand that was stamped by changes wrought "by the philanthropic spirit of the British Nation."[241]

In later years, the Archbishop of Canterbury would praise Darwin as a supporter of the South American Missionary Society.[242] The fact was, as his old *Beagle* shipmate B. J. Sulivan put on record, Darwin supported this effort monetarily because their work improved the Fuegians in ways Darwin had not thought possible of so-called savages.[243] His support for this missionary society began in the late 1860s and continued for the rest of his life. In 1870, Darwin told Sulivan he was delighted to be made an honorary member of their organization. That a man of such deep faith as Sulivan and a secularist like Darwin could cooperate in this way was a remarkable development.[244] Darwin's financial support also aided the orphan dubbed "Jemmy FitzRoy Button."[245] Darwin ended his travelogue on a hopeful note regarding the missions, but the mission among the Fuegians was not without its problems. FitzRoy had, in fact, failed in his attempt to install Matthews and his westernized Fuegians on the ground.[246] The well-intentioned donors in England had provisioned Matthews with finery that in Darwin's estimation "showed the most culpable folly & negligence."[247] Wine glasses, soup tureens, elegant white linens, and beaver hats indicated "how little was thought about the country where they were going to." The disastrous nature of this misadventure was compounded in subsequent years after the Patagonian Missionary Society began luring small groups of Fuegians to live and work at their missionary station in the region. Deteriorating relations eventually led to a massacre of several missionaries and fellow crew members. Jemmy Button narrowly escaped being held accountable for these killings. The Society changed its name to the South American Missionary Society to distance itself from this debacle. After Jemmy died of illness, his son "Threeboys" became one of four Fuegians brought to England by the Society. Threeboys met FitzRoy during that visit in 1865. Threeboys died shortly after his return to Tierra del Fuego, apparently from an ailment contracted as a result of his English contacts.[248] These failures notwithstanding, Darwin looked to the English missions as the beacon of the world's moral and religious future. Writing to Caroline late in the voyage, he praised the work of the missions to Tahiti and New Zealand. "The Missionaries have done much," he wrote, "in improving their moral character & still more in teaching them the arts of civilization." He added, "It is something < to > boast of, that Europæans may here, amongst men who, so lately were the most ferocious savages probably on the face of the earth, walk with as much safety as in England."[249] Darwin would later express the same judgment to Sulivan about the work of the South American Missionary Society. In Darwin's estimation, the great Christian successes lay in the moral improvements brought by the English missions, a reality that stood in sharp contrast to the bloody conflicts reigning in Catholic South America. Not only were the Christians of Waimate the "one bright spot" in New Zealand but for Darwin the English missions were the one great light amid the horrors of Christendom he encountered elsewhere in his travels.

The sublime powers of life

On his voyage, Darwin unearthed the various strata of human religiosity. Moral monotheism with its English missionaries stood proudly at the peak, as Catholicism fell short of the summit. The noble Hindus were next. The religious layers descended down through the humble Tahitians, the tribal primitives in New Zealand and Australia, and finally hit bedrock with the crude Fuegians. But there was yet one more element resting beneath all these layers. Darwin discerned the ultimate source of religiosity in the human sense of wonder at Nature's grandeur. Early on in his *Journal of Researches*, Darwin observed that Nature stirs "higher feelings of wonder, astonishment, and devotion, which fill and elevate the mind."[250] During his voyage, he encountered the sublime powers of the world that stood at the root of the human religious sense. This subterranean layer is perhaps Darwin's most important discovery.

In his most powerful reflections on the subject, Darwin spoke of the "sublimity" of "the primeval forests undefiled by the hand of man."[251] The experience left him at a loss for words, explaining that "it is nearly impossible to give an adequate idea of the higher feelings which are excited; wonder astonishment & sublime devotion fill & elevate the mind."[252] Darwin associated "sublimity" with the work of the Italian Renaissance artist Sebastian del Piombo, in particular his dramatic *Raising of Lazarus* housed in the National Gallery in London.[253] The religious associations of "sublimity" were felt deeply in the tropics. His utter astonishment at the sight was captured most directly in his Rio de Janeiro field notebook with the simple exclamation: "silence hosannah."[254] The phrase tells us that this was truly a religious experience for Darwin. The spiritual richness of Nature overwhelmed him as he stood in awe of the "powers of life" in the Brazilian rainforests and shuddered at the furious tempests of Tierra del Fuego "where Death and Decay prevail."[255] Concerning such places of life and death, Darwin wrote, "Both are temples filled with the varied productions of the

God of Nature: no one can stand in these solitudes unmoved, and not feel that there is more in man than the mere breath of his body."[256] Writing to his sister Caroline about the tropics, he said, "No disciple of Mahomet ever looked to his seventh heaven, with greater zeal, than I do to those regions."[257]

Nature's luminous beauty left Darwin enthralled. On one "pitch dark" night, when the *Beagle* plowed forward off the eastern coast of South America, Darwin was entranced as "the vessel drove before her two billows of liquid phosphorus, & in her wake was a milky train."[258] The scene presented a captivating marvel. "As far as the eye reached," recounts Darwin, "the crest of every wave was bright; & from the reflected light, the sky just above the horizon was not so utterly dark as the rest of the Heavens."[259] To put his experience into words, Darwin was inspired by the book he carried everywhere on his voyage: Milton's *Paradise Lost*. Later, when working on the species question, Darwin would also turn to the poetry of Wordsworth and Coleridge, but "in my excursions during the voyage of the Beagle, when I could take only a single small volume, I always chose Milton."[260] Milton became a lens for Darwin's experience of nature's wonders. The sea's magic demanded the heightened language of religious poetry. "It was impossible to behold this plain of matter, as it were melted & consuming by heat," he explained, "without being reminded of Milton's description of the regions of Chaos & Anarchy."[261] Such words justify Douglas Burton-Christie's contention that Darwin deserves to be called a "contemplative naturalist."[262] Whether it was St Elmo's fire streaming around the *Beagle*'s mast, frogs singing in "harmony," or the stars glistening in the southern sky, Darwin found countless reasons to be astonished.[263] Nature played delightful games, as on the sea to Patagonia, where swarms of butterflies engulfed the ship. One seaman cried out that "it was snowing butterflies."[264] Then there was the sheer scale on which Nature operates, dwarfing human achievements. At Chonos harbor, ascending a nearby mountain, Darwin exulted in his "triumph and pride" at conquering the hill to take in the "grand view."[265] He admitted a bit of "vanity" in thinking himself the first to ascend such a hill. Elsewhere, speaking again of mountains, Darwin was caught by staggering images. "How opposite are the sensations," he wrote, "when viewing black mountains half enveloped in clouds, and seeing another range through the blue haze of a fine day! The one for a time may be very sublime; the other is all gaiety and happy life."[266] That mix of dark and light gave Nature a special allure. Of a bad storm and subsequent rainbow, Darwin said, "White massive clouds were piled up against a dark blue sky, and across them black ragged sheets of vapour were rapidly driven. The successive mountain ranges appeared like dim shadows; . . . it was an ominous, sublime scene."[267] Elsewhere, the clear air, a sky of "intense blue," a region of "profound valleys," and "quiet mountains of snow" called forth Darwin's poetic sensibilities. "I felt glad I was alone," he reflected, "it was like watching a thunderstorm, or hearing in full orchestra a chorus of the Messiah."[268] In the Antipodes, Darwin recalled his "childish doubt and wonder." For the older adventurer, such "resting-places for the imagination" were like "shadows, which a man moving onwards cannot catch."[269] Nature's untamable power was also seen, said Darwin, in earthquakes, particularly "in seeing the laboured works of man in a moment overthrown."[270] He added, "we feel the insignificance of his boasted power."[271]

Such wonders unleashed the deepest wellsprings of awe in Darwin. This sense of the sublime was the ultimate ground for the human religious sense. It was this experience, felt so often on his voyage, which created the conviction that humans are more than the playthings of chance adrift in a purposeless universe. Of course, the later Darwin would remain puzzled whether or not this transcendent awareness constituted genuine evidence for belief in God. In his autobiographical recollections, he professed having become "colour-blind" to these realities.[272] But we can be certain that the Darwin of the voyage had a deep appreciation for life's grandeur. To a young man whose naturalist studies had been framed by hikes in Wales, such sublime images were jarring. Witnessing the staggering spectacles of "hundreds of thousands" of birds flying in the sky, as on the Island of Chiloe, or observing nature's little oddities, such as the Guid-guid, Chiloe's "barking bird," exposed Darwin to nature's marvelous diversity.[273] The puzzle had far more pieces than he initially imagined. Seeing Nature's marvels engendered a new kind of thinking about creation that in turn challenged long-held dogma about the fixity of species and the necessity of invoking "special creation" to account for nature's infinite variability. These facts would weigh heavily on Darwin after his return, when he poured out his thoughts in his secret notebooks and as he updated his *Journal of Researches* for its second edition.

Conclusion

After his voyage, Darwin's religious and cultural experiences would cause him to continue to wrestle with an astonishing range of religious and moral questions, ranging from the origins of human moral awareness to the time-honored problem of evil. His global journey and his encounters with the varieties of human religious experience encouraged Darwin to "take all chances."[274] Religion, like life itself, Darwin was beginning to realize, had evolved. It was a breath-taking realization. Far from thinking that he was simply a tortured evolutionist plagued by a fracturing faith, we should see in his voyage the first of many steps in which Darwin would learn to rewrite our understanding of the rise and progress of religious belief. While we have only scratched the surface when it comes to the central religious questions raised by his voyage—primitive religion; Catholicism and heresy; natural disasters and the problem of evil; just war theory; Christian missions; and the sublime—we have seen enough to demonstrate that the *Beagle* voyage altered Darwin's understanding of religion. Far from simply frittering away his faith as he lost a naïve Biblicism, the voyage had the effect of opening Darwin to new ways of thinking about religious belief and practice. To focus on Darwin's loss of faith is to narrow the scope of Darwin's religious explorations. A more powerful construct suggests that we see in his journey the starting point of an intellectual trajectory that would lead to a multifaceted appreciation of religion's place in the evolutionary Web. While Darwin's *Descent of Man* would spell out this vision in greater detail, especially in reference to the evolution of morality, his *Journal of Researches* laid the essential groundwork for an evolutionary view of religion. Between the voyage and his much later *Descent of Man*, Darwin struggled to find a theory to explain how religion evolved. To that story, we now turn.

A Disposition to Doubt: Darwin as Skeptical Seeker

Darwin credited his voyage on H. M. S. *Beagle* as "the first real training or education of my mind."[1] While the trip may have raised doubts about the Bible and Christian belief, threatening to halt his ministerial career, the journey was also key to his scientific and religious awakening. Darwin returned a changed man. Indeed, when his father first set eyes on him after his homecoming, he exclaimed to his daughters, "Why the shape of his head is quite altered."[2] But his new views were far from settled. So, the period between October, 1836 and January, 1839 became a time when he "was led to think much about religion."[3] His global voyage had brought a sea change in his thinking about belief, while leaving many questions still unanswered. The biblically minded sportsman who left England on December 27, 1831 returned to England a scientifically minded seeker on October 2, 1836. Fearing a change of heart about the ministerial path, with its promise of a cozy parsonage, the women in Darwin's life still held out the hope that he would choose the Church— mostly because they saw in this way of life assurances of wedded bliss for their brother. Against this backdrop of jarring travel experiences, biblical skepticism, scientific probing, and family piety, we find Darwin entering the next phase of his quest to understand religion's evolutionary dimensions. In this chapter, we take up his abandonment of a clerical career amid growing doubts about traditional religion. In the following chapter, we turn to consider Darwin's covert effort to find a theory to explain religion's rise and function. Through it all, we see Darwin as much more than a fractured believer. He was rethinking the religion question in earnest.

A snug parsonage

Darwin's older sister Caroline, ever the protectress, repeatedly pressed her brother with little nudges to embrace the clergyman's life: "I often make a day dream of seeing you so happy in your Parsonage."[4] She held out that "snug parsonage" as a beacon for her brother's journey, offering the parson's domicile as a haven of happiness to the weary world-traveler. For his part, Darwin fostered the family's fantasy. Writing from Botofogo Bay (Rio de Janeiro) early in the voyage, he told Caroline that the end of the journey would see him taking up the cloth. "I find," he forecasted, "I steadily have a distant prospect of a very quiet parsonage, & I can see it even through a grove of Palms."[5]

Caroline continued to recommend books on the Bible, just as she had recommended Gospel readings several years before. Mid-voyage she shipped off the Rev Richard Whately's *A View of Scripture Revelations Concerning a Future State*, a book by the Archbishop of Dublin that she liked "so very much."[6] With wisps of nostalgia, she reminded her brother of their meeting of the minds in days gone by: "I think we often used to find we liked the same kind of books."[7] She may have suspected that seeing a bigger world might cause Charles to lose interest in the clerical life, but she still tried to keep him to that path both intellectually and spiritually.

Catherine Wedgwood, Darwin's aunt, shared Caroline's hopes and fears for Charles. At the outset of the voyage, she expressed her sorrow that a third year had already been added to the trip's itinerary: "I do confess that that third year makes me tremble much more than I did before for the country parish & parsonage house where I should be very sorry not to see you established."[8] She imagined the clergyman's life the best for molding one's character: "I think it is the happiest kind of life & one which would almost oblige one to be good, & something to oblige one to be good is what one feels the want of every day of one's life."[9] She had mixed feelings about the value of the voyage. She acknowledged the healthy demands of sea-life but in the next breath cautioned, "I am very much afraid that ship board is not a good place for working" since it required "a great deal of resolution & perseverance."[10]

It was not uncommon for women of the time to see themselves as the religious and moral force of the family even as the men of the family became adventurers of the mind. As Paul White observes in his *Thomas Huxley: Making the "Man of Science,"* Victorian males profited from navigating between woman's domestic piety and the wider world of science. Huxley, who was Darwin's champion in later years, faced the same entanglements as Darwin. Henrietta Heathorn, Huxley's future wife, "gathered evidence from scriptural accounts of creation to parry her fiancé's skepticism" and "proudly displayed the importance of Christian virtues for her command of the household."[11] White tells the story of "how, returning home one evening to find the staff all 'tipsy', the horse escaped, the kitchen on fire, and the nurse hurling abuse, she astonished a friend by her forceful manner of reproving the servants. In a measured tone, she quelled the inferno, restored order to chaos, and admonished the intemperate creatures for intemperance."[12] The women in Darwin's life imagined a great gulf separating the parish world from the world of adventure. While that larger world had its admitted attractions, in the end they preferred to offer their brother the promise of wedded stability in a parsonage. They hoped he would see the good sense of their choice for him.

All they required to make the picture complete was actually finding a worthy wife for their future parson. Catherine Darwin recognized that one of the real dangers of a global tour was that a man on such a journey would be pulled out of the social network that would ensure him a wife fit for the parson's life. "I can conceive nothing more extraordinary and interesting," she acknowledged, "than to be quietly living in a Brazilian Cottage."[13] But, she remonstrates, "do not let the cottage put the Parsonage out of your head."[14] From his younger sister's perspective, a multiyear worldwide scientific venture was simply a temporary holiday from a sensibly constituted domestic life. Making the most out of feeble signs that Charles might still have the clergyman's life in mind, she reported that "we were rejoiced" to hear that parish living "continued to be a vista to your prospects."[15] To keep her brother on track, Catherine was not shy about playing matchmaker. For a suitable marriage partner, she suggested Fanny Wedgwood, the cousin she trusted Darwin would find "*disengaged* and **sobered** into an excellent Clergyman's wife by the time you return, a nice little invaluable Wife she would be."[16] She expressed the concern that in Fanny's case another clergyman was already "paying her very sedulous attention."[17] She told Charles that she found this fellow "such a vulgar, fat, horrid man" and that she did "not think it possible she will have him." Catherine went on to relate an embarrassing incident to ease any anxiousness about winning Fanny that she may have caused her brother. While some of the relatives were visiting a greenhouse and admiring the flowers, Fanny's bumbling suitor pulled a scrap of paper out of his pocket and presented in triumph to her a sketch of "some little flowers" he had "scrawled." He solemnly declared that he had drawn "some far prettier flowers" than those in the greenhouse. The suitor's boorish behavior gave the family a good laugh: "Emma was by, and was near choking with laughing at the man's odd manner, and Fanny's amazement."[18] Fanny Wedgwood, in fact, never did marry, tragically dying the very next month after a sudden illness. Darwin's marital prospects were dimming.

This same feminine preference for the parish life with a proper wife was most forcefully presented to Charles by Charlotte Wedgwood, sister to Emma and Fanny. Eager to see who would be married first, Charlotte wrote Darwin on the occasion of Charles Langton's proposal to her of marriage: "I looked forward to seeing you established in your parsonage but now I suppose I shall receive you first in mine."[19] To Charlotte, a marriage that led straight to the doors of a country parsonage was "the happiest life in the world."[20] She sketched her life plan for herself and Charles: "I hope dear Charles that we shall hereafter compare notes upon it when we have both tried it & found it as happy or nearly as happy as we expect."[21] She imagined herself a coconspirator in the religious life, as if life with a marriage partner in a parish setting was a greater adventure than world travel. As she told Darwin: "In looking forward to it myself & thinking of its advantages I feel more anxious that you should finish all your wanderings by settling down as a clergyman but it must be as a really good active religious clergyman (you know you gave me leave to preach) in that only can the happiness consist."[22] She adhered to such a high standard for clerical life that, "If I did not think Mr. Langton would be all that, I think I would rather he were any thing but a clergyman."[23] Comparing the clergyman's life to Charles's trip Charlotte attempted to link the two ventures but privileged the life of a parish minister—provided Darwin could find a good parson's wife. But Charles would have to leave behind his worldly pursuits to obtain this more worthy prize. She told him, "I am sure that in one respect being going to be married is very like going on a voyage round the world—it makes one love all one's friends more than ever."[24] Would he not prefer a parish, with a good wife, surrounded by friends rather than live aimlessly after his return?

At one point, Darwin lamented the prospect of missing out on the parson's life. His flirtatious trysts with Fanny Owen before the voyage had crashed on the shoals of her decision to marry while Darwin was still away at sea. Hearing the news, he cried, "by the fates, at this pace I have no chance for the parsonage."[25] Later, Fanny held out the hope that after Darwin was "cured of your *roving* turn," he would "settle quietly with the *little Wife* in the *little Parsonage*!!"[26] But Darwin's world was no longer so little. In fact, he would find in his *Beagle* voyage far greater benefits than the "feeling of security" that his sisters, relations, and acquaintances so earnestly sought for him. He had come to see that he was ill-suited to the narrow world of the country cleric, a claustrophobic existence captured so starkly in George Eliot's *Scenes of Clerical Life* (1858).[27] Eliot (Mary Ann Evans) portrays snobbish parishioners caught up in a Web of cheap gossip, even as their beleaguered preachers falter under the weight of failed personal hopes and dreams. In one of her "scenes," Rev Amos Barton naively took into his home the freeloading Countess Czerlaski, earning him the scorn of suspicious townsfolk. Only when Barton's wife Milly died in childbirth did he gain the sympathy of his "flock," as they together learned to read "that terrible handwriting of human destiny, illness and death."[28] Writing in the late 1880s, T. E. Kepple took stock of the changing lifestyle of the country parson. He identified the period from 1828 to 1833, Darwin's last years at Cambridge and the first of his voyage, as the time of a titanic shift in the idea of the parson. Darwin would have been schooled in the old ways, fitted with "a very broad-skirted black tail coat . . . a black single-breasted waistcoat, black knee-breeches, shoes, and gaiters."[29] As pillars of the village system, the parson and squire would preside over the parish's farmers and laborers as if they were lords of a small empire. The Church, before the social quake, was settled and confident—keeping Catholics in their place and holding Dissenters at bay. Making the cottage rounds, the parson would dispense neighborly advice about crops and hunting. In this era prior to modernist "spiritual warfare," the country parson would assuage doubts with timeless theological chestnuts.[30] As the world moved away from this vision of the parson's life, Darwin would have been left out of step at his return. With the repeal of laws that for so long limited Catholic and Dissenter participation in public life, as well as the establishment of the new Poor Law of 1834 that disrupted the settled relations between parsons and peasants, Darwin returned to a changing political and religious landscape. Finding themselves in competition with other Christian churches, country parsons came to fear their ecclesial rivals and grew weary making themselves appear relevant to disaffected locals. As railways replaced stage-coaches and farm machines displaced field laborers, so too the country parson of Darwin's student days was ill-suited for the brave new world dawning in the mid-1830s. Darwin was, however, not destined for this career path. His younger sister Catherine noted the shift in Darwin's career direction midway through the *Beagle* voyage. She wrote, "I cannot help being rather grieved when you speak so rapturously of the Tropics, as I am afraid it is a still stronger sign, how very long it will be, before we shall have you again, and I have great fears how far you will stand the quiet clerical life you used to say you would return to."[31] Eventually Darwin would find a quiet family life in the countryside, but it would be a life of science and not a clerical career. Still, as we shall see, this environment would bring no relief from the religion question. He would learn, however, how to tackle those questions on his own terms.

Darwin's own doubts about the clerical life began to percolate many years before at Cambridge. He later recalled that midway through his studies he could not honestly take Holy Orders because he did not feel "inwardly moved by the Holy Spirit."[32] Yet the correspondence from his student days paints an ambiguous picture. As late as 1830, he expressed an earnest desire to read divinity with John Stevens Henslow "the summer after next," which would have been the summer before the *Beagle* voyage. Pangs about the workings of the Holy Spirit had not turned Darwin into a freethinker or atheist. We find him fretting over whether or not his mentor Henslow might have "some curious religious opinions." He asks Fox, "I never perceived anything of it. Have you?"[33] When the *Beagle* was in Buenos Aires, Darwin and Robert

Hamond sought out Holy Communion before heading out to Tierra del Fuego.[34] Had the prospect of a world voyage not presented itself, Darwin may well have become a country cleric who continued mulling over theological verities for the rest of his life. What we should not overlook, however, is that the abandonment of a clerical career did not mean the abandonment of interest in religious questions.

Darwin's wrestling over his future career path took on a markedly changed tone in August 1835, late in the *Beagle* voyage, just one month before the trip to the Galapagos Islands. Darwin confessed to his second cousin William Darwin Fox, "This voyage is terribly long."[35] Now that the end was in sight, he was anxious about his plans for life after the voyage: "I dare hardly look forward to the future, for I do not know what will become of me."[36] Certainly the clergyman's life had its attractions and he says as much to Fox: "Your situation is above envy; I do not even venture to frame such happy visions— To a person fit to take the office, the life of a Clergyman is a type of all that is respectable & happy: & if he is a Naturalist . . ., ave Maria; I do not know what to say."[37] Many of the ordained had combined the clergyman's life with an itinerant career in natural science, puttering with plants or collecting fossils. Indeed, he would find himself urging Fox to become a first-rate "naturalist": "it is a **shame** that you are not so **now**. recollect that Sir—."[38] But by the end of his voyage, Darwin could not imagine a part-time commitment to the sciences nor a full-time career in the Church.

Not that everyone in the family was convinced that ministerial life was best for Darwin. He earned his brother Erasmus's stinging rebuke at all this talk of a ministry career. Tempting Charles with a life back in England split between science experiments and smoking all day, Erasmus pooh-poohed the clerical career.[39] "I am sorry," he snarled, "to see in your last letter that you still look forward to the horrid little parsonage in the desert. I was beginning to hope I should have you set up in London in lodgings somewhere near the British Museum or some other learned place."[40] "My only chance," he added sarcastically, "is the Established Church being abolished."[41] Yet nothing so catastrophic would be required to alter Darwin's career plans, inasmuch as he was already experiencing the gradual collapse of any orthodox Christian commitment in his own life. While not as extreme in his views as his brother, nonetheless as his journey ended, Charles could not easily imagine a life that combined his family's dream of the parsonage with his own growing desire to make his way in the world of science. Other naturalists might be country parsons, but Darwin could not conflate the two.

By the end of the trip, family members were well aware of Charles's shifting career intentions, even if Darwin's mind was not entirely settled. Susan Darwin, his elder sister by six years who styled herself "Granny," coupled her prediction of the "future prospect of distinguishing yourself in Geology" with her "fear there are but small hopes of your still going into the Church."[42] Her fears about his church career were well-founded. Yet she was right to surmise that he would make his mark in science. What she could never have imagined was that Darwin would eventually challenge the substance of Christian teaching through his science. She charted out a future in academia instead: "I think you must turn Professor at Cambridge & marry a Miss Jenner if there is one to be had.—"[43] Darwin's "Miss Jenner" turned out to be Emma Wedgwood.

A painful void

Though their courtship was brief and their wedding came fairly quickly, enough time elapsed for Darwin's religious doubts to raise troubling conversations between the two. The courtship lasted a scant three days, taking place in July, 1838 at Maer.[44] But the Wedgwoods and the Darwins had been long intertwined and the cousins' engagement, while not inevitable, was not out of the ordinary. The formal marriage proposal came in November, 1838, just two months after his breakthrough reading of Malthus (a work that we shall consider in the next chapter). The following January brought a flurry of activity with a move to 12 Upper Gower Street in London (the so-called Macaw Cottage dubbed so for its "gaudy" walls and furniture), Darwin's election as a Fellow of the Royal Society, and his marriage to Emma on January 29, 1839, at Maer Church.[45] "It is very like a marriage of Miss Austen's, can I say more?," exuded Georgina Tollet to Emma about the sudden surprise and speed of her marriage to Darwin.[46] When the marriage was just over a week away, Darwin wrote Emma about his hopes for a life beyond the *"brute"* existence of the *Beagle*.[47] "I think you will humanize me," he told her, "& soon you will teach me there is greater happiness, than building theories, & accumulating facts in silence and solitude."[48] From that time onward, Darwin's life would be split between science and family.[49] As he told Emma soon after the engagement, she need not bother to read Lyell's *Principles of Geology* "for depend upon it you will hereafter have plenty of geology." For Darwin, the scholarly flurry reached its peak in the summer of 1839 with the publication of his *Journal of Researches* based on his voyage, a work issued in multiple editions under different titles.[50] The personal side of things was capped by the birth of the blue-eyed baby with the "harmless" nose, William Erasmus Darwin, on December 27, 1839.[51] In documenting the expressions and behavior of this boy nicknamed Hoddy-Doddy, Darwin even found ways to blend science and family life.[52] Needless to say, the years

1837 to 1841 were a time of transition and new directions. They were also years of great theological doubt and redirected seeking for Charles Darwin. It was a struggle and a search that now had a marital dimension.

Before his marriage, Darwin fretted about the limitations of family life. He feared such obligations would cut into his travel time. His dreams of trips to America and France would surely go up in smoke. Likewise, he feared his scientific activity would be severely curtailed. No reading time in the evenings, no money for books, no trips to the clubs to chat with "clever men," no "Freedom to go where one liked," no scientific experiments, in short no great achievements.[53] The terrors of marriage mounted in his mind. Financially strapped by hungry children and a quarrelsome wife, he imagined that life in London would become terribly difficult. Perhaps he would have to end up as a professor at Cambridge just to make ends meet. The alternative—country life—looked more likely but was even more troublesome. A kind of "hibernating," thought Darwin.[54] He still was not ready to abandon the hustle and bustle of life in London with its scientific gatherings and gentlemen's clubs like the Athenaeum. By contrast, marriage seemed like slavery. "You will be worse than a negro," he told himself.[55] For all that, marriage had its advantages. He found that a "constant companion" was an asset. A wife would serve as an "object to be beloved & played with."[56] "Better than a dog," he humorously confessed.[57] There would be "someone to take care of house" and offer "female chit-chat."[58] Certainly there would be "Children—(if it Please God)."[59] The temptations of marital bliss flitted through Darwin's mind. "Only picture to yourself a nice soft wife on a sofa with good fire, & books & music perhaps."[60] Marriage certainly looked far more appealing to Darwin than the "dingy reality" of his digs at Great Marlborough Street just off Carnaby Street where he lived before his marriage. Overall, Darwin was won over by the obvious benefits of marriage. "There is many a happy slave," he mused.[61] So, his marital calculus finally concluded, "Marry- Mar[r]y-Marry Q.E.D." With "it being proved necessary to Marry," the only question that remained was "When? Soon or Late?"[62]

Darwin's doubts about marriage were far easier to resolve than his private qualms about religion. Not content to hide his theological views from Emma as his father had counseled, Darwin's courtship and marriage brought to the surface his theological dilemmas.[63] His skepticism worried Emma, both as bride-to-be and newly wedded wife. She was well established in the Church of England. Darwin's biographer Janet Browne tells us that Emma and her sisters "ran a Church of England Sunday school for local children, distributed food and basic medicines to villagers, and made useful items for charity bazaars."[64] Emma, as her daughter Henrietta remembered, "was not only sincerely religious—this she always was in the true sense of the word—but definite in her beliefs."[65] She regularly attended church services and partook of the sacrament, taught her children "a simple Unitarian Creed," and had them baptized and confirmed in the Anglican Church.[66] Her son Frank would later recall his "unwilling" attendance at church, finding some relief in the fact that the family attended the shorter evening worship service.[67] At St. Mary the Virgin Church in Down, Kent, where the Darwins took up residence in 1842, the family "had a large pew, lined with green baize, close beneath the clergyman's desk, and so near the clerk that we got the full flavour of his tremendous amens."[68] Young Frank distracted himself by playing with his boot threads, plucking them as if they were "miniature harp-strings." Emma, given her Unitarian background, directed the children to turn away from the altar when the congregation recited the Trinitarian Creed. Inasmuch as the Darwins were neither Low Church nor particularly anti-Rome, Frank later commented that it was rather pointless to "sternly" stare the congregants in the eye over theological nit-picking.[69] Emma's piety went so far as making lists of rules for how to keep Sunday sacred, "whether she might rightly embroider, knit, or play patience."[70] For a time, she insisted on holding a family prayer ceremony at home on Sundays, only to abandon the practice when she found that "the servants took no especial interest in it."[71] The children, Frank recalled, were all glad "when, on rainy Sundays, we escaped church altogether." In later years, she lamented to Henrietta that she felt her faith was "less vivid than it had been in her youth," nonetheless works of charity toward those in need "gave her rest, peace and happiness."[72] Late in life, this kindness extended to the animal world as she campaigned vigorously for more humane animal traps to replace the "cruel steel trap in common use."[73]

Darwin's correspondence with Emma during the period of their engagement affords a most moving and poignant expression of doubt and of the desire for faith. Emma pressed the issue because she valued a marriage built on shared religious sentiments: "When I am with you I think all melancholy thoughts keep out of my head but since you are gone some sad thoughts have forced themselves in."[74] Her sadness was rooted in her "fear that our opinions on the most important subject should differ widely."[75] She did not want to appear "foolish" but she felt compelled to address the issue openly because "my own dear Charley we now do belong to each other & I cannot help being open with you."[76] Like a doctor announcing a difficult diagnosis, she named the problem: "My reason tells me that honest & conscientious doubts cannot be a sin, but I feel it would be a painful void between us."[77]

Since, for Emma, doubt about God was an affair of the heart, she skillfully probed more deeply out of concern that he might not be completely candid about his views: "I thank you from my heart for your openness with me & I should dread the feeling that you were concealing your opinions from the fear of giving me pain."[78] The antidote she offered to this disease of doubt was the thirteenth chapter of the Gospel of John—the "part of the New Testament I love best"—namely Jesus's farewell discourse to his disciples regarding the promise of God's love.[79] Love casts out doubt. Her heart told her so. She did not seek an intellectual discussion on this point. As she said, "I don't wish you to give me your opinion about it."[80] She wanted him to take her prescription to heart. Her "whim" was to have him read Jesus's discourse. She indicated that this would give her "great pleasure, though I can hardly tell why."[81] That pleasure would be enhanced, one presumes, if only he would embrace the Gospel's teaching and overcome his inner religious turmoil. Shortly thereafter he replied to her letter, having read this Gospel passage, although unfortunately his response is now lost. Yet his reading clearly set Emma at ease, at least for a time, and she thanked him "for complying with my fancy." "To see you in earnest on the subject," she told him, "will be my greatest comfort & that I am sure you are." He seems to have indicated that he would treat these religious discussions with seriousness. For the moment, they had reached an understanding. "I believe I agree with every word you say," she added, "& it pleased me that you sh^d have felt inclined to enter a little more on the subject."[82]

Soon after their wedding, however, her concern over her husband's doubts surfaced once again. She returned to these worries in a letter that Darwin later termed "her beautiful letter to me."[83] Her counsel came now not as an apprehensive fiancée but as a supportive wife. Her missive is perceptive, thoroughly respectful of his need to be an independent thinker. She recognized that he was immersed in "the most interesting subjects & thoughts of the most absorbing kind."[84] But this absorption, she pressed, may have caused him to overlook the full scope of the questions he was considering, namely the religious implications of his views. She worried that his brother Erasmus's agnosticism may have rubbed off, serving "to have taken off some of the dread & fear which the feeling of doubting first gives."[85] Though she admitted that there was a kind of superstitiousness in her reaction, she nonetheless was concerned that the scientific approach might not be adequate for handling religious questions: "May not the habit in scientific pursuits of believing nothing till it is proved, influence your mind too much in other things which cannot be proved in the same way, & which if true are likely to be above our comprehension."[86] Emma raised a difficult issue. If religious truth was indeed a different sort of truth, then science's very method would short-circuit the search for that truth. The stakes were high if his doubt destroyed faith, for the consequences in her mind were eternal. Who could not help but be pained to hear her distress when she agonized, "I should be most unhappy if I thought we did not belong to each other forever."[87] No doubt Emma's deep sense of loss at the far too young death of her sister Fanny a few years previous—a painful time when she redoubled her commitment to God—was an event that no doubt increased her anxiousness over her husband's religious doubts.[88] Darwin's response to Emma's letter tells us less about his intellectual struggle than of the personal toll her fears created. At the end of her letter he penned these simple words, "When I am dead, know that many times, I have kissed & cryed over this."[89] His insistence on rational scientific investigation was a source of discomfort to his wife despite her respect for his candor in "conscientiously & sincerely wishing, & trying to learn the truth." Although she saw in his dedication to the truth a source of encouragement, she summed up the source of her unease: "There are some reasons that force themselves upon me & prevent my being always able to give myself to this comfort."[90]

In an earlier letter, written on the eve of their marriage, Emma held out an olive branch: "I do hope that though our opinions may not agree upon all points of religion we may sympathize a good deal in our *feelings* on the subject."[91] Perhaps that is all either of them could expect, given the age in which they lived and his intellectual trajectory. In many ways, it seems that Darwin did find that suitable wife his sisters had so earnestly desired for him, but Emma was more than a cleric's companion. She was an intelligent partner who could stand beside him on the road of doubt, despite the challenges his thinking would ever after raise for her. Fortunately, they were not alone in that struggle. Rev Charles Langton, the husband of Emma's sister Charlotte, had his own "crisis of doubt," which, as Emma's daughter Henrietta Litchfield explained, meant that "he could not conscientiously continue in the Church."[92] In the fall of 1842, Langton and Charlotte returned to live at Maer Hall, the Wedgwood family estate, where they cared for Emma's ailing mother Bessy. In Darwin's family circle, the home provided the needed cushion against the blows of religious doubt.

For Darwin, the struggle over such momentous questions remained at that time a private affair tempered by Emma's presence. There were evenings spent listening to her piano music, reading novels out loud, playing games of whist and backgammon—Darwin held the edge with 2,795 wins to Emma's 2,490 in 1875—billiards, and at least for a time, attending church together.[93] On occasion she would join him on his journeys to scientific meetings, though her tastes were not always his. During one lecture at the British Association for the Advancement of Science, Darwin said to her, "I am afraid this is very wearisome to you." She replied, "Not more than all the rest."[94] It was his sensitivity to her feelings and her "comfort to him"—not religion as such— that kept them together through his illnesses and life's challenges. Emma appreciated her husband's openness, an affection which she told her aunt Jessie was "not like the rest of the Darwins, who will not say how they really are."[95]

FitzRoy and the flood

Darwin certainly distrusted overblown religious enthusiasm. He wrote to his sister Caroline, now married to Josiah Wedgwood III, "Thank Katty [referring to his sister Catherine] for her very amusing letter.—it is wonderful how Marlborough St [Darwin's London residence at the time] & Shrewsbury [the Darwin family home] agree in thinking good sound sense about the nonsense of all the spiritual-minded people who believe they live in a world of spirits."[96] His religious restraint surfaced on the occasion of the birth of William Darwin Fox's son. Fox, a second cousin to Darwin, sought him out to be the godfather of his child. Darwin resisted, explaining that he and his wife did not have godparents for their own children since, "We both disliked the statement of believing anything for another."[97] If nothing else, Darwin was a person of great integrity, perhaps doubly so in this case because of his closeness to his cousin Fox and since he knew Fox's "deep feelings on religion."[98] His integrity and critical mind led him far from the Biblicism of many of his contemporaries, including the Captain of H. M. S. *Beagle*.

Could the Bible be believed as it stands? Many natural theologians, among whom one may number Darwin's Cambridge mentors, found ways to reinterpret Genesis in light of new scientific and historical discoveries while still retaining their belief in the God of the Bible.[99] Darwin and Caroline were aware of these perspectives and we find them playing the game as well. Their banter about the Bible included Charles's sniping comment to his sister that "You will be amused with FitzRoy's Deluge Chapter."[100] After the *Beagle* voyage, Capt. FitzRoy was holding up the Bible to be "the Record of truth" concerning the world's creation and Noah's Flood.[101]

Like Darwin, FitzRoy once had his doubts about the Bible. "I suffered much anxiety in former years," he wrote, "from a disposition to doubt, if not disbelieve, the inspired History written by Moses."[102] What once seemed "mythological or fabulous" became for FitzRoy a book of capital importance for the reconstruction of the earth's geological past as confirmed by the *Beagle* voyage.[103] He wrote of his change of heart about the Bible, he said, for the benefit of "young persons of my own profession"—perhaps he had in mind conversations with Darwin—who were being misled by Bible-denying modern geological theories such as those propounded by Charles Lyell. Lyell did not believe that the fossil record and the earth's strata offered proof of a global flood as related in Genesis, electing instead to argue "that the earth is in a continual though gradual state of change."[104] Against Lyell, the geological picture painted by the Bible, according to FitzRoy, was of a world created in six days, not over successive epochs.[105] And just as the Bible declares, the entire earth suffered a great catastrophe that left its mark in the shell beds of Patagonia and Concepcion.[106] Part miracle and part result of secondary causes, the biblical Flood which seems so vast to us was nothing on God's cosmic scale. FitzRoy observed that if the earth were reduced to a sixteen-inch diameter globe, the Flood was hardly more than the "thickness of ordinary drawing paper," merely a "coat of varnish."[107] Miracles abound in FitzRoy's depiction of the great Flood. God assembled a "heterogenous mixture of animals," which, were it not for the divine intervention that tamed them for the voyage on board Noah's Ark, might easily have killed each other.[108] Against those who thought this additional miracle unlikely, FitzRoy contended, "He who made, could surely manage."[109] Curiously, FitzRoy claimed that God did not include the dinosaurs. They were among the "few that quitted the ark."[110] God inexplicably could not manage that circumstance. After many pages devoted to a discussion of the density of the flood water, the sinking of creatures into layers that reflected their specific gravities, and the vast tides unleashed by the "war of elements," FitzRoy brought the Ark to rest on a "mountain of middle height" because the higher mountains would have frozen at their tops. Post flood the animals migrated "till they reached places suited to them," thereby explaining why "we find no kangaroos in Europe."[111] This shaken world continued to be rocked by "volcanic eruptions and earthquakes" until the earth achieved its present form.[112] Modern geology took up where the Bible left off: "Such changes are said to be going on even now, though on a small scale (Lyell, Darwin, &c.)."[113] Thus, FitzRoy made the case for a scriptural geology, written to "warn" young men "against assenting hastily to new theories."[114] Freethinkers were put on notice.

Needless to say, Lyell and Darwin were amused and appalled at FitzRoy's remarks about the Flood. Darwin told Caroline, "Lyell, who was here to-day, has just read it, & he says it beats all the other nonsense he has ever read on the subject."[115] Charles Lyell's harsh rebuke of FitzRoy came as no surprise. He embraced a "uniformitarian" view of geologic history that rested on long-term mechanistic processes churning away in the earth, not miracles or biblical floods. Lyell once quipped in jest to Darwin that his *Beagle* discoveries were made on that "new continent, which was heaved up, *à un seul jet* ['with a single surge'], Anno mundi 1656," a mocking reference to the commonly held date for Noah's flood after the creation of the world in 4004 B.C.[116] Like Lyell, Darwin came to see the geological data from the Beagle voyage in an entirely different light. His growing distance from FitzRoy's brand of literalism put him in an awkward spot. As he told Caroline, "Although I owe very much to Fitz R[oy,] I, for many reasons, am anxious to avoid seeing much of him." He felt equally awkward about FitzRoy's wife, confessing, "I called, the other day, on Mrs. Fitz Roy & paid her rather a long call—She was looking thin but very gracious—rather too patronizing but then this cannot be wondered at from so very beautiful & religious a lady."[117] Intellectually and socially, by the fall of 1839, Darwin's thinking had moved far away from Capt. FitzRoy's literalism.

Both Caroline and her brother Charles had taken up the theories FitzRoy feared most. When she, elsewhere, casually broached the topic of the impact of modern geology on scriptural interpretation, she readily trumpeted the more progressive view of the text: "I thought that Lyell & all modern Geologists disbelieved, or thought we did not understand rightly, the chronology of the Old Testament—so I do not see how what Sir J. Herschel says is new."[118] Sir John Herschel (1792–1871), the noted astronomer, had observed that the period of time required for the Chinese, Hebrew, Delaware Indian, and Malesass (Madagascar) languages to diverge from their common parent must have been much greater than the 6,000 years spoken of in Genesis, since "we see what amount of change 2000 years has been able to produce in the languages of Greece & Italy or 1000 in those of Germany France & Spain." Merging linguistic history with the Bible, Herschel explained, "we must not impugn the Scripture Chronology, but we *must* interpret it in accordance with *whatever* shall appear on fair enquiry to be the *truth* for there cannot be two truths."[119]

Conclusion

As they haggled over the subtleties of this debate, both Caroline and Charles were walking on the productive side of doubt in search of a reasoned faith. Sifting the Bible in light of modern science and history expanded the scope of biblical and religious truth. The guiding principle here, as Herschel so aptly stated, was that truth must be one. If the Bible was true, it had to be in agreement with the best ideas of modern science. In his reply, Darwin revealed that he was quite conversant with these more progressive interpretations. He spoke about Herschel's new way of understanding Old Testament chronology, namely that the "six thousand odd years" commonly thought to date man's creation was far short of the number of years suggested by other records such as those of the Chinese.[120] Doubt and questioning led to a new religious truth. It was a lesson that Darwin was beginning to take to heart. For him, there was no returning to the Bible for scientific knowledge. With this revelation, the door stood open for him to seek a naturalistic explanation behind the rise and function of religion. For this side of the story, we now turn to Darwin's secret notebooks.

Did Religion Evolve?: The Search for a Theory

"Till the Renaissance," writes Darwin's niece Julia Wedgwood, "Nature had been the invading, disturbing influence in Creation; she is now enthroned as Creator."[1] For medieval Christians the focus was on God in Heaven. With the European Renaissance and Enlightenment, the tables were turned. The English poet Alexander Pope (1688–1744) summed up the spirit of the age when he wrote, "The proper study of mankind is man." The Enlightenment cast aside the biblical God to focus on celestial mechanics, fossil ages, natural law, and human economy. Even before Pope's day, the chief question, said Sir Thomas Browne in his *Religio Medici* (1642), was whether "Nature is the art of God"?[2] Darwin embraced Browne's maxim that "Natura nihil agit frustra ["nature does nothing in vain"] is the only indisputable axiom in Philosophy." Reading *Religio Medici*, Darwin may have felt an affinity for Browne, who also labored in secret as he puzzled over the existence of God and the workings of nature, risking the charge of atheism.[3] He may also have been impressed by Browne's loose attachment to religious dogma and his deep commitment to follow "the dictates of my own reason."[4] As Browne uncovered "many things, untouched, unimagined, wherein the liberty of an honest reason may play," so too did Charles Darwin clear fresh pathways in his notebooks where he allowed his scientific imagination to run free.[5] Yet where Browne thought it devilish to explain the Bible's miracles naturalistically, Darwin sought to unlock the natural workings of all things—even religion.

The rough-and-tumble character of Darwin's private notebooks, written in 1837–1840, permits us to peer over the shoulder of an intellectual giant as he teased out the secrets of life's laws of development and religion's fundamental ground. Darwin considered this one of the "most active" periods of his life.[6] As he put to paper his first musings on evolution—with all his quirky spellings, awkward grammar, and racing conjectures—his thought took him far from the sterile landscape of biblical literalism into theological and philosophic terra incognita. Sequestering himself from public view, he confronted the complexities of species development, nature's reproductive pleasures, the world's suffering, and the workings of the moral and religious sense.[7] He sketched programmatic views regarding the function of ethics and the place of religion in the scheme of things. The suspicions about the multilayered character of religion that were stirred by his world voyage became the fodder for new thinking about human religiosity. Let us consider now Darwin's secret search for a theory to explain religion's rise and function, beginning with his thoughts about the "Religion Instinct."

The religion instinct

After initially settling at Cambridge upon his return and then in March, 1837, moving to London to reside on Great Marlborough Street, Darwin began to take stock of all the data he collected. It was in July of 1837, he later recalled, that "I opened my first note-book for facts in relation to the Origin of Species."[8] The month before, 18-year-old Victoria had ascended the throne. Darwin and England were on the cusp of a new age. As his notebooks unfolded, he moved beyond geology, botany, and the animal world to search for a theory that could help him make sense of the human religious diversity he encountered on his *Beagle* voyage. As he did so, the workings of the religion instinct came into focus.

Darwin's interest in the possible evolution of religion was hardly an afterthought, despite the fact that metaphysics and morals are taken up after geology and the transmutation question in the notebooks. What most scholars overlook is the fact that Darwin was already at work on the question of human religiosity in his *Beagle* volume, which he readied for publication between January and September of 1837.[9] What we see in Notebooks M and N is the *continuation* of his interest in religion. Darwin was well along the way in his search of a credible *theory* to explain the rise and function of religion and ethics, just as he had been at work struggling to find a theory for the transmutation of life forms. The human dimension of evolution was already on the table in Notebook B from late 1837: "Each species changes. does it progress. Man gains ideas. the simplest cannot help.—becoming more complicated,; & if we look to first origin there must be progress."[10] The possibility of cultural evolution—the evolution of ideas—is certainly in Darwin's calculations.

Likewise, the common descent of man and primates was on the table: "If all men were dead then monkeys make men.—Men make angels—."[11]During the spring of 1838, he argued in Notebook C against the view that humans were separable from the rest of the animal world. Man, he said, was "not a deity" and formed "no exception."[12] He added, "how dredfully we are deceived" when in fact the human form "possesses some of the same general instincts, < as > & < moral > feelings as animals."[13] He urged his imaginary interlocutor to observe the orangutan's "expressive whine, see its intelligence when spoken; as if it understood every word said— see its affection.— to those it knows.— see its passion & rage, sulkiness, & very extreme of despair."[14] How could anyone continue to claim that humans stood apart from the rest of the animal kingdom? To drive home his point, he invoked his memory of the Fuegian savages who left such a deep impression on his voyage: " << let him look at savage, roasting his parent, naked, artless, not improving yet improvable >> and then let him dare to boast of his proud preeminence." The continuum was clear, marked by gradations from the higher mammals and savages to civilized humans. There were no breaks in the developmental line from animals to humans and between human groups.

The later notebooks M and N deepen this theoretical trajectory by focusing on the animalistic and savage roots of morality and religion. Thus, while working on his third notebook on the transmutation of species during the summer of 1838 (Notebook D), Darwin was also reading books on "Metaphysical subjects" (Notebook M) and in September of 1838 reported: "*All September* read a good deal on many subject; thought much upon religion."[15] This was the very month that he read the book that would put teeth into his theorizing about species, Malthus's *An Essay on the Principle of Population*. The Fall saw more of the same with further notebooks on transmutation (Notebook E) and continued discussion of the "metaphysics" of morals (Notebook N), the latter work running from October of 1838 until the spring of 1840. With notebooks M and N, Darwin took a more serious look at the perplexities regarding religion and morals raised by his global voyage.

From his first glimpses of natural selection and his first diagram of the tree of life to his more serious musings about the moral and religious implications of evolution, the questions ran fast and furious in his notebooks.[16] What is it that makes us human? Is the world designed for us? Is there a Creator who instills our lives with a greater purpose? Natural theology, the belief that nature's design gave evidence of a divine designer, was under interrogation everywhere in these notebooks. As John Hedley Brooke explains, "Darwin was experimenting with his own variant of natural theology which was decidedly more positive than a mere negation of Paley."[17] Spiriting us away from sacred scripture and miracles, however, Darwin tweaked Alexander Pope's maxim to claim that the proper study of mankind was the ape and the dog: "He who understands baboon < will > would do more towards metaphysics than Locke [:] A dog *whines*, & so does man.— dogs laughs for joy, so does dog bark. (not shout) when opening his mouth in romps, < so > he smiles."[18] When it came to the question of religion, the notebooks vented Darwin's gnawing doubts about natural theology's miracles, revealing his increased interest in materialist explanations. If there was a God, this God was not a micromanager caught up in the day-to-day minutiae of creation. Rather, the universe ran on laws established by the Creator from the beginning, laws that accounted for the motion of the planets and the mechanics of life. But if so, whence religion?

Religion has a past

It is well known that when Darwin read the work of Robert Malthus on population pressure and the fierce competition for resources, he engaged a writer who helped him discern the mechanism of Natural Selection.[19] However, what most scholars do not notice is that just prior to his reading of Malthus, he ran across quite by accident another theorist who helped him understand the evolutionary rise and function of religion. Spending the day at the Athenaeum Club in London in August, 1838, a month before his momentous reading of Malthus, he read a substantial review article summarizing the work of the French positivist philosopher Auguste Comte (1798–1857) that left him with an "intense headache" but which caused him to "remember, & to think deeply" about religion.[20] Reading one of Charles Dickens's humorous "Sketches by Boz" cured the headache, but Comte's ideas wormed their way into Darwin's notebooks. This serendipitous discovery led Darwin to see that religion went through developmental stages. We might well argue that Darwin's curiosity about the evolution of religion and his reading of Comte paved the way for his reception of Malthus.

Darwin found in Comte's three-stage division of history a compelling account of the rise and development of religious belief, enabling him to place the "religion instinct" into a historical framework. The first stage—the age of theology—was the period when people imagined the world having been "first caused by will of Gods. << or God >> ."[21] This was a crude stage in which the "savage attribute thunder & lightening to Gods anger," a stage that gave rise to "the *theological* age of science in every nation."[22] Darwin characterized this primitive mentality as one with "more poetry in that state of mind."[23] Instead of thinking in terms of natural causes, the savage invoked God as the sole cause: "the Chileno says the mountains are as God made them."[24] The second stage advances toward "metaphysical abstractions."[25] In this phase, the mind seeks to tease out the principles by which the world operates while still "tracing facts to laws. without any attempt to know their nature."[26] In other words, the universe's mechanisms of operation are uncovered but they are still ascribed to the work of a Deity and not understood as natural processes in their own right: "Now it is not a little remarkable that the fixed laws of nature should be << universally >> thought to be the *will* of a superior being; whose natures can only be rudely traced out."[27] Nonetheless, although God is still invoked at this stage, the understanding of how nature works has taken a giant leap beyond the primitive conceptions of the savage's poetic mentality. In the third stage—the stage of science—the fixed laws of nature are seen to function on their own, operating apart from divine influence. In this phase, the practitioner of science perceives that our spiritual awareness, our capacity to reason, and our will to choose are functions of the material structures and history of the world.

The enduring bone of contention for Darwin, of course, was the deleterious legacy of stage two, a legacy that ensured that thoughtful religionists might obstruct scientific progress in the name of outmoded theological ideas. Darwin took inspiration from Charles Lyell who heralded scientific progress in the face of clerical sneering. Of Galileo, he wrote that his "sufferings in the cause of truth did not extinguish the spirit of the Inquisition, but gave a death-blow to its power, and set posterity free, at least from all open and avowed opposition, to enlarge the boundaries of the experimental sciences."[28] The progression from stage one to stage three was not a placid stream but turbulent rapids in which the tiny craft of scientific progress tumbled dangerously along the rocky outcrops of theological intransigence and primitive ignorance. Darwin looked to Lyell for guidance: "If I want some good passages against opposition of divines to progress of knowledge."[29]

Darwin understood that he was charting a new course through treacherous theological waters. The "savages" and the so-called "philosopher," he wrote, both "make the same mistake" when they say an "innate knowledge of creator < is ><< has been >> implanted in us (< by > ˀindividually or in race?) by a separate act of God."[30] He resisted the thought that in a one-time creative moment God injected theological ideas into our brains. If not from God, then how did religious belief arise in the first place? How can we not be struck, he asked, by the variation in divine ideas between the Greeks, whose views were "mystical but sublime," and those of the Australian savages or the tribes of Tierra del Fuego who were imprisoned by "wretched fears & strange superstitions"?[31] How could such divergent religious beliefs emerge among human cultures? Were different gods giving different messages to different peoples? Is the true God's message just not getting through? Or does religion branch out in the world like a an evolving species, taking different shapes according to cultural laws of Natural Selection?

Rather than a singular and static revelation from Heaven, Darwin explained the history of religious belief as a process of evolution and diffusion, making religion "a necessary integrant part of his most magnificent laws."[32]

He adds, " $<<$ it would be difficult to prove that $>>$ this innate idea of God in civilized nations has not been improved by culture."[33] If religion improves with age, this can only mean that the forces of history conspire to modify the idea of God. The history of religion, just like the speciation of animals and plants, has produced—by variation and selection—the diversity and progress in religious belief that has occurred down through the centuries. As Desmond and Moore observe, "It was a grand instinct, developed because of its social utility."[34]

Reading George Staunton's account of river rituals in China, Darwin gained an insight into the historical processes that took the obeisance originally given to kings and transformed these honors into the "cruel" sacrifices enjoyed by the gods.[35] Staunton had joined Britain's first diplomatic mission to China in 1792 and wrote about his experiences. He speculated on the origins of sacrifices to the gods. As royal subjects reflected on their dependent relation to their Sovereign, says Staunton, "it was inferred, that physical events were directed likewise by a personified being, however invisible, whose favours were to be gained, and protection granted, by the same means which were practised in the moral conduct of the world."[36] Staunton's speculations about the roots of religion left Darwin uncertain. He wondered, "Origin is certainly curious. Chinese, S. American. Polynesians, Jews, African all sacrifices. How completely men must have personified the deity."[37] Did the reverencing of belligerent kings serve as the launching point for the worship of blood-drinking gods? Darwin was unsure. Yet some such historical view was needed.

To explain the widespread character of religion, Darwin did not resort to metaphysical speculation or the Bible. Rather, he placed religion inside a historical process that stamped all human cultures, much as his tree of life branched around the planet yet joined all species at the root. But religion was more than a set of historical stages. This progression had psychological underpinnings. Having read the philosopher David Hume's *Dialogues Concerning Natural Religion* and *The Natural History of Religion*, he took note of Hume's view that modern religion developed from ancient polytheism.[38] But Darwin was also intrigued by Hume's suggestion that religion owed "its origin in Human mind."[39] As Hume explained, "the first ideas of religion arose, not from a contemplation of the works of nature, but from a concern with regards to the events of life, and from the incessant hopes and fears which actuate the human mind."[40] Hume's writings would have enabled Darwin to recognize two intertwined dimensions of religion's evolution, namely that religion has a staged developmental history (reinforcing a view gained from Comte) and that religion had an inner psychological core.[41] For Hume, religion developed historically from polytheism to monotheism, not the other way around, because the "mind rises gradually, from the inferior to the superior."[42] Since the ancient Greeks and Romans were polytheists just like the "savage" tribes in the Americas, Africa, and Asia, all the evidence suggested that monotheism was a secondary development.[43] As for the initial psychological prompting behind religious awareness, Hume argued that the hopes and fears sparked by the chaos of life caused people's imaginations to attribute human qualities to natural objects. In this way, the belief arose that a multitude of gods ruled every aspect of the material world. Psychologically, however, religion was a projection of the mind onto nature.[44] These twin dimensions of religion's development would be worked out more fully in Darwin's *Descent of Man* but already they find their place in Darwin's early theorizing about religion. When it came to a more psychological understanding of religion, in his notebooks he speculated that our idea of God was a spatial concept. We connect God with height, thinking he is "living in lofty regions."[45] There was also a strong emotional tone to belief in God. In particular, the chief emotions tied to God are "terror & wonderment."[46] Thus, the effect of our encounter with this "vast ocean" of size, time, and emotion was "an inward pride & glorying."[47] If there were "causes" behind this longing for the sublime, this experience did not derive from God but from the "vastness of Eternity" that wrenches human awareness.[48] Yet he did not oversimplify this longing for eternity, concurring with Steward that our sense of the sublime does not arise from a single cause.[49]

A universal longing?

Was this religious sensibility truly universal to humans? Darwin credited his relative Hensleigh Wedgwood with the statement "The love of the deity & thought of him << or eternity >> only difference between the mind of man & animals."[50] Darwin's travels told him otherwise. While western Europeans had been caught up in pietistic certitudes and lofty musings about the one true God, Darwin could not help but notice "how faint" such conceptions were to "a Fuegian or Australian!"[51] His global travels strongly suggested that there was no universal awareness of the Christian God, much less a universal rational speculative theology or philosophy regarding this Higher Power. The most that one could say was that there is a broad "gradation" of divine awareness across the human race. Darwin imagined the difficulties this gradation posed as God readied his creatures for the afterlife: "no greater difficulty for Deity to choose, when perfect enough for future state, that when good enough for Heaven or bad enough for Hell.—"[52]

Perhaps the better explanation was that this gradation signaled that these religious feelings had no divine source. The very existence of diverse ideas of the gods would seem to indicate they were a function of our evolving monkey minds. Was it not the case, Darwin asked, that we humans are given to the "wildest imagination & superstitions" when it comes to talk of the supernatural?[53] Would this fact not speak to our lack of connectedness to the divine, rather in favor of such a connection? Would such mental habits not more sensibly be seen to have their roots in our animalistic fears, rather than in a fear of a real God? Darwin was reminded of the Beagle voyage and "York's Minster story of storm of snow after his brothers murder."[54] The Fuegians provided Darwin insight into the ground layer—historically and psychologically—of religion's rise and development. The tribal mind was governed not by philosophic thoughts of a divine presence but by abject terror at the meteorological fierceness of the world. This was the ultimate source of our idea of God. Animalistic fears and passions, then, unite us as human beings. There is no universal monotheistic awareness that separates us from the animals. In the primitive state, humans were plagued by a swirl of fears and delusions, with only occasional rational musings when it came to supernatural matters. They were more like cowering dogs than heady Greek philosophers. Seen from its animalistic side, this awareness of the divine is faulty and mistaken. Yet it is an intelligible response to the hostile world in which primitives found themselves.

Fear alone, however, was not the only emotion grounding religion. God had long been associated with a heavenly abode in the sky. Perhaps the experience of "height" and "ascension" helped spark our image of the lofty God.[55] As we deepened this image, supernatural loftiness translated into other divine attributes such as "Infinity eternity. darkness, power."[56] The root of all religious feeling, then, was the product of a complex set of associations between height, terror, and wonder. Darwin was led to conclude: "It appears to me, that we may often trace the source of this 'inward glorying' to the greatness of an object itself or to the ideas excited & associated with it. as the idea of Deity. with vastness of Eternity. which superiority we transfer to ourselves in the same manner as we are acted on by sympathy."[57]

This oceanic feeling—our awareness of God—is a very human response to the cosmos: "A man shivers, from fear, sublimity, sexual ardour.—a man cries from grief, joy. & sublimity."[58] To be human is to know the sublime and wonder at its source—within ourselves. From this standpoint, Darwin upended received religious explanations for belief in God. He even turned the Lord's prayer inside out. The petition "deliver us from temptation" ought no longer to be said to God.[59] Rather, we should speak such words to ourselves to influence the shape of our bodily organization for good, so that humility and the improvement of the self might arise through a sense of the free will surging through our beings. We ought to marvel at the sublime within, not looking beyond our animal urges for the source of this overwhelming sensation.[60]

Belief and the brain

Having traced our religious instincts and yearnings back to their animalistic roots and emotive counterparts, the final step for Darwin was to put our idea of God onto a thoroughly materialist basis: "Thought (or desires more properly) being heredetary $<$) $>$.—it is difficult to imagine it anything but structure of brain heredetary,. analogy points out to this."[61] If, in other words, our desires are passed on, it makes sense to say that the brain's structure and resultant thinking processes are hereditary. Evolution has equipped us with a God instinct. Can it be that our idea of God is hereditary? Darwin's materialism forced the conclusion that the origin and transmission of the idea of God was simply a function of the brain's inheritance: "—love of the deity effect of organization."[62] To which Darwin added both furtively and a bit deliciously: "oh you Materialist!" Similarly, in the so-called "Old & Useless Notes," Darwin wrestled with the Bridgewater Treatise of creationist William Kirby. Kirby railed against the French naturalist Jean-Baptiste Lamarck who because of his developmentalist theories said that the human mind was not "a spiritual substance derived from heaven."[63] However, Darwin found himself in the Lamarckian developmentalist camp, arguing that our physical makeup and habits were the natural ground of our God instinct. Animals exhibited the same fears that ultimately gave rise to religion, in their case the "fear of man."[64] Since such behaviors and responses were inherited, they were clearly a function of the "organization of brain."[65] These mental states and behaviors were "produced as soon as brain developed," confirming their material basis.[66] The key in the case of both animals and humans was for Darwin to demonstrate that soul was not "superadded."[67] Of course, he was well aware that he was challenging a central tenet of religious belief regarding the human soul. Yet he was puzzled why such an objection should be lodged against him. "Why," asked Darwin, "is thought being a secretion of brain, more wonderful than gravity a property of matter?" For one reason only: "It is our arrogance, it our admiration of ourselves.—"[68] Darwin anticipated the religious arguments against his views. Although many conservative Christians in his day made allowances in the Bible for an ancient earth and extinct fossil creatures, they were unable to accept purely mechanical and animalistic explanations for human nature. Christians, who liked to think of humans as a little lower than angels, would no doubt bristle at the thought that they were little higher than the apes.

Darwin's biology of belief carried profound implications. According to him, we should not grant "religious feelings" a different status than other feelings. If feelings in general are somehow functions of the brain, nothing differentiates religious feelings from all the rest of our emotions and urges: "It is an argument for materialism. that cold water brings on suddenly in head, a frame of mind, analogous to those feelings. which may be considered as truly spiritual.—"[69] In this case, the sensations some might call religious are in fact feelings that have a concrete cause that is identifiable. As a consequence, such feelings are not accorded the status of special knowledge into God's creative workings in the universe. Darwin drew the reasonable conclusion that our God instinct was a function of our brains. For all this, he did not claim to have completely undermined religious belief. When it came to the ultimate truth value of religion, his views were not fully formed at this time. Against the claims of the creationist Kirby, Darwin denied the charge of full-fledged unbelief: "This Materialism does not tend to Atheism."[70] Even Kirby had to acknowledge that Lamarck's developmentalism still allowed room for a Deity. To expose the material side of religion was not to deny the validity of religious belief entirely. As this section of his notebooks falls away into fragments about "steps towards some final end" and a "reward in good life," it is apparent Darwin had not yet sorted out the God question despite the bold way his materialist thesis sought to explain religious feelings.[71] Thirty years on from John Dalton's *A New System of Chemical Philosophy* (1810), which pulled back the veil on the atomic character of the elements, Darwin was still compelled to say, "What is matter? The whole a mystery.—"[72] Science, at least at this juncture for Darwin, had to acknowledge its limits. Perhaps there was a God and perhaps this material process was how belief in that God came to be. The jury was still out.

Ethics without God

Throughout this period, despite great strides, Darwin struggled to find a purely natural explanation for our higher faculties, what he called the "inutility of so high a mind without further end."[73] Were humans without any purpose? In natural theology, the search for final causes or ends focused on identifying the overarching reason God had created humans. Our purpose for existing rested above and beyond any purely material causes or natural processes that were at work in the world or which may have been employed by the Creator to fashion his creatures. Everything existed to serve higher ends, especially for humans to live for God. But Darwin was led to wonder if indeed we were the *"one* great object, for which the world was brought into present state"?[74] Certainly, the natural theologians had no explanation for the "purpose" of all the lost fossil epochs. Was God stumbling by trial and error in his creative activity before succeeding in making humans? If the moon was uninhabited and so much of geological history left us out of the picture, Darwin came to think it was impossible to keep humans at the center of the story. With undirected evolution, all this sort of thinking comes to an abrupt halt: "Progressive development gives final cause for enormous periods anterior to Man."[75] No additional "purpose" beyond Natural Selection was needed to justify or explain the existence of life's many forms. By removing both God and humans from the means and the goal of creation, Darwin identified the ongoing evolutionary process itself as the only "end" that governed life. The mechanism of natural selection alone gave "meaning" to life's patterning, nothing more. Yet the ethical question remained palpable. How was one to live morally in the evolutionary world that Darwin was creating? Could there be a zoological basis for ethics?

Traveling by carriage back to his family home in Shrewsbury in April, 1840, Darwin found himself riding with a collection of religious relics. There was the old gentleman with the "portentously purple nose" intently reading the *Christian Herald*. Next to him was "the primmest she-Quaker I have ever seen."[76] Also stuffed in the carriage was an indomitably "loud" woman with her "pious" companion. The boisterous woman intoned on the subject of prayer, telling to all within the reach of her voice how she always held household prayers at 10:30 in the evening so as "not to keep the servants up." She insisted that her friend not write her letters on Sundays. The friend submitted most solemnly, "Yes, Eliza, I will write on Saturday night or on Monday morning." Then, says Darwin, "our virtuous female" took out a religious tract which she proceeded to read to the group, marking the best bits with a "thick lead-pencil." "Was not I in good company?" he asked Emma. Harboring much more radical ideas about God, Darwin held his tongue. "I never opened my mouth," he told Emma, "and therefore enjoyed my journey." Keeping his religious opinions to himself proved a valuable strategy throughout Darwin's lifetime; doubly so when it came to the question of ethics and morality. As Darwin's secret notebooks sparked a rethinking of nature's design, fanning the flames of skepticism toward natural theology, he steadied himself to light the powder keg that would explode traditional religious ideas about human morality. The far-reaching power of Darwin's theory of life can be seen in the compelling way he constructs a biologically centered ethic. Notebooks M, N, and the so-called "Old and Useless Notes" provide clues to Darwin's alternative biological moral vision.[77] He charted this new ground for ethics in reflective dialogue with natural theologians (Abercrombie, Bell, Browne, Brougham, Fleming, Kirby, MacCulloch, Paley, Spence, and Wells) and other writers such as the social critic Harriett Martineau and the political historian James Mackintosh.[78] It was a vision that would have given his pious carriage companions a collective heart attack.

The starting point for Darwin's evolutionary ethic was the fact that what we label free will and choice, just like the religion instinct, owe as much to our bodily constitutions as they do to anything else. "The common remark that fat men are good natured, & vice versa," he reflected, implies a belief that bodily "organization & mind" are connected.[79] Darwin briefly entertained the phrenology craze: "One is tempted to believe phrenologists are right about habitual exercise of the mind, altering form of head, & thus these qualities become heredetary."[80] At first glance, this reshaping of one's head by exercising mental powers under the direction of a phrenologist might just look like evidence for the power of free will, but Darwin was careful to tie this activity back to an exercise of the appetites.[81] In a continual loop, the mind and appetites answer to a deeper law: "Shake ten thousand grains of sand together & one will be uppermost:—so in thoughts, one will rise according to law."[82] However much "free will" bubbles to the surface of the mind, the body's machinery feeds on "circumstances & education, & by the choice which at that time organization gave me to will."[83] We say we are free to choose, but our bodies call the ethical shots. By making bodily constitution and physical circumstance fundamental to moral action, Darwin modernized the old biblical notion of sin's taint: "Verily the faults of the fathers, corporeal and bodily are visited upon the children.—"[84] For Darwin, this was a "predestinarian" doctrine of a "new kind."[85] Law-like processes govern moral action. No divine foresight or set of commands propels us through life's maze of moral perplexities. We dance to a higher moral law, one instilled in our bodies, not a legal code such as the Ten Commandments.

Ultimately, we answer to the law of pleasure. Darwin defined "the good" in these terms: "I am tempted to say that those actions which have been found necessary for long generation, (as friendship to fellow animals in social animals) are those which are good & consequently give pleasure."[86] Pleasure as such, though, is not our sole guide, for pleasure can be seen and valued from radically different vantage points: the child, the peasant, the philosopher, and the baboon. As with so much else in Darwin's system, variation has its role to play in the realm of pleasure. The "healthy child," in Darwin's estimation, "is << more >> entirely happy."[87] Peasants know both pleasures and pains, but, since they are caught up in daily toil, they are the ones "whom sensual enjoyments of the minute make large < parts > portion of daily < happines > << pleasure >> ."[88] At the level of immediate sensual experience, the happiness of the "peasant" would seem to be a function of the "contingency of good food, no pain."[89] But there is a deeper or more substantive pleasure that tips the balance in favor of the intellectual and moral life, namely the pleasure of conscience. Such happiness arises when "thoughts are most pleasant. When the conscience tells our good has been done."[90] These pleasures are so deep and significant that life's moral fundamental imperative presents itself through them: "Therefore do these & be happy— & these pleasures are so very great, that every one who has tested them, will think the sum total of happiness greater. even if mixed with some pain."[91] Darwin credited the "well << regulated >> philosopher" with the better lot in life due to "a much more intense happiness."[92] In this connection, he wrestled with whether we should focus on happiness as the "object of living" or concern ourselves to "obey literally New Testament future life" as the "sole object" and for that reason to "mortify" ourselves.[93] At some level, Darwin thought that when it came to a choice between present happiness and the Bible's focus on the afterlife, "The two rules come very near each other."[94] However, he had his doubts about the utility of mortification. For some, he wondered if "*believing* it [mortification] to be true, & *then acting* on it, will add to happiness.—"[95] Yet he hesitated, "I doubt whether the last be right."[96] Better to pursue the pleasures that are given by Nature and philosophy than the potentially false afterlife promises tendered by the New Testament.

Darwin certainly recognized that not all instincts were conducive to happiness. The "instincts" for "revenge << & anger >>" threatened to destroy the person who succumbed to them. To be happy, he counseled, we must learn to check these instincts despite their past evolutionary value: "with lesser instinct they might be necessary & no doubt were preservative, & are now, like other structures slowly vanishing."[97] These powerful yet destructive primordial tendencies have gradually been giving way to more civilized sensibilities. We stand, however, between epochs. From our modern moral high ground, we can discern our origins in a jungle of emotions: "Our descent, then, is the origin of our evil passions!!"[98] We can understand our darker character as humans as we unearth the animalistic side of our moral machinery: "The Devil under form of Baboon is our grandfather!"[99] Without the interposition of a refined intellect, we might continue to be prisoners of animalistic passions and suffer from their tyranny. The way out, according to Darwin, was to cultivate conscience: "A man, who perfectly obeys his conscience or instinct, would probably feel but little that of anger or revenge."[100] Perfection on the road to happiness might be beyond our reach, so Darwin opted for juggling "degrees of happiness."[101] Our choice in life may not be "*Entire happiness*" so much as "*intense* happiness even with some pain."[102]

Downplaying free will and accenting the biological drive, Darwin came to believe that crime and moral turpitude were the unfortunate by-products of human evolution. In the past, Christianity explained bad behavior by the inner flaw of original sin, a flaw that generated crimes that deserved divine punishment. However, Christian tradition also held people responsible for their choices despite this unavoidable inner flaw. The contradiction between original sin and free will created something of a theological and moral muddle. Darwin, however, claimed we were simply victims of an inner biological turmoil that prompted us to do things outside our control. Where religionists would use threats of eternal punishment and promises of heavenly reward to shape behavior, Darwin, while not entirely excluding the idea of the afterlife, did not think that "reward or retribution" of the eternal sort could effectively reshape human behavior. "These views," he claimed, "are directly opposed & inexplicable if we suppose that the sins of a man, are under his control, & that a future life is a reward or retribution.—it may be a consequence but nothing further."[103] The alternative? Darwin issued his moral prescription for his immoral patient, "One must view a wicked man, like a sickly one."[104] We ought not to treat biologically flawed actors as sinners who deserve punishment. "We cannot help loathing a diseased offensive object," observes Darwin, but we must learn to regard a person's moral failings as lapses that result from a troubled psyche. He suggests profoundly different regimen for sin: "it would however be more proper to pity than to hate."[105]

What happens to the old ground for ethics, namely the foundations of morality in a divine metaphysics? Darwin summarily banished God and philosophy from the realm of evolutionary moral discourse. Concerning God, he simply reduced the concept: "Notion of deity effect of reason acting on (< not social instinct >) but a *causation*. & << perhaps >> an instinct of conscience, feeling in his heart those rules, which he will to give his child.—"[106] God was a projection of the inner life of moral reason, the crystallization of the rules we wished to hand on to posterity. As for philosophic speculation, Darwin also brought metaphysics back down from its Platonic pedestal: "To study Metaphysic, as they have always been studied appears to me to be like puzzling at Astronomy without Mechanics."[107] In order to understand the human moral sense, we must take stock of its biological moorings, if we hope to make genuine progress in theology or moral philosophy. Abstract speculation about ethics severed from morality's biological roots invariably distorts one's view of human nature. By making biology central to a discussion of ethics, Darwin refused to get lost in philosophic speculation about moral systems apart from their physical embodiment in the human person.

In reflecting on deep biological instincts, social pressures, and emotive passions, Darwin's evolutionary ethic ultimately looked to the faculty of conscience for guidance. Conscience draws on reason and memory to mold the sense of *ought* that governs moral action. At the center of our moral life resides conscience: "Conscience is one of these instinctive feelings"[108] But conscience is a many-layered organ with deep neural pathways: "I believe that certain feelings & actions are implanted in us."[109] Implanted by nature, not by God. Between the inner biological workings of human nature and the surface "feeling of right & wrong," Darwin recognized the connective tissues of pain and pleasure. These fibers carry the impulses to act, while the pleasure or pain which results tell us if our actions are right or wrong. As he observed, "doing them gives pleasure & being prevented uneasiness."[110] In the Darwinian view, moral action is not guided by abstract principles or divine commands but inner biological feelings that operate in tandem with the moral sense regulator we call "conscience."[111] Any other view of ethics stuck Darwin as so much "rigmarole."[112]

Acting for others

If conscience is in the driver's seat, sympathy is the fuel propelling Darwin's evolutionary ethic. Whether we think of dogs or humans, nature has built into its creatures the pleasure that comes from aiding others. For the dog, "we see a struggle between its appetite, or love of exercise & its love of its puppies: the latter generally soon conquers, & the dog probably thinks no more of it."[113] Humans, too, know such other-directed pleasures as well as the forgetfulness of assisting, defending, and acting for others: "Therefore in man we should expect that acts of benevolence towards fellow < living > creatures, or of kindness to wife and children would give him pleasure, without any regard to his own interest."[114] Indeed, if such outer-directed care is thwarted, Darwin surmised, pain ensued in the form of anger or remorse. All creatures, in other words, are outer-directed in their orientation based on their inner biological endowment. The difference between other animals and humans rests in this: Where animals act out of passion and instinct, humans must rely on memory and their ability to reflect on their choices. We possess, in other words, a potentially more refined altruistic awareness. Where a Spaniel guards a house due to its trained instincts and where young children are governed by passions, the adult who has attained the "power (reason) obtained by age" learns how to select from among the instincts to be guided by a sense of "*ought*." [115]

Humans in their maturity, in other words, know how to "follow certain lines of conduct, < although > even when tempted not to do so, by other natural appetites."[116] What is the "rule" here? How do we know which path to follow? For Darwin, the guiding moral rule was that "the passions & appetites should << almost >> always be sacrificed to the instincts."[117] The deepest instincts for Darwin were conscience and filial attachment, the latter representing the sort of other-directed action already found in a dog's care for its young: "Which as I hope to show is << probably >> the foundation of all that is most beautiful in the moral sentiments of the animated beings."[118] Darwin's speculation about canine behavior opened a window into the complexities of human moral action. What if a dog were to "hesitate to jump to save his masters life"? If the dog "meditated on this, it would be conscience." Such hesitation was more rudimentary, but it was the animalistic base on which the superstructure of human conscience has been built. Humans complexify this hesitation: "A man, might not < to > do so even to save a friend, or wife.—yet he would ever repent, & wished he had lost his life in doing so."[119] In our struggle to make moral choices, as in so much else in life, Darwin imagined a battleground. Dogs and humans were warriors on the moral battlefield of animalistic passions. Hesitation, conscience, remorse, and sympathy all play a role in that conflict. Yet in this battle one virtue stood out for Darwin. In his evolutionary scheme, the common good was to be the goal of moral action. From Plato onward, moral reflection had been one long discussion of "the good." Darwin gave "the good" a biological spin. The highest aim for Darwin was the "general good" and it would seem we exhibit such conduct because it has become "instinctive."[120] Natural selection has fitted us to be the purveyors of the common good.

As with religion, Darwin did wonder to what extent the moral sense was shared across all groups. He was well aware that Harriett Martineau's *How to Observe: Morals and Manners* "argues << with examples >> very justly there is no universal moral sense."[121] Yet he came to think otherwise because of James Mackintosh's *On the Progress of Ethical Philosophy*. Mackintosh, a relative of Darwin by marriage to the sister-in-law of Emma's father, took a different tack by arguing that all tribes display at the very least some "faint perception of a difference between right and wrong."[122] Putting these two views together, Darwin argued that "the conscience varies in different races" much as dogs have different instincts. Yet inasmuch as even Martineau allowed "*some* universal feelings of right & wrong," he could imagine that conscience was "firmly fixed" in a general way inside everyone.[123] What Martineau found to be universal were the social instincts that were so crucial to Darwin's theory. Thus even she was forced to admit that "charity is found everywhere."[124] However, Darwin still had his lingering doubts about the

Fuegians, who were said to devour their old women in times of famine rather than eat their dogs.[125] Yet in some strange way, he realized that the Fuegians showed a measure of charity toward their animals. Conscience, however rudimentary, was at the heart of what it means to be human. Of that Darwin was certain.

Darwin's zoological morality may have fallen short of the absolutism of the Ten Commandments, but his was a robust vision nonetheless.[126] However much he departed from the religious beliefs and ethical systems of his mentors and contemporaries, it is fair to say that his twin interests in the mechanics of life and the roots of ethics addressed the key concerns of natural theology, namely the question of nature's creative design and the moral character of God. Darwin, however, stepped outside this theological frame by offering a naturalistic account of both the evolution of life and the rise of the religious and moral sense. Even as he turned the tables on natural theology's view of creation, he also put religion and ethics on a compelling biological footing. Eventually, he would make public his views on the evolution of religion and morality. To this unveiling, we now turn.

The Golden Rule: An Evolutionary Vision of Religion and Morality

Darwin knew from as early as 1837 or 1838 that he "could not avoid the belief that man must come under the same law."[1] He even alluded to this fact in his *Origin of Species*, saying that "Light will be thrown on the origin of man and his history."[2] Darwin added these words so that "no honourable man should accuse me of concealing my views."[3] But, as he explained to Fritz Müller in 1867, having been "taunted with concealing my opinions," Darwin steeled himself to come clean "on the origin of Mankind."[4] As the 1870s dawned, Darwin presented the world a provocative understanding of the evolution of the Golden Rule, bringing together science and religion in unexpected and illuminating ways.

Darwin's delay in publishing on the human side of evolution left him open to misunderstanding. When translator Clémence Royer tackled Darwin's text, she used the preface to the French version of the *Origin of Species* to trumpet a veritable revolution in human society based on Darwin's ideas.[5] Fuming to Asa Gray about Royer, Darwin suggested she "must be one of the cleverest & oddest women in Europe."[6] He complained that she was an "ardent Deist & hates Christianity, & declares that natural selection & the struggle for life will explain all morality, nature of man, politicks &c &c!!!"[7] At that moment, he was not ready to declare his own views on the human implications of evolution. A decade after publishing his *Origin of Species*, Darwin finally went public with this side of the evolution question. When his response appeared in the form of *The Descent of Man, and Selection in Relation to Sex* (1871), he argued that evolutionary theory not only accounted for man's ape-like form but could also be used to explain the rise and function of religion and the moral sense. Apparently, Royer had been right after all.

There are many ways to read Darwin's *Descent of Man*. It is certainly a "wonderful period-piece of Victorian upper-middle-class male scientific rationalizing about human nature, sex and civilization, and how the socio-economic world works."[8] Indeed, the *Edinburgh Review* reported, "In the drawing room it is competing with the last new novel, and in the study it is troubling alike the man of science, the moralist, and the theologian. On every side it is raising a storm of mingled wrath, wonder, and admiration."[9] But when it came to the question of the evolution of religion and morality, Darwin's *Descent of Man* also served as a remarkable contribution to the then raging debates over the very nature and function of religion. Darwin used the anthropological and sociological discussions of the day to frame his own *Beagle* observations about religion, thereby completing his revolution of ideas. If his *Origin of Species* marked a turning point in our understanding of the forms of life, then his *Descent of Man* signaled an advance in our understanding of ethics and the workings of religion. Darwin dealt special creationism a mortal blow in his *Origin of Species*, putting many religionists on the defensive. His *Descent of Man* served as creationism's obituary. Yet this was not the end of religion for Darwin. In fact, religion and morality were now placed on a zoological basis to stand at the very heart of the human evolutionary journey.

Darwin's wife was anxious over the theological impact of the book, telling her daughter Henrietta who was helping to edit the work, "I think it will be very interesting, but that I shall dislike it very much as again putting God further off."[10] Darwin seemed to confirm his wife's misgivings when he wrote to his old *Beagle* shipmate Lieutenant B. J. Sulivan, "I shall this autumn publish another book partly on Man, which I dare say many will decry as very wicked."[11] On the other hand, he told his daughter Henrietta, "I fear parts are too like a Sermon: who w^d ever have thought that I sh.^{d} turn parson?"[12] The *Descent of Man* was Darwin's sermon on an evolutionary view of religion and morality.

Of baboons and brandy

Darwin's first move in his *Descent of Man* was to apply the lessons of his *Origin of Species* to the human species by showing that the human physical structure had evolved and was not created by an instantaneous miracle. Defending his view that the human form descended from a common ancestor with apes and other mammals, Darwin marshaled "three great classes of facts" from his *Origin of Species* and applied them to the human form.[13]

In the first place, he pointed to homologous structures that signaled animal roots for humans. Humans shared brain structures with the orangutan and suffered diseases similar to those that beset monkeys because of kindred tissues and blood types. Humans shared with primates the same processes of reproduction and systems for healing. Humans even had the same taste for tea, coffee, tobacco, and alcohol. As proof, Darwin noted that people in Africa would commonly set out beer to catch baboons. Apes that drank alcohol were known to suffer hangovers. He also told the story of one monkey who decided to give up on brandy, thereby making this monkey "wiser than many men."[14]

As a second line of evidence, Darwin pointed to embryonic development. Human embryos start off looking like those of any other vertebrate, diverging from apes only at a late stage. The fact that human embryos shared traits with lower animals and other mammals suggested their common ancestry. Darwin found it significant, for example, that the human brain at seven months resembled that of a baboon.[15] He endorsed Huxley's judgment that "the mode of origin and the early stages of the development of man are identical with those of the animals immediately below him in the scale: without a doubt in these respects, he is far nearer to apes, than the apes are to the dog."[16]

But the strongest line of evidence was found in all those rudimentary parts humans carry about in their bodies. Such structures and organs were at one time functional in human ancestors but have since fallen into disuse. Head muscles, once truly useful, now evoke strange looks, as in the case of the man who won bets by pitching heavy books off his head merely by twitching his powerful scalp muscles.[17] As pointed out to Darwin by the sculptor Woolner, human ears still carry that odd "little blunt point" on the upper side of the inner rim, a relic of former bat-like ears.[18] While currently our sense of smell lags far behind that of other animals, Darwin doubted that our ancestors were always so poorly equipped. The hair on our bodies was likewise merely a pale reflection of once vibrant fur. Human wisdom teeth have become so useless that Darwin reported that it had become quite the fashion in the United States to remove children's back molars. Of course, the clearest signal of our animal roots—our tailbones—serve as a telling reminder of long-ago primate days.

These three groups of facts—homologies, embryos, and rudimentary parts—were sufficient in Darwin's mind to overturn the separate creation view. Regarding homologies, for example, he says, "On any other view the similarity of pattern between the hand of a man or monkey, the foot of a horse, the flipper of a seal, the wing of a bat, & c., is utterly inexplicable."[19] Countering the natural theologians, Darwin put his foot down by insisting, "It is no scientific explanation to assert that they have all been formed on the same ideal plan."[20] While Biblicists were content to imagine that humans were created intact in a single instant and that larger-than-life heroes were our forbearers, Darwin argued that it was the height of "arrogance" to trace our lineage to "demi-gods."[21] All these lines of thought led to one conclusion, said Darwin, namely that we are intimately tied to the animal kingdom by common descent from ape-like ancestors. Unless we are prepared to say God has trumped up this evidence as a "snare laid to entrap our judgment," then we are forced to conclude that the belief in the separate creation of the human species was quite mistaken.[22] Darwin anticipated the day when people would be astonished to learn that naturalists had ever believed in separate creationism.

Having dispensed with the special creation of the human form in a matter of a few pages, Darwin was ready to upend the common view of religion and the moral sense. His colleagues, such as Lyell and Wallace, had raised doubts about the evolution of human intellectual capacities by pointing to the gap between humans and other animals in this regard, so Darwin decided it was time to defend the force and scope of his natural selection view by outlining a theory of the evolution of religion and ethics.[23]

Monkey minds and God

Having long taught that man was created in the image of God, Christian theologians insisted this endowment signified that humans were unique among God's creatures in their mental capacity and abilities. Darwin acknowledged the challenge these differences raised for his theory. A separate mental structure for humans would cause his theory of common descent to break down.

Was the human intellect fundamentally different than that of apes and other animals? No, says Darwin. When it comes to our emotional life, humans are excited by the same feelings as animals. Terror sparks the same gut-level response in humans and other creatures. Horses are just as ill-tempered and sulky as we are. Monkeys seek revenge. Dogs display love for their masters. Baboons have been known to adopt and affectionately care for young monkeys. Animals play together like little children and monkeys delight in teasing dogs. Even complex emotions like jealousy and shame are found in dogs. The range and quality of these emotions suggest that human emotions have their animal roots. Darwin would investigate further many of these matters in a separate volume, *The Expression of the Emotions in Man and Animals* (1872).

Intellect, too, has its animalistic counterparts. Dogs and monkeys know excitement and boredom. Many animals exhibit wonder and curiosity. Monkeys are "ridiculous mockers," great imitators of behavior.[24] Cats display tremendous powers of attention, patiently waiting for their prey to pop out of a hole. Baboons can recognize people after many months. Ants remember their fellows after several weeks. Who could doubt that the dreams of dogs, cats, horses, and even birds signal the presence of an active imagination? Even human reason, the supposed "summit" of the mind, was found wherever animals deliberate and resolve to take action. Monkeys learn from their experience, especially after touching sharp tools, cracking eggs, or getting stung by a wasp hidden in paper.[25]

Whether one considered the emotions or the intellect, the building blocks of the human mind can be found in the animal kingdom. So why did some religious believers insist on erecting an "impassable barrier" between animals and humans?[26] Archbishop Sumner and the Duke of Argyll claimed that only humans made progress in knowledge. But Darwin knew that chimps and baboons learned and passed on their knowledge of tools for cracking nuts, constructing levers, and making weapons.

Nor could language be seen as an exclusively human preserve. All the components of language can be found in nature in the form of dog barks, ape gestures, bird songs, or monkey cries of danger. Humans may be unique in affixing definite meanings to specific sounds, said Darwin, but the inarticulate cries of many creatures signal fear, pain, surprise, and anger. Language was no divine insertion into the heads of humans. Rather, brain damage revealed that language was purely a function of the brain's anatomy. Once up and running, languages evolve by means of struggle, natural selection, and extinction. Darwin's vision was far removed from the Bible's story of the Tower of Babel, where the world's languages were said to have resulted from God's confusion of human speech as a result of divine wrath.

What about those higher levels of consciousness? Darwin reminded his readers that dogs show self-awareness. As for a sense of beauty, Darwin pointed to female birds who admire male plumage and mating songs, suggesting that humans were not alone in enjoying these delights. Having heard the "hideous music" of savages on his world travels, Darwin exclaimed that many birds exhibited a better taste in music![27]

Neither do the mental underpinnings of religion escape animalistic roots. Darwin asked whether the savage's awareness of "unseen or spiritual agencies," often thought to animate the natural world, shared some counterpart in animal consciousness.[28] He admitted that a dog's dreaming was not the same as humans ascribing unseen spiritual powers to nature, inasmuch as the latter human activity required a complex triangulation of imagination, curiosity, and reason, but he suggested that when a dog mistakenly growls at a parasol that has been stirred by a breeze, we can glimpse the very process by which human progenitors ascribed spiritual agency to the unseen hand of nature. The Fuegian belief that Nature employs rain and snow as retributive forces was not too far from the dog's misplaced growl. Again, Darwin admitted that religious feeling was more complex, insofar as this sense joined together love, submission, and dependence, but the ground of religious belief could be found in a dog's devotion to its master, even if the trappings of religion required higher intellectual processes. In Darwin's mind, there was a clear series of gradations running from a dog's groveling to the human obedience to an unseen God. From an animalistic and savage perspective, the "same mental faculties" have led humans along the evolutionary path from a vague belief in "spiritual agencies" toward "fetishism, polytheism, and ultimately in monotheism."[29] Religion, in other words, has evolved in stages and complexity from animalistic fears and perceptions.

But Darwin needed more than anecdotes from his travels and tales about the animals from his estate to substantiate his ideas, so he turned to anthropologists and sociologists for confirmation of his views.[30] From them he learned three things, namely that belief in God was not innate to the human race, that the religious sense was prompted by still more fundamental human experiences, and that the psyche played a key role in shaping human religious awareness. Let us consider these elements in turn.

Regarding the non-universality of religious views, Darwin drew on the Rev Frederic William Farrar for proof that belief in God was hardly innate. Farrar's *An Essay on the Origin of Language* came to Darwin's attention in 1865, after which they were in occasional correspondence. It was Farrar who was later instrumental in securing Darwin's burial in Westminster Abbey.[31] In thinking about the evolution of religion, Darwin took note of Farrar's essay "On the Universality of Belief in God, and in a Future State." In this presentation before the Anthropological Society of London in April, 1864, Farrar asked those present whether or not they had evidence to prove or deny a universal belief in God.[32] He then proceeded in his own paper to cite reports from travelers to all parts of the world who indicated quite clearly that such a belief appeared to be far from universal. The aboriginal Australians were said to have "no idea of a superior Divinity" and showed "no trace of any religion." There were peoples in Africa who did not have in their language "*any word to use as the name, or to denote the being, of a God*—of any God." The Eskimo had "*no knowledge of a God.*" Residents of the Andaman Islands in the Bay of Bengal were said to have "no conception of a Cause, and are not even polytheists." Finally, the Vedda peoples in Ceylon (modern Sri Lanka) were reported to "have no religion of any kind,—*no knowledge of a God or of a future state;* no temples, idols, altars, prayers, or charms." Farrar's comments sparked a lively debate, with some arguing that travelers often misunderstood the religion and customs of their informants while others claimed that in fact even in England right under the church towers one could find people ignorant of religion. During the discussion period, Alfred Russel Wallace confirmed Farrar's views, saying that the tribal groups he had encountered in the Moluccan Islands and in New Guinea had no concept of a Creator of the universe. For Darwin, such evidence was terribly important, underscoring his own travel experience that suggested there was no universal belief in God.

If there was no innate belief in God, then one had to wonder how religion arose in the first place. For key considerations, Darwin looked to John McLennan, E. B. Tylor, and Herbert Spencer.[33] From the Scottish sociologist John Ferguson McLennan, he learned that primitive encounters with forces in nature gave rise to a belief in spirits.[34] In a series of articles on "The Worship of Animals and Plants" published in the *Fortnightly Review* (1869–1870), McLennan sought to characterize the "totem stage" of religion's evolution.[35] Drawing on reports from European travelers concerning the American Indians, Australian aborigines, and Pacific Islanders, he observed that tribes regularly bound themselves to animals and plants as protective spirits. These "totems" were either powers in nature (the tribe's favored animal, tree, or heavenly object) or they were the sacred relics associated with such powers. McLennan suspected that the first steps toward totemism occurred when primitives attempted to explain natural phenomena in familiar anthropomorphic terms. "This animation hypothesis," he claimed, "held as faith, is at the root of all the mythologies."[36] McLennan sketched, but did not develop, an evolutionary history for religion, treating the Fuegians as among the most primitive, followed by the Australian aborigine belief in spirits, and then the fuller animism of the American Indians. At the next higher level or phase, he placed the New Zealand tribes alongside the Greeks and Romans, followed by the more advanced "pantheism" of the Hindus which incorporated actual doctrines about cosmogony and ethics not found in earlier stages. Islam, likewise, was seen to be doctrinally more advanced but still carried remnants of earlier stages in the form of genii and amulets. The ground or origin of all these developments, McLennan argued, was the primitive tendency to ascribe humanlike qualities to animals, plants, and heavenly bodies. For Darwin, McLennan's analysis helped to confirm his own suspicion that a "belief in unseen or spiritual agencies" was the universal ground for religion's evolution.[37] Still, the question remained as to how these beliefs were generated in the first place.

From the anthropologist, E. B. Tylor, Darwin learned that the experience of dreams could also give rise to a belief in spirits.[38] In his classic *Researches into the Early History of Mankind and the Development of Civilization* (1865), Tylor explained that since primitives failed to separate their subjective experiences from objective sense data, they assumed that their dreams were the products of actual out-of-the body travels by their souls at night.[39] For Darwin, this observation helped to identify one of the earliest phases in religion's evolution. A belief in souls or spirits was key. Yet he added that until human reason, imagination, and curiosity developed sufficiently, dreams alone would not produce a belief in spirits "any more than in the case of a dog."[40] There must be other processes that explain the development of religion. The problem was how to isolate these elements.

The social philosopher Herbert Spencer offered a fairly complex scheme for the rise of religion. His essay on "The Origin of Animal Worship" (1870), written as a response to McLennan's essay, argued that "the rudimentary form of all religion is the propitiation of dead ancestors."[41] Spencer speculated that a primitive's experience of the body's shadow, reflections in water, dreams, fainting, epilepsy, and corpses suggested to them the existence of a spirit that lived on after death. Now, if the deceased bore some metaphorical name or nickname such as "Wolf" or "Star," over time their descendants would misapprehend the name and assume that their great ancestor was an actual wolf or star. The next step was for the community to imbue the living counterpart, in this case actual wolves and stars, with human qualities, thereby anthropomorphizing the natural world. The lack of abstract terms in most primitive languages, said Spencer, led naturally to this confusion. In other words, Fetishism (ascribing objects and agents in nature with human qualities) was a secondary step and not the origin of religion, which could be traced to a metaphorical mistake regarding deceased ancestors. As tribes mingled in ancient times, the number of metaphorical figures increased, resulting in the development of composite deities (half human and half animal). Polytheist mythology was only steps away. As Spencer saw it, this scheme "conforms to the general law of evolution: showing us how, out of one simple, vague, aboriginal form of belief, there have arisen by continuous differentiations, the many heterogeneous forms of belief which have existed and do exist."[42] Darwin could not have said it better. He found this essay "ingenious," but suggested, based on his own experience of tribal religion, that there was "a still earlier and ruder stage," namely that we must first ascribe life and mind to objects in nature when we see these objects display power and movement.[43] For Darwin, this initial intellectual projection, rather than assumptions about deceased bodies and talk of spirits, sparked the process that gradually produced the great religions of the world.[44]

There was also an emotive side to religion of which Darwin was well aware not only from his family relations but also from his experience of the sublime during his world travels. The sublime, he discovers, is the flip side of a more basic cosmic fear. Darwin, as we have seen, traced the roots of religion's emotions to a primordial layer of animalistic fears and behaviors inherited by humans from their evolutionary past. For this aspect, his anthropology and sociology research was not the best guide, so Darwin turned to mental philosophy.[45] In particular, he consulted legal historian and barrister Luke Owen Pike's essay "On the Psychical Elements of Religion," presented before the Anthropological Society of London in 1870.[46] "In their own frames, and in everything external to them," Pike stated, "there is something to remind human beings of their weakness."[47] Ultimately, argued Pike, religion is rooted in fear. "The proudest and the strongest, the bravest and the wisest," he observed, "are made to feel the humiliation of dependence, and that sense of dependence or of weakness is the foundation of all religion."[48] This pervasive fear operated in tandem with the projection of humanlike qualities onto the heavens or other natural objects.[49] As Pike observed, "the average human being has a dread of certain unknown powers because he likens them to himself."[50] This combination of fear and projections gave rise to a belief in deities who needed to be propitiated.[51] As Pike observed, "Through ram-worship and bull-worship, through sun-worship, and star-worship, through storm-worship and water-worship, through prayers to all the good gods, and bribes to all the bad gods, may be seen the worship of a magnified humanity."[52] Pike, thus, presented the fundamental starting point of all religion: "fear is the great emotional basis of all popular religions."[53] He had uncovered the key for constructing a history of religion, namely its psychological aspects. "Mythology and superstition," said Pike, "are the mirrors of mankind; they reflect all the knowledge, and all the feelings, and all the motives of the people to which they belong."[54] Pike's article on the emotive roots of religion helped to ground Darwin's view that there is an evolutionary link between human submission to the divine and a dog's obedience to its owner. The "feeling of religious devotion," Darwin wrote, finds its counterpart and precursor in an animalistic layer that is reflected in "the deep love of a dog for his master, associated with complete submission, some fear, and perhaps other feelings."[55] While Darwin acknowledged that the human religious sense was "highly complex," consisting as it did of a combination of love, fear, reverence, hope, gratitude, and submission, nevertheless he found the essential components of this sense already at work in animal emotions and behaviors.[56]

Implied in Darwin's use of this anthropological, sociological, and psychological research was the view that religion had a chronological development. In his notebooks, as we have seen, Darwin looked to the French sociologist Auguste Comte for such a historical perspective. Spencer, as noted above, also made a complicated attempt at such an analysis. However, for the chronological dimension, Darwin was particularly indebted to the studies of his colleague and friend John Lubbock. The oldest of eleven children in a prominent banking family, Lubbock had the good fortune to grow up in Darwin's neighborhood.[57] His father was something of an amateur astronomer who had become good friends with Darwin. The younger Lubbock was blessed having Darwin as his "informal tutor in natural history."[58] Lubbock was swept up into the scientific circles of his day. Among men of science, he made his mark in archeology, sorting out the tools used by paleolithic and neolithic peoples.[59] Applying Darwinian ideas to human cultural evolution, Lubbock believed that primitives provided clues to the primal stages of human development. His book, *The Origin of Civilization and the Primitive Condition of Man*, documented a theory of the evolution of religion in "three striking chapters" that greatly impacted Darwin.[60] Darwin's work on the *Descent of Man* was well underway by the time Lubbock's work came into his hands, leaving him to "groan" that he wished Lubbock had "published 4 or 5 months ago: I sh[d] have so profited & saved so much work."[61]

Lubbock's views on the evolution of religion helped bolster Darwin's case. Surveying the many "savage" cultures of the world, Lubbock detected evidence for the evolution of religion. He organized that evidence into a series of stages of development and adaptation that moves from the lowest religious practices to the higher conceptions of belief. The lowest stage was a kind of practical Atheism, where beliefs about religion were unformed and almost nonexistent. The prevalence of religious unknowing in so many primitive cultures suggested to Lubbock that religion was not universal or innate, a view shared by Darwin. At best, a "sensation of fear" was common.[62] This feeling, he said, was more like the attitude of a horse to its master or of a dog howling at the moon. For Lubbock, "atheism is the natural condition of the savage."[63] There were no deep religious theories or doctrines at work in the primitive mind. The dreams of savages appeared to be one root of religion, for they commonly believed that they exited their bodies at night. A person's shadow was another root, since shadows were regarded as a person's soul or life. At these lowest levels of religion, spirits, if they could be said to exist at all, were considered evil, bringing disease, eclipses, and other calamities. Although at death an individual's ghost might linger for a few days, there was "no hope beyond the grave."[64] At this lowest level, there were no forms of prayer, no ideas about creation, and no ceremonies or temples as places of worship. Of this stage, said Lubbock, the savage tribes looked more like "herds of wild swine, which run about according to their liking."[65] Speaking of the Indians of California, he wrote: "In one word, the Californians lived . . . as though they had been freethinkers and materialists."[66] Religion sprang from this ground of original Atheism.

The next step up the evolutionary ladder was Fetishism. A fetish was an object that could be used to catch the deity and coerce it to heed the fetish maker's demands. Any object was suitable for this purpose, whether a stone or stick, a cat or dog, and the like. If the fetish proved useless, it was either threatened or destroyed. Since Fetishism was more like an antireligion, additional steps were needed to arrive at higher views. A sophisticated development of Fetishism could lead, according to Lubbock, to Totemism.

In Totemism, the natural order came to be worshipped as a repository of spirits, both good and evil. Trees, stones, rivers, mountains, planets, animals, and plants were imbued with a divine aura. Indian totems, for example, included turtles, bears, and wolves. The serpent was also widely worshipped the world over. Other cases of what Lubbock deemed "zoolatry" included the Peruvian reverence of the llama and condor, the Tahitian adoration of the heron and woodpecker, and the Maori esteem for the spider. The latter believed that the souls of the dead ascended to heaven on gossamer threads, and so the natives were wary of breaking spider's webs.[67] At this stage, savages would apologize to the animals they killed during a hunt. This reverencing of nature was one factor that separated the lower and higher religions, said Lubbock, for the higher religions understood God to stand beyond nature in a supernatural realm.[68] Thus, tree-worship was widespread in the totemic phase, not because the practice had been passed down by "common origin" but because each group had to pass through this phase if it was to move to a higher level of religiosity.[69] At this stage, too, lakes, rivers, and springs served as objects of worship, as reflected even as late as the holy wells of Scotland. Likewise, stones were a focus, with columns dabbed in blood appearing as a regular feature. Lastly, fire was worshipped, and the need arose to maintain a perpetual fire within the tribe. The worship of heavenly bodies, as emblems of fire, was nothing more than an extension of totem worship, not a sign of a higher level of religiosity as some might imagine.

As each stage complexified through a process of development and adaptation, religion's deep roots gave rise to the next stage of Shamanism. Whereas in the lower religions the deities were localized in nature, for Shamanism the deities reposed in a heavenly realm to which the Shaman alone had direct access. Through shivering fits and trances, the deity entered the Shaman to address the tribe. While there was no system of theology in Shamanism, to Lubbock this stage marked the typical transit point to the higher religions among the world's tribes.

In the subsequent stage of Idolatry, religion centered on statues of gods that were cast in human form. Not to be confused with Fetishism, which used any natural object to attract the deity, Idolatry chiseled anthropomorphic images as an act of submission to a higher power. Lubbock suspected that Idolatry arose from two factors. In the first place, he said, Idolatry depended on the prior development of a monarchy. Idolatry also appeared to be connected to ancestor worship, where deceased individuals were elevated to the status of deities who needed to be fed and who could bestow favors. Fusing monarchy and ancestor worship together, kings, both living and dead, would function as the primary focus of these traditions. As the king's wealth increased, Lubbock speculated, the tribe learned to associate royal power with divine power and at his death they identified the deceased king with the gods. If a society went directly from Totemism to Idolatry without passing through the stage of Shamanism, reasoned Lubbock, then that religion would be dominated more by animal figures than would otherwise be the case.

Theological conceptions advanced as the stages proceeded. Initially, savages had no concept of the soul, but religious practitioners gradually arrived at a belief in "universal, independent, and endless" existence.[70] Thus, while "a very intelligent docile Australian black" regarded talk of immortality as nonsense, the Tongans treated their ruling chief as an immortal.[71] The Tongan conception represented an advance on Lubbock's scale. Nonetheless, the Tongan idea fell short inasmuch as the people continued to regard the realm of the dead as simply another region of the earth which could be reached by canoe if one only tried hard enough. Ideas of the afterlife remained vague at the lower levels of religion. The lower levels also lacked any idea of a Creator or of religion as the foundation of morality, these being the centerpieces of the higher religions.

Although he did not say so explicitly, it is clear that Lubbock regarded Christianity as a product of religion's evolution. He repeatedly placed the Old Testament with its ritual dance and sacrifices among the secondary levels of religion, totemic in its orientation and superstitions.[72] He specifically linked the story of the prophet Elijah calling fire down from heaven with a similar tribal tale of dancing in a frenzy to bring rain.[73] Nor did Lubbock imagine later Christian Europe to be free of the vestiges of the earlier levels. Stone worship was only denounced during the Middle Ages, while popular superstitions lingered on in Europe and "spirit-rappers and table-turners" were still at work in the late nineteenth century.[74] It was only with the advent of science, argued Lubbock, that "true religion" had become possible.[75] While some "narrow-minded" people regarded science as "hostile to religious truth," Lubbock said the fact was that science "is only opposed to religious error."[76] In the modern period, the truths of religion stand or fall in direct relation to emerging scientific knowledge. The religion of the future will be a religion sifted by science.

Darwin endorsed Lubbock's view of the evolution of religion. The march toward monotheism from its savage roots had its noble aspects, but he was bothered by the fact that human religious evolution included the "terrible to think of" ritual of human sacrifice to a "blood-loving god" as well as painful trials by ordeal and the practice of witchcraft.[77] Nonetheless, Darwin's animalistic and evolutionary assessment of religion was sweeping, as he traced both our noblest religious concepts and our most disturbing ritual practices back to their roots in the loves and fears of our primate progenitor and their savage heirs. It is good to reflect, says Darwin, on these roots, if only to appreciate the strides and benefits offered to us by science, reason, and the advance of human knowledge.[78]

Philosopher apes?

Yet no matter how many links Darwin might attempt to forge between humans and animals, the immense gulf between the human moral sense and the mentality of the rest of the animal kingdom looked to most religionists like a bedrock truth. Darwin found himself at odds with George Douglas Campbell, the Duke of Argyll, author of *The Reign of Law* and self-appointed guardian of his own version of creationist religious truth. This clash had its roots in the British Association meeting at Dundee (1867), where Lubbock laid out his theory of the savage origins of religion and morality, after which Campbell clubbed Lubbock with his *Primeval Man* (1868).[79] Darwin took up the cudgels against the Duke in his *Descent of Man*. Let us consider Argyll's argument and then turn to Darwin's rejoinder. This debate and Darwin's response helped clarify his position on the rise and function of morality, shaping the case he would make in the *Descent of Man*.

Earlier in the decade, Argyll tried to turn Darwin's book on orchids (1862) into proof for natural theology, arguing that the complex reproductive structures of orchids identified by Darwin, together with their relation to the pollinating actions of a moth's proboscis, reflected God's purposive arrangements in nature.[80] These intricate arrangements signaled divine design to Argyll, regardless of whether God used instantaneous creation or evolution to achieve this result. Here Argyll tried to commandeer Darwin's work for his own theological purposes.[81] Darwin was unimpressed at the time, telling Gray, "I do not see that it really removes any of the difficulties of Theology.—"[82] When he read the essay, Hooker accused Argyll of straining at a gnat and swallowing a camel for claiming that God performs "superhuman" works and not magical "supernatural" deeds.[83] He told Darwin that Argyll "had found the desiderated difference between *tweedledum* & *tweedledee*."

In his pithy volume *Primeval Man*, however, Argyll went on the offensive against both Lubbock and Darwin on human origins and the evolution of religion. He categorically denied the theory that primitive tribes offer us evidence of the earliest phases of human thought and religious practice. He attacked Lubbock and Darwin on three fronts, namely the how, when, and why of human origins. Argyll's first line of attack concerned the "how" of human origins. Could Darwin's view of creation by development alone account for the unique combination of the human body and mind? Despite our similarity to apes in form, Argyll believed the "chasm" between humans and the apes was not simply a matter of a few more cubic centimeters of skull size. Darwinian evolution, he argued, could not account for the miraculous leap in the human intellect.[84] Argyll's second line of attack examined the "when" of human origins. Here he says that the Book of Genesis, though correct to claim that the creation of humans was a "special act," did not give a clear date for the precise moment of creation.[85] While the life of Abraham was fixed at 2000 B.C., the Bible was unconcerned with many races in China and elsewhere that were known to be very ancient. Unless blacks constituted a separate creation as a pre-Adamite race, the Bible's doctrine of the unity of mankind led to the belief that human origins must be quite ancient. Regardless of how ancient man is, he argued, the evolution of the human species from apes was ruled out by the sharp geologic breaks in the fossil record. These breaks clearly demarcated a succession of creations and total destructions. Humans did not arise from more primitive life forms. With the creation of man, the cycles of God's creative activity were now complete. Though the date of man's creation was obscure, the fossil record supported the Bible's view that humans were the last of God's unique and separate creations.[86] Argyll's third line of attack concerned the "why" or ultimate purpose driving the creation of humans, especially with regard to their mental and moral capacities. While Lubbock and Darwin thought humans arose from "utter barbarism," Argyll believed quite the opposite. History told us, he said, that humans regularly fell into decline, corruption, and decay.[87] Far from rising from a savage state to high civilization, Argyll claimed we were created from the start as intellectually capable and morally conscious persons who through migration and warfare lapsed into barbarism. Argyll argued that Lubbock and Darwin should not use the "outcasts of the human family" as evidence for the upward progress of humankind's development.[88] Humans did not start off as cannibals, but fell from great heights into such ignorance and corrupt practices. The Tasmanians didn't walk on water to Tasmania, they lost the art of making canoes. As for religion, he said, we did not start out in ignorance of God but lost that precious knowledge, much as the Hindus declined from the noble Vedas into their contemporary degraded customs and practices.

For Argyll, this combination punch of the "how," "when," and "why" landed a decisive blow against Darwinism. But Darwin had his own counter arguments to offer. He used his *Descent of Man,* in part, as a way to silence this formidable critic and establish the evolutionary foundations of morality. To some extent, Darwin had to agree with Argyll: the moral sense was the "most important" difference between humans and animals. Whether it was the capacity to do metaphysics or mathematics, Darwin agreed that the gap between humans and apes was "immense."[89] The question was, however, whether animals were entirely devoid of the rudiments of human moral sense.[90] On that score, Darwin discovered a multitude of connections. While many philosophers, such as Kant, had tried to tackle these questions philosophically through reasoned arguments, Darwin presented himself as the first person to adopt a natural history approach to human moral sense. He began by wondering "how far the study of the lower animals could throw light on one of the highest psychical faculties of man."[91] Animals, it turned out, displayed all the building blocks of human moral sense.

Darwin saw in animal social instincts the first steps toward human moral awareness. Many species, such as monkeys and birds, live together. They might post sentinels to warn each other of danger and in other ways aid each other. Benefits accrue as monkeys extract thorns and burrs from each other or as baboons move rocks together in a quest for insects. Wolves will hunt in packs and monkeys have been known to band together against a pesky eagle. It looked to Darwin as if "associated animals have a feeling of love for each other."[92] Blind birds will be fed by others, suggesting a kind of "sympathy" in distress.[93] When a little monkey intervened to save its zoo keeper from a baboon attack, suffering terribly for its courageous act of assistance, we see that such sympathy can cross species lines. This sociability among animals, with its mutual aid and sympathy, looked to Darwin like a precursor to human moral sense.[94] While sympathy was central for humans, we were not unique in this regard. Like lions or tigers who care for their young, we know the "feeling of pleasure from society" that is "an extension of the parental or filial affections."[95] This feeling, over time and through the influence of natural selection and habit, has made sympathy a kind of instinct in humans and other animals. Darwin considered sympathy rather than selfishness to be the cornerstone of his moral vision. Adam Smith, said Darwin, linked sympathy to an awareness of the pains of others in the "first and striking chapter" of his *Theory of Moral Sentiments*.[96] "How selfish so ever man may be supposed," wrote Smith, "there are evidently some principles in his nature, which interest him in the fortune of others, and render their happiness necessary to him, though he derives nothing from it, except the pleasure of seeing it."[97] Smith thought that our desire to aid others was tied directly to our ability to remember our own pain in similar circumstances but Darwin thought the kinship bond was the governing factor, since sympathy is almost always first directed to relatives rather than strangers. In any case, sympathy's reciprocal character means that one creature is able to enter into the suffering of another in order to relieve that suffering. Natural selection, said Darwin, works at the group level, both among animals and humans, to refine and extend such a beneficial trait. He concluded that "those communities, which included the greatest number of the most sympathetic members, would flourish best and rear the greatest number of offspring."[98] So if the building blocks of morality are available in the animalistic landscape, how did our sociability come to serve as the glue to bind these elements together? Since humans are social animals, then it is likely, he argued, that our "early ape-like progenitor" was one of the social animals.[99] And we know how much sociability means to us, says Darwin, by the fact that "solitary confinement is one of the severest punishments which can be inflicted."[100] This social bond led to the preservation of all sorts of animal traits that comprise our moral sense. From its primordial roots to its highest levels, Darwin saw in the human moral sense the refining of our animalistic social instincts.

Given his emphasis on sociability, Darwin resisted those philosophers who rooted morality in selfishness or who, such as John Stuart Mill, traced morality to the "Greatest Happiness principle."[101] Instead, Darwin asserted that the moral sense had its roots in the "general good of the community," linking morality to the promotion of society's welfare and not something as fleeting as happiness.[102] The social instincts and their related affections, not self-interested happiness, stood at the foundations of morality in Darwin's view. Darwin did not think his emphasis was entirely new. He ascribed to the emperor Marcus Aurelius the philosophic insight that our social instincts are "the prime principle of man's moral constitution."[103] He also claimed that our animalistic instincts have given rise "naturally" to the "Golden Rule" known well from the teachings of Jesus and moral philosophy: "As ye would that men should do to you, do ye to them likewise."[104] In a later chapter he wrote, "To do good unto others—to do unto others as ye would they should do unto you,—is the foundation-stone of morality."[105] Darwin dared to trace to our ape-like progenitors the altruistic tendencies later enshrined in biblical morality. This is not to say that biblical morality was beastly, but that the Bible conformed its moral voice to a fundamental aspect of Darwin's theory of human evolution. Drawing the threads of his argument together, he spelled out the relation between morality and religion: "Ultimately a highly complex sentiment, having its first origin in the social instincts, largely guided by the approbation of our fellow-men, ruled by reason, self-interest and in later times by deep religious feelings, confirmed our moral sense or conscience."[106] Ironically, Darwin found a way for religion and science to converge on a ground usually thought to be a battlefield. "With the more civilised races," he explained, "the conviction of the existence of an all-seeing Deity has had a potent influence on the advancement of morality."[107] Reinforcing this judgment, he stated elsewhere that "religious feelings" along with education and social approval are factors that bring about the "advance of morality."[108] Indeed, he placed "the founders of beneficent religions" on a par with "great philosophers and discoverers in science" as aiding in the "progress of mankind in a far higher degree by their words than by leaving a numerous progeny."[109]

On Darwin's evolutionary reading, the Golden Rule represented the latest phase in a moral evolution that harked back to our common descent from ape-like progenitors who instinctively acted with sympathy and mutual aid. While Darwin's *Descent of Man* had radically rewritten the history of human moral development and the values once deemed solely biblical, the discerning reader might be heartened to know that the central pillar of biblical morality was at one with Darwin's evolutionary ethics in its focus on the impulse to aid our fellow creatures.

Ethics and the biological imperative

With inherited traits such as loyalty, obedience, mutual defense, and sympathy forming the animalistic contours of human moral thought, the philosophic question inevitably arises as to what obligation we have to follow a system of ethics that has nothing more than a biological imperative at its core. As Darwin framed the question, "Why should a man feel that he ought to obey one instinctive desire rather than another?"[110] In the first place, Darwin would have us consider the "different degrees of strength" of the instincts that have shaped us as a species. Instincts such as mothering, courage, and self-sacrifice run deep, and we deceive ourselves about moral choice if we overlook the biological roots of these qualities under the assumption that they are unique to humans. A "young and timid mother," he observed, "will, without a moment's hestitation, run the greatest danger for her infant, but not for a mere fellow-creature." Likewise, in a moment of crisis a man will disregard his own "instinct for self-preservation" to "plunge into a torrent to save a drowning fellow-creature." The monkey who saved his keeper from a baboon attack shows us the biological precursor to these acts and they are not rendered any less moral or imperative because of their animalistic underlayer. When an Indian prisoner would rather die than betray his fellow warriors, he says, we see evidence of an impulse that is older and deeper than any abstract philosophic quality. For Darwin, the noblest acts are those done on impulse and not by way of detached deliberation. Deeds such as the self-sacrifice of the Indian prisoner, said Darwin, "ought to be considered as moral," despite not being motivated by abstractions such as a "general benevolence towards mankind" or by "any religious motive."[111] By implication, religion and moral philosophy would need to take into account this biological inheritance in order to construct a compelling and scientifically informed system of ethics for the modern world.

Yet in humans the variety and intensity of these impulses play out in complex and conflicting ways. How shall we choose among the impulses that propel us to action? Darwin recognized that we "struggle with opposing motives" as a result of our biological inheritance.[112] Humans, unlike animals, suffer inner moral conflicts, especially when we betray our higher qualities by yielding to baser instincts such as vengeance. Our powers of reflection and memory, likewise, leave us with a deeper sense of remorse than we find in any other creature. The question then arises as to how we are to make our way forward in this evolutionary moral wilderness. If we are merely presented with a bewildering array of instincts and impulses, how can we make ethical choices when our animal makeup has such a profound effect on us? Offering a biological way out of this philosophic conundrum, Darwin suggested that our sense of "ought" should be defined as a "persistent instinct." In his view, the "bad man" is seen as one in whom such higher instincts fail to prevail.[113] Some are only held in check by a fear of divine wrath or a desire to gain God's approval. The truly moral person, he said, was one who tamed the baser impulses to follow the higher instincts. Yet the road from lower instincts to civilization's highest impulses made for a long and arduous journey. Savage tribes reveal the first crude steps on the path toward a higher moral awareness and conscience. At the primitive level, the virtual enslavement of women prevails along with the robbing of strangers and the torturing of enemies outside of the tribe. Virtues such as courage and sympathy are limited to one's own group. Darwin found no high morality among primitive tribes. Over time, savage licentiousness gave way to marriage, whether polygamous or monogamous, burdening women with the protection of their feminine virtue and leading to the "senseless" practice of celibacy among some men.[114] Morality's advance, in other words, has come in fits and starts. The law of "honor" and sense of "shame" has led to the "strangest customs and superstitions, in complete opposition to the true welfare and happiness of mankind."[115] By way of example, Darwin pointed to the feelings of dishonor that might torment a Hindu who elects to break with his caste or the shame felt by a Muslim woman who exposes her face. "How so many absurd rules of conduct, as well as so many absurd religious beliefs, have originated we do not know," says Darwin. Such developments, he argued, resulted from distortions in the evolution of human moral sense, as odd beliefs become nearly instinctive.[116] Moral conflicts, for the near term, remain the norm.

Despite these regressions in human moral progress, Darwin believed a higher stage was emerging. He saw signs of this in the fact that the extension of human sympathy beyond one's tribe toward all nations had finally become a possibility in human history. He also saw indications of progress in the fact that sympathy for animals had at last arrived. While savages might keep few pets and the Gauchos found Darwin's talk of the humane treatment of horses quite bizarre, the day of our sympathetic kinship with animals had finally dawned. This broadening of our sympathies to those beyond our kin group and to the animal world heralded the evolution of a higher morality. Darwin looked to a time when "virtue will be triumphant."[117]

Darwin concluded his discussion of the evolution of religion and morality with a grand vision: "It is apparently a truer and more cheerful view that progress has been much more general than retrogression; that man has risen, though by slow and interrupted steps, from a lowly condition to the highest standard as yet attained by him in knowledge, morals, and religion."[118] Lest anyone think this stance to be "irreligious," he pointed to the liberal Congregational minister Rev James Allanson Picton's *New Theories and the Old Faith* (1870) for a theological acceptance of the gradual evolution of human "God-consciousness" from animalistic roots.[119] Darwin had opened the door to new ways of thinking about religion. However, despite the fact that he regarded the "belief in all-pervading spiritual agencies" to be "universal," resulting from advances in the human reasoning and the "faculties of imagination, curiosity and wonder," he doubted that the major monotheistic religions could claim much from this evidence.[120] As he explained toward the end of his *Descent of Man*, "The idea of a universal and beneficent Creator of the universe does not seem to arise in the mind of man, until he has been elevated by long-continued culture." With the *Descent of Man*, Darwin made a compelling case for the evolution of religion and morality. Whether these views ultimately lead to atheism, agnosticism, or a new kind of theism is the subject of the next chapter.

A Certain Sympathy: Darwin and the Creed of Science

While the *Descent of Man* represented Darwin's major public contribution to the question of the evolution of human religious awareness, it would be a mistake to think that he lost interest in religious matters after the publication of this volume. Indeed, the last ten years of his life would witness more sparring over religion, many attempts at bringing Darwin back into the traditional religious fold, and further private musing concerning the religious sense. This period allowed Darwin to take stock of his own thinking on religion as he struggled to decide whether his views led to theism, atheism, or agnosticism. In coming to the conviction that religion's rise and function are natural products of human evolution, the question remained whether this sense had any transcendent validity. Did science have the last word on this matter or could religion and science learn to live in a productive symbiotic relationship? We begin this chapter on the negative side, as Mivart, a Catholic and lapsed Darwinian, attacks Darwin's ideas. We then turn to consider the efforts of those who sought to pin down Darwin regarding traditional Christian belief, taking note of the more receptive positions of figures like Kingsley and Conway. For some, at least, Darwin was a kind of sage ushering in a new way to think about religion. Next, we will explore Darwin's own autobiographical musings on religion, penned late in life, as he sifted the theistic wheat from the theological chaff in an effort to discern religion's proper place in a scientific age. Finally, we will look at Darwin's hearty response to Graham's provocative *Creed of Science*, a work which argued that religion could benefit from an engagement with Darwinian ideas. As Darwin and others wrestled with the implications of his evolutionary ideas for modern religious belief, we find that his perspectives on religion and morality afforded vital new starting points for theological reflection.

A catholic rejoinder

Among the many religious critics of Darwin's *Descent of Man,* one lapsed Darwinian launched a sharp attack that sought to negate Darwin's forward thrust.[1] That writer—St George Jackson Mivart—had been an ardent disciple of Huxley, making his mark in the 1860s as the leading researcher on primate skeletal structures.[2] Turning the tables, Mivart came to defend a liberal Catholic spin on speciation and human origins, hoping to "harmonize . . . the teachings of science, philosophy, and religion."[3] Appearing as they do about the same time, Mivart's *On the Genesis of Species* and Darwin's *Descent of Man* present very different visions of religion and science.[4] Despite the fact that Mivart was actually attacking Darwin's *Origin of Species,* what was at stake in both works was the question of what it means to be human. Darwin, as we shall see, was particularly agitated by Mivart's critique.

After challenging Darwin's Natural Selection theory's reliance on gradualism to explain the evolution of physical forms apart from a Creator's guidance, Mivart spoke out against the implications of Darwinism for ethics. He resisted the idea that "right" was nothing more than the "gradual acceleration of useful predilections which, from time to time, arose in a series of ancestors naturally selected."[5] How, asked Mivart, did higher values gradually arise out of the "brutal desires and appetites" that mark ape and savage life?[6] Humans, he said, appeared to have been endowed with an innate moral awareness that belied Darwinian talk of the gradualist origins of human moral sense from ape behaviors.[7] To accept the utilitarian ethic of Herbert Spencer, John Stuart Mill, or Charles Darwin on this count "would be disastrous indeed!"[8] For Mivart, the religionist could accept a kind of evolution, provided that one also accepted the divine creation of the inner forces that drove the evolutionary process. God worked through a combination of divinely instituted laws and inner vital forces to shape life.

Mivart's book was a theological answer to what he perceived to be the atheistic trends in Darwinism. He challenged Darwin's rejection of Gray's theistic evolutionary view, as Darwin had done in his *Variation of Plants and Animals under Domestication* (1868).[9] There, Darwin tried to poke holes in Gray's belief that "variation has been led along certain beneficial lines."[10] While Darwin could see no way around the conflict between Natural Selection and divine foresight (preordination), Mivart postulated a harmonious interplay of the Divine mind with innate forces and external life conditions.[11] As far as Mivart was concerned, Darwin had not knocked down true theism but simply a "dummy, helpless and deformed."[12] Inasmuch as evolution's cofounder Alfred Russel Wallace had already argued that Natural Selection could not account for the human brain, the human hand, musical abilities, and the moral sense, Mivart simply used Wallace against Darwin by affirming that "the whole universe is not merely dependent on, but actually *is*, the WILL of higher intelligences, or of one Supreme Intelligence."[13] Wallace's own review of the *Descent of Man* had only hinted at "unknown causes" and "unknown laws," thereby masking his spiritualist ideas. However, Mivart wrote more bluntly, arguing that only a divinely derived creation could account for the "harmony, the beauty, and the order of the physical universe."[14]

Soon after Darwin's *Descent of Man* was published, Mivart followed up his *Genesis of Species* with attempts to engage Darwin via post. Although their exchange had a surface civility, with Mivart tempering his tone and Darwin struggling to make his case, Mivart could not resist getting in a jab at Darwin's view of morality. He wrote, "Unhappily the acceptance of your views means with many the abandonment of belief in God and in the immortality of the soul together with future rewards & punishments."[15] While he said that he did not "blame" Darwin "*personally*" for this situation, he nonetheless did fault him for not doing enough to stop those who drew "irreligious deductions" from his work. Mivart only made matters worse by issuing a rather caustic anonymous review of Darwin's *Descent of Man* in the *Quarterly Review*. In this review, which left Darwin and his colleagues guessing the name of the author, Mivart opined that he expected much more from "Mr. Darwin's biological treasure house."[16] At times, Mivart grumbled, Darwin was merely stating the obvious—that man has an animal side. But to say "that he is *no more* than an animal" was one of Darwin's numerous gratuitous assumptions. Mivart blamed Darwin for sloppy argumentation, having based much of the *Descent of Man* on hearsay, anecdotes, and over-hasty assertions about the power of sexual selection. In overstating the links in form between humans and animals, Mivart claimed Darwin had grossly underplayed the difference between the mental powers of animals and humans. Human rationality and morality were hardly equivalent to the grunts of gibbons or the sociability of swallows. Darwin "utterly failed" to make sense of man, he said, because his theorizing had become "entangled" in a "false metaphysical system."[17]

Of all his critics, Mivart was the one who got under Darwin's skin.[18] While Darwin imagined that most of his critics, however misguided, responded to his ideas in good faith, he felt otherwise about Mivart because he "acted towards me 'like a pettifogger', or as Huxley has said 'like an Old Bailey Lawyer.'"[19] Yet Darwin knew he could not ignore Mivart's book. The man's stature as a former Darwinian sent Darwin into action. He penned an entire chapter's rebuttal against Mivart in his sixth and final edition of the *Origin of Species*. There, Darwin hacked away at Mivart's claim that Natural Selection could not account for the incipient stages in the evolution of beneficial structures.[20] He left it to Huxley to skewer Mivart's theology. In his article "Mr. Darwin's Critics," Huxley mocked Mivart's claim that the Catholic Church had long embraced a kind of evolutionary view. He put to the test Mivart's hero Fr. Francisco Suarez (1548–1617), the renowned Spanish Jesuit metaphysician. Mivart had claimed that Suarez embraced evolutionary ideas long before Darwin. Huxley disagreed. "But in these days," Huxley mused, "when Judas Iscariot and Robespierre, Henry VIII., and Cataline, have all been shown to be men of admirable virtue, far in advance of their age, and consequently the victims of prejudice, it was obviously possible that Jesuit Suarez might be in like case."[21] But Huxley smelled a rat. Doing his homework at the library of St Andrews University, Huxley astonished the librarian by diving into the Suarez folios "as the careful Robin eyes the delvers toil," he later told Darwin.[22] Drawing on an astonishing array of original Latin quotes from Fr. Suarez's work, Huxley demonstrated that Suarez was just as mired in Genesis literalism as other Catholics. Incensed by this betrayal on the part of his former disciple, Huxley offered Mivart a good theological slap in the face. He pointed out that "the belief that the universe was created in six natural days is hopelessly inconsistent with the doctrine of evolution."[23] Therefore, "the contradiction between Catholic verity and Scientific verity is complete and absolute."[24] One could not be a good Catholic and a good Darwinian. Papal authority did not trump the facts of science. Wagging his finger at Mivart, Huxley snarled, "let him not imagine he is, or can be, both a true son of the Church and a loyal soldier of science."[25] "A hell of honest men," he fumed, was "more endurable than a paradise full of angelic shams."[26]

Mivart was stung by Huxley's criticism. "I felt," he complained, "that I was being severely reprimanded by my superior officer."[27] In effect, Huxley had threatened Mivart with "expulsion from the service" for "treasonable communication." And what, moaned Mivart, was the "unpardonable sin"? Merely suggesting that "there is no real antagonism between the Christian religion and evolution!" Yet the kind of evolution Mivart defended, namely "derivative" creation, with its reliance on miracles, inner forces, and talk of a soul, hardly meshed with Darwin's materialist stance.[28] Despite Mivart's protests of innocence, Huxley's charges stuck. Attacking Darwin in the name of Catholicism, Mivart had crossed the line. He would never be welcomed back into the Darwinian fold.[29] Darwin's praise for Huxley's hammering of Mivart was unequivocal. "I have been delighted with it," he wrote Huxley, adding, "How you do smash Mivart's theology."[30] Huxley had been reluctant to go after Mivart's book but having become certain that the anonymous article in the *Quarterly Review* was penned by Mivart, he felt that Mivart got the "pounding" he deserved.[31] He relished his "slaughter of the Amalekite."[32] Mivart would be shunned by the Darwinians, not only for his arrogant manhandling of Darwin's system but also for his ill-advised attacks on Darwin's son George over eugenics.[33] Blocked from membership in the Athenaeum Club, Mivart's expulsion by the Darwinians was complete. Ironically, Mivart would eventually be excommunicated by the very Church he sought to keep in dialogue with science. The concept of a miracle-laden theistic evolution pleased neither the Darwinian skeptics nor an ecclesiastical authority bent on reigning in modernism.[34]

Fundamental differences

While Mivart's critique rankled Darwin, another family acquaintance received a more patient if still not terribly sympathetic hearing. The Irish religious writer Francis Power Cobbe, who became noted for her opposition to live animal experiments (vivisection) and her support of women's rights, received advanced copies of the *Descent of Man* from Darwin, promising to write a response for the *Theological Review*.[35] Although Darwin facilitated the review, indeed he was eager to read religious reactions to his publication, he urged Cobbe not to offer her appraisal of the work "too soon."[36] While Cobbe was receptive to the idea of evolution, she was quite critical of Darwin's view of morals. "Mr. Darwin," she complained, "will leave us only the sad assurance that our idea of Justice is all our own, and may mean nothing to any other intelligent being in the universe."[37] She viewed Darwinism as a threat. "These doctrines," she warned, "appear to me simply the most dangerous which have ever been set forth since the days of [Bernard] Mandeville," referring to the cynical philosopher and social satirist from the Netherlands. She added, "must we not hold that this Simious Theory of Morals is wholly inadequate and unsatisfactory?"[38] She found Darwin's thinking destructive of religious morality, especially the virtues of remorse for sin, penitence for righting wrongs, and pity for the weak. In reading her review, Emma Darwin told Cobbe that her husband did appreciate the positives of her assessment, but of course he had to address her criticisms of his book. "Mr Darwin," wrote Emma, "has been much interested in your article as he likes to read all that you have to say against his views."[39] Although he told Fanny Wedgwood that he later "read over again a large part & like it much," he found his disagreements with Cobbe's essay "too fundamental" for him to cooperate with her in a follow-up review of the work.[40] In the second edition of his *Descent of Man,* in fact, he took her to task for her negative evaluation of his evolutionary ethics. In one place in the article, Cobbe objected when Darwin claimed that if humans grew up under the same conditions that govern the hive bee, then "our unmarried females would, like the worker-bees, think it a sacred duty to kill their brothers, and mothers would strive to kill their fertile daughters; and no one would think of interfering."[41] Cobbe said that in such a disastrous state of affairs not merely the "*acts* of social duty would have been different, but its *principles* would have been transformed or reversed."[42] Darwin, however, argued that the underlying principle would still be the same both for humans and bees, namely that individuals in each group seek the "good of the community," however different that good might be for bees and humans. While Cobbe regarded Darwin's system as the demise of human virtue, Darwin strongly disagreed. "It is to be hoped," he argued in response, "that the belief in the permanence of virtue on this earth is not held by many persons on so weak a tenure."

Mivart and Cobbe were not the only attempts to bring Darwin around to a Christian belief. To the end of his days, he was pestered by letter writers who wished to bring him back to biblical truth. Long letters instructed Darwin in the doctrines of creation and immorality. For example, a self-styled "child of God" heckled Darwin by shouting, "Oh Man, Man, Man, why wrap yourself up in the dark *theories* of your own imagination; and spend your days in striving to prove 'God' a liar?"[43] Such letters went unanswered. However, some of the more thoughtful inquirers received an informative reply.

One such inquirer, James Grant, may have warmed Darwin's heart with the comments that his letter was coming from a "comparatively young man" who admired Darwin's "civility and candour."[44] Grant did a little name dropping by mentioning Paley's *Natural Theology*, a work that had influenced Darwin as a young student. Hoping to gain insight concerning evolution on the God question, Grant wrote directly to Darwin as disciple to teacher, placing Darwin on a pedestal with the words: "you, who are so much acquainted with nature, so disciplined in intellect, and have doubtless looked at the bearing of your principles upon this idea."[45] Perhaps seeing a younger version of himself in Grant, Darwin candidly confessed that at this stage of his life and beset by ill health the God question was too taxing, adding that the subject would be difficult to tackle "with any amount of strength."[46] Then, he told this inquirer that the "strongest argument for the existence of God, as it seems to me, is the instinct or intuition which we all (as I suppose) feel that there must have been an intelligent beginner (*sic*) of the Universe." But, he was compelled to admit, "then comes the doubt and difficulty whether such intuitions are trustworthy." The question, in the end, remains "insoluble." Darwin did not doubt there was a god instinct, but he did question whether this instinct was a reliable indicator of transcendent truths.

A year later, Darwin explained to a Congregational minister, the Rev John Fordyce of Grimsby, that the word "theist" was subject to differing interpretations.[47] "In my most extreme fluctuations," he reflected, "I have never been an atheist in the sense of denying the existence of a God."[48] He went on to tell Fordyce, who after Darwin's death authored *Aspects of Scepticism,* that it was "absurd to doubt that a man may be an ardent Theist & an evolutionist," offering the well-known Cambridge professor and novelist Rev Charles Kingsley and Harvard botanist Asa Gray as prime examples of evolutionists who were religious believers.[49] Kingsley, who embraced Darwin's ideas from the very start, predicted that in future centuries Darwin would be "esteemed as a prophet."[50] Gazing in his crystal ball, he once told Darwin that in "500 years hence, men will know what you have done for them."[51] In a lecture to Anglican clerics at Sion College in 1871, Kingsley decried the fruitless "war" that had arisen between religion and science.[52] Rather than despise the earth as the "devil's planet," he urged the clergy to engage science with a view to reweaving the tattered theologies of George Berkeley, Bishop Butler, and William Paley.[53] When it came to the design of the world, he suggested that science tells us "how" nature works while theology reveals the moral "why."[54] He went so far as to recommend the study of science as an ordination requirement, so that the clergy would no longer fear science's investigations into the ever-widening mystery of the universe. Kingsley's views were captured more playfully in an earlier letter to Huxley, which he dutifully passed on to Darwin. Half in jest, Kingsley sent to Huxley a fable he concocted to illustrate the profound effect that Darwin had on the reshaping of his natural theology.[55] The fable concerned a heathenish Khan in Tartary who worshipped a horse's skull. One day, so the fable goes, two religious teachers came to visit the old Khan. The trouble was that these mullahs worshipped different gods. Despising one another and each believing the other was headed to Hell, the mullahs sought to convert the Khan to their particular deity. The Khan spoke frankly. He had no further use for the horse's skull since it had let him down on several occasions. He was in the market for a real God. So the Khan asked the mullahs which of their gods was the cleverest. The first replied, "Oh Khan, worship my God. He is so wise, that he made all things." "Wah!," exclaimed the Khan. "He is a wise builder. But what can thy God do, oh Moollah number two?" The second teacher replied, "Oh Khan, it is a light thing for a God to make all things . . . .But, Oh Khan, my God is a God indeed; *For he is so wise, that he makes all things make themselves.*" To which the Khan stammered in amazement, "WahWah! . . . He is the wisest of all Master-builders. He is the God for me henceforth, if he be wise enough to make things make themselves." These words were also put on the lips of Mother Carey, a fairy symbol of nature, in Kingsley's *Water Babies* as an attempt to playfully impart to children (and adults) the new sensibilities of science and theology.[56] When Darwin heard the fable of the Khan, he was delighted at "the sound sense of an Eastern potentate."[57] He was also pleased to hear a theologian he respected embrace evolutionary views unabashedly, even if he himself might not go the whole way theologically with Kingsley.

The Rev Moncure Conway, the American Unitarian who became Minister to the progressive South Place Chapel in London in 1863 and who visited Darwin in January 1873, went farther than Kingsley. One of Conway's sermons caught Charles and Emma's attention. "We have just been reading a very grand sermon of his on Darwinism," Emma wrote to her aunt Fanny Allen, adding, "I sometimes feel it very odd that anyone belonging to me should be making such a noise in the world."[58] Yet in Conway's estimation Darwin had every reason to be making noise. In his sermon, Conway distinguished between the Pre-Darwinite and Post-Darwinite ages of thought. Darwin's theory, he said, upended all the "crude fancies" of the past.[59] The Bible's science had been exposed as the "speculation of an ignorant tribe in an ignorant age of the world,"[60] Though many religionists had greeted Darwin with predictable fear, Conway saw no great loss in abandoning an outmoded idea of God as a "gigantic man" who governed creation by means of the "seven-planet theory." The fall of such folly was just someone's "little idol" that has been toppled, not the entire universe.[61] Darwin's revolution, according to Conway, "has given the world new eyes with which to look at nearly everything."[62] Religion could not stand still in such a moment. Understanding that humans were the offspring not simply of the apes but the entire "animated universe," Conway moved beyond belief in God as the miracle worker and "Almighty Mechanic" to a theistic view that embraced the Darwinian view that "pain is a beneficent agent . . . under which the whole world has progressed."[63] More than the Sufi, says Conway, the Darwinian believer feels himself "walking through life in the perilous scimitar-edged bridge, Al-Sirat."[64] Having been "emancipated from fables," Conway characterized the history of mental, moral, and religious ideas as a struggle that had progressively yielded to new and refined views of God.[65] Darwin not only tells the religious crowd, said Conway, "once more you have been found wrong in your speculation as to God's relation to this universe," his theories also provided clues to God's real workings in the world.[66] What was the moral of the Darwinian story? Survival of the fittest was not "survival of the strongest"—the great dinosaurs perished long ago—but it was the story of the survival of humility, sympathy, and justice.[67] The moral evolution of man is one of the great truths revealed by Darwin. "The whole tendency and evolution of the world," explains Conway, "has been to the end of unfolding in man a power to overcome all the selfishness of brute nature."[68] Religion in a Darwinian key ought to be seen as "the power that frees man from low motives and makes his action flow straight from reason and conscience."[69] When Darwin spoke at times of being a Theist, surely something of Conway's approach was what he had in mind even if he wouldn't follow him all the way.[70]

On other occasions, Darwin would tell inquirers that he was more an agnostic than a theist or an atheist. A 17-year-old Russian student at Jena, Nicolai Alexandrovitch von Mengden, wrote to Darwin in June, 1879, to confess his conflicted doubts over the relation between evolution and traditional religious belief. Assisting her aging husband with the reply, Emma Darwin told the questioner that her husband "begs me to say that he receives so many letters that he cannot answer them all."[71] But she added that her husband "considers that the theory of Evolution is quite compatible with the belief in a God; but that you must remember that different persons have different definitions of what they mean by God." Seeking clarity, Mengden pressed Darwin on the fact that the German evolutionist Ernst Häckel rejected any talk of the supernatural. Darwin took pen in hand to respond. "Science has nothing to do with Christ," he insisted, "except in so far, as the habit of scientific research makes a man cautious in admitting evidence."[72] Then he cut to the chase by affirming, "For myself, I do not believe, that there ever has been any Revelation." This letter was made public by Häckel just a few months after Darwin's death, an "unauthorized" gesture that created consternation for the Darwin family and stirred up the British press. For Häckel, the letter was proof positive that Darwin had abandoned the Church of England in favor of the "monistic religion of Humanity" espoused by Goethe, Lessing, Lamarck, and Spinoza.[73] While Darwin, as we have seen, had clear ideas about the evolution of religion, he would hardly have embraced Häckel's view.

On one occasion Darwin's response was quite pointed about traditional Christianity. Writing to the barrister Frederick A. McDermott of London's Middle Temple in 1880, he penned a one-line reply: "I am sorry to have to inform you that I do not believe in the Bible as a divine revelation, & therefore not in Jesus Christ as the son of God."[74] A generalized belief in theism was one thing; biblical religion quite another.

Not all queries elicited a negative response. When Darwin was sympathetic with the letter writer's query, he would return to the theme of his uncertainty. Francis Ellingwood Abbot, editor of the Toledo, Ohio periodical *The Index*, wrote Darwin to solicit support for his free-thought journal. Abbot praised Darwin for laboring on behalf of "true religion," hoping that Darwin would endorse his effort "to show my fellow-men that science must shape their ideas of God."[75] In reply, Darwin was a bit skittish. He praised Abbot's "zeal & exertions in the noble cause of truth."[76] But he added, "I can never make up my mind how far an inward conviction that there must be some Creator or First Cause is really trustworthy evidence."[77] In a subsequent letter, Darwin opened up a bit more. He told Abbot that he had "never systematically thought much on religion in relation to science, or on morals in relation to society."[78] He went on to explain that he had once been advised by a colleague to leave religion out of his writings if he wanted to promote the cause of science in England. And so, said Darwin, "this led me not to consider the mutual bearings of the two subjects."[79] As a result, scattered in his books and letters were brilliant but often half-formed ideas about the religious implications of his own scientific insights. While his discussion of religion and morality was much more extensive in his *Descent of Man*, he still proceeded with a sense of reserve and caution. "Had I foreseen, how much more liberal the world would become," he told Abbot, "I should perhaps have acted differently."

There were those who wished he had said more and had been more outspoken against religious belief. On one occasion, Darwin was taken to task by a secularist inquirer for his religious ambiguities. Nicolaas Dirk Doedes was a history student and son of a Dutch Reformed professor of theology at Utrecht University. He was also a self-professed atheist who was puzzled by comments in Darwin's works that led him to imagine Darwin was more of a Deist than an atheist.[80] He wrote Darwin wishing to know "*on what grounds* you believe in God?" He added, "Is your chief ground for your belief in God perhaps *this,* that you think a first cause, a Creator, needed for the universe?" In his reply, Darwin confessed "the impossibility of conceiving that this grand and wondrous universe, with our conscious selves, arose through chance."[81] This, for Darwin, was the "chief argument for the existence of God."[82] But other considerations clouded this view. First, whether these convictions about chance constituted "an argument of real value."[83] Secondly, supposing the Creator existed, where did this so-called "first cause" come from?[84] Thirdly, the "immense amount of suffering" in the world weighed against belief in God.[85] Darwin said he was quite willing to defer judgment on theological matters to the "many able men who have fully believed in God; but here again I see how poor an argument this is."[86] Darwin elected the "safest conclusion," namely that "the whole subject is beyond the scope of man's intellect."[87] Rather than lapse into despair, Darwin reminded Doedes that "man can do his duty."[88] In response, this young student berated Darwin for mentioning the Creator at the end of the *Origin of Species* and in the second chapter of the *Descent of Man*. He urged Darwin to stand with those equally "able men" who take up the cause of unbelief, reminding him that "there are some who make use of those passages from your works as an authority, for their belief in God; others who regard them as your feeble point, or as an accommodation."[89]

Darwin's brand of agnosticism pleased neither conservative believers nor the absolute atheists. Yet there was a virtue to this stance. A letter of advice to his son George, who was preparing an essay on morality and religion for publication, provides a clue as to Darwin's thinking. He told his son that he had recently read John Morley's *Voltaire*. He suggested that "direct attacks on Christianity, (even when written with the wonderful force & vigour of Voltaire) produce little permanent effect: real good seems only to follow from slow & silent side attacks."[90] On the previous evening, as Darwin recounted to his son, he had had a conversation at home with some of their relatives on this very subject. He was reminded by his guests that the philosopher John Stuart Mill had been counseled by his father to keep his skepticism under wraps so as not to risk damaging his reputation. Mill's writings, Darwin advised his son, would never have become textbooks at Oxford had the man's religious views been generally known. He also held out Lyell's geological work as an example for his son to follow. Lyell was "most firmly convinced that he has shaken the faith in the Deluge &c far more effectively by never having said a word against the Bible, than if he had acted otherwise."[91] In his later years, Darwin took the same line with Edward Aveling, a popular biology lecturer in London whose later liaison with Karl Marx's daughter Eleanor ended in her tragic suicide. In his correspondence, Darwin cautioned Aveling that much as he supported free thought, he felt "direct arguments against christianity & theism produce hardly any effect on the public."[92] Darwin insisted that "freedom of thought is best promoted by the gradual illumination of men's minds, which follows from the advance of science." He told Aveling that he tried to avoid writing on religion to focus on science and to keep from causing pain to his family by aiding "direct attacks" on religion. Aveling tried to pin Darwin down in a face-to-face meeting the year before he died. The thought that the atheist Aveling and his collaborator Ludwig Büchner would be dining at the Darwin residence rankled Emma. Both Aveling and Büchner were in London for the Congress of the International Federation of Freethinkers, with Büchner as its President. During lunch, Darwin affirmed his cordial relationship with the local parson, the Rev Brodie Innes, who was present at the gathering. Afterward over cigarettes in the study, he prodded his guests by inquiring, "Why do you call yourselves atheists?" Aveling explained that " 'Agnostic' was but 'Atheist' writ respectable, and 'Atheist' was only 'Agnostic' writ aggressive." But Darwin challenged their assertiveness. "Is anything to be gained," he pressed, "by forcing new ideas on people?"[93]

While Darwin was generally circumspect about matters of faith, the topic of religion refused to go away for his fellow Darwinians. As rivals sought to gain control over the scientific institutions of the day, the X-Club, an elite scientific dining club built around Huxley's colleagues, showed its influence by capturing the Presidency of the British Association for the Advancement of Science. Hooker was president of the BAAS in 1868, Huxley in 1870, and John Tyndall in 1874. The BAAS served as John Tyndall's bully pulpit. It was Tyndall's address at the Belfast meeting that drew the line in the sand between science and the old faith.[94] "We cannot, without shutting our eyes through fear or prejudice, fail to see that Darwin is here dealing, not with imaginary, but true causes," trumpeted Tyndall.[95] Tyndall had made his mark debunking séances, questioning miracles, and challenging the efficacy of prayer.[96] Now he championed Darwin as the latest in a long line of trailblazers who rejected superstitious views of nature's workings in favor of mechanisms, laws, and atoms. The line of worthies he hailed included Democritus, Epicurus, Lucretius, Copernicus, Giordano Bruno, Francis Bacon, Pierre Gassendi, Isaac Newton, and James Clerk Maxwell. Against this onward march of scientific insight stood the "drought of the Middle Ages" brought on by Christianity's negation of the world, biblical obsessions, and a reliance on philosophic "authorities" such as Aristotle rather than the rational investigation of nature. Rejecting talk of a divine Artificer and special acts of creation, the trailblazers overturned the narrow and prejudiced views of the religionists of their time.[97] What of religion? Tyndall did not wish to ignore this "deep-set feeling."[98] We must, he says, recognize that beyond the world constructed by our minds from sense data lies an "insoluble mystery" that governs life.[99] His was no "rank materialism."[100] Provided that religion yielded to the free investigations of science, religion could work with science to "raise life."[101] Religion had its role to play, said Tyndall, in nurturing the emotional life of man—our awe, reverence, and wonder.[102] He envisioned a future in which religion would learn to follow science's lead, supporting free inquiry and being enlivened by the expanding horizons of knowledge and truth.

More than breath?

While Tyndall elected to clear the deck publicly regarding the relation between religion and science, Darwin remained privately troubled. Taking a quieter approach to the burning issue of the day, he used his own autobiographical reflections to sort out these questions once and for all. While Darwin often claimed he never thought systematically about religious topics, his life and works such as the *Origin of Species* and the *Descent of Man* tell a different story. The *Origin* picked apart the creation idea. The *Descent* underscored the evolutionary roots of religion and the Golden Rule. Toward the end of his days, Darwin produced yet another statement on religion, a wide-ranging piece that he included in his private autobiography. During the late spring and summer of 1876 (with some minor later additions), when Darwin was in his late 60s, he penned his "Recollections of the Development of my mind and character."[103] In this work, he offered an extended discourse on theological matters, proving once again that he did indeed think deeply and read widely in questions of religion.

After a lifetime of exploration, Darwin's view of the Bible had been transformed. We saw earlier that while as a young man he might quote the sacred text as a source of moral truth, during his voyage he began to doubt the Old Testament's historical character with its "manifestly false history of the world."[104] Specifically, he said that he took issue with the Flood story with its rainbow, the tale of the confusion of languages at the Tower of Babel, and the Bible's portrait of God as a "revengeful tyrant."[105] These fanciful tales conspired in Darwin's mind to make the Bible "no more to be trusted than the sacred books of the Hindoos" or the beliefs of any barbarian.[106] Not surprisingly, the Bible's miracles were denied by Darwin. As the science-minded Darwin explained, "the more we know of the fixed laws of nature the more incredible do miracles become."[107]

The Gospels of the New Testament as historical records fared poorly under Darwin's withering gaze. Texts that were not simultaneous with the events they recount and which conflicted in major points with each other, well beyond the simple contradictions of "eye-witnesses," were texts that lacked trustworthiness as historical accounts. Darwin's understanding of the historical criticism of the Gospels had certainly come a long way since the days when he read Andrews Norton's *The Evidence of the Genuineness of the Gospels*. Norton sought to demonstrate that the Gospels were authentic records straight from the hands of those whom early church tradition regarded as their authors. In 1848, such a view sounded "good" to Darwin, but late in life his skepticism about the credibility of the New Testament had grown.[108] Presumably Darwin had been influenced by the critique of Francis Newman's *Phases of Faith* and other critical authors. This is not to say that Darwin gave up the search for the history behind the Gospels. "I can well remember," he recalled, "often & often inventing day-dreams of old letters between distinguished Romans & manuscripts being discovered at Pompeii or elsewhere which confirmed in the most striking manner all that was written in the Gospels."[109] He confessed, "I was very unwilling to give up my belief."[110]

Christian teaching also earned Darwin's stinging rebuke. He could not tolerate the doctrine of everlasting punishment. Speaking for many of his contemporaries, he labeled this "a damnable doctrine."[111] Finding it unimaginable to consign his own "Father, Brother & almost all my best friends" to such a cruel fate, Darwin could "hardly see how anyone ought to wish Christianity to be true."[112] After his death, Darwin's wife sought to expunge this passage from the autobiography before allowing the work to be published.[113] She felt that such a doctrine had already been supplanted in many modern believer's minds, although she did have to admit "the words are there" in the Bible.[114] She succeeded over the protests of her son Frank in having several such offending passages purged from the initial publication of the autobiography.

Darwin's main sparring partner in his autobiographical reflections, of course, was natural theology. He acknowledged that William Paley's argument from design "formerly seemed to me so conclusive."[115] But with the discovery of Natural Selection, Paley's argument failed. No longer did people have to think that bivalve hinges were designed by an "intelligent being, like the hinge of a door by man."[116] There was no more design in nature's variability or in the process of Natural Selection "than in the course which the wind blows."[117] For Darwin, the question of design in nature was more than a matter of nature's mechanics, it was also a question of the value of creation. Natural theology treated nature as a repository of God's goodness. "How," wondered Darwin, "can the generally beneficent arrangement of the world be accounted for?"[118] In natural theology, God was not merely a Designer but a beneficent Designer who has arranged all things for the good of Man. But Darwin was acutely aware that suffering drove nature's machinery. He wrestled with the relation between life's sufferings and nature's obvious rewards. Acting as if he were the last great natural theologian, Darwin scanned the balance sheet to weigh these factors, asking if happiness did indeed win out over the evils of this world. Some skeptics were so "impressed with the amount of suffering in the world," he said, "that they doubt if we look to all sentient beings—whether there is more of misery or of happiness, whether the world as a whole is a good or a bad one."[119] Yet the aging Darwin, who had suffered so much illness and even the loss of his beloved daughter Annie, was nonetheless able to affirm: "According to my judgment happiness decidedly prevails."[120] In nature's pleasure factory, claimed Darwin, we have been "formed so as to enjoy as a general rule happiness."[121] If suffering prevailed, no creature would ever seek to propagate. Given that our organs are set up to help us "compete successfully," we aid our species not merely through enduring "pain, hunger, thirst & fear" but also by our pursuit of pleasure in "eating & drinking."[122] Such pleasures ensure the victory of "happiness over misery, although many occasionally suffer much."[123]

Although accenting the pleasure principle, Darwin was hardly blind to the evils of the world. Indeed, one of natural theology's greatest challenges received from Darwin a new solution, namely the vexing problem of evil. There was a time, observed Darwin, when religionists would claim that the world's suffering had been sent by God for our "moral improvement."[124] Even if this were the case for humans, he argued, this belief hardly accounted for the vast suffering of the animal world, where we see no sign of moral improvement despite all their pain. The concept of God insists there exists a Being who is "omnipotent & omniscient" and thus "it revolts our understanding to suppose that his benevolence is not unbounded."[125] He wondered, "what advantage can there be in the sufferings of millions of the lower animals throughout almost endless time?"[126] But in a Darwinian universe there was no need to continue blaming God for nature's evils. As he explained, "This very old argument from the existence of suffering against the existence of an intelligent first cause seems to me a strong one."[127] Get rid of supernatural interference and the age-old problem of evil is solved. Suffering accords well with Natural Selection, even as the theory clashes with a belief in a benevolent Designer. On Darwin's scheme, God is off the hook. Pain can be endured. Pleasure is our guide. Darwin the free-thinking Epicurean took aim at Paley the supernaturalist Stoic in the debate over theodicy and divine design. For Darwin, his views had clear theological implications, albeit negative ones. Yet his thinking on the problem of evil did point in a new direction for an old theological conundrum.

Likewise, just as Epicurus freed his followers from the fear of the gods and from evil, Darwin freed himself from false religion. Having traveled the world, Darwin came to think that "many false religions have spread over large portions of the Earth like wild-fire."[128] He understood the dangers of forced conversions and missionizing by conquest. In each culture and in every pious family, Darwin suspected that "the constant inculcation of a belief in God" had a mind-altering effect, perhaps leading to changes that could be inherited.[129] For children reared on such brainwashing, "it would be as difficult for them to throw off their belief in God, as for a monkey to throw off its instinctive fear & hatred of a snake."[130] Darwin's analysis cut Emma to the heart. As she later told her son Francis, "where this sentence comes in, it gives one a sort of shock."[131]

Whether religion is an instinct or a product of indoctrination, must we think that this fact negates the oceanic feeling of transcendence so many experience and which has long served as evidence for a belief in God? On his voyage around the world, Darwin knew this sense of wonder firsthand. "In my Journal," he recalled, "I wrote that whilst standing in the midst of the grandeur of a Brazilian forest, 'it is not possible to give an adequate idea of the higher feelings of wonder, admiration & devotion, which fill & elevate the mind.'"[132] Surely belief in God was justified by our experience of the sublime powers of Nature. Unfortunately, this profound sense of awe did not reveal specifically which god to believe in. Darwin rightly realized that many different religions used this "deep inward conviction" as a starting point in their self-defense.[133] Hindus could invoke this evidence as proof of their belief in a multitude of gods while Muslims could claim support for belief in just one God. Darwin also realized that Buddhists could likewise tap the same evidence, marshaling it to support their philosophy of no God. Pointing to the anthropological work of Tylor and the sociological speculations of Spencer, works considered by Darwin in his *Descent of Man*, he observed that "barbarian tribes" were led by such uncanny experiences, not toward belief in a monotheist God but simply toward a belief in spirits and ghosts.[134] The oceanic experience, profound as it was, offered little clue as to what kind of a deity, if any, stood behind these profound yet purely subjective feelings. Darwin confessed that these sentiments, while not "strongly developed," once undergirded his own belief in God and an immortal soul.[135] But after his travels brought an awareness of religion's evolution, Darwin understood that the link between the oceanic feeling and particular religious belief systems was tenuous at best. If a singular belief in God were shared by all people, then the "argument would be a valid one."[136] The fact was that there is no universal religious belief led him to conclude, "I cannot see that such inward convictions & feelings are of any weight as evidence of what really exists."[137] The "sense of sublimity," he added, "can hardly be advanced as an argument for the existence of God."[138] We may not know how this sacred awareness evolved, but for Darwin the door to belief on this basis was closed. When it came to religious feelings, Darwin admitted he had become like a "colour-blind" person.[139]

Darwin gave the idea of immortality a little more credence. He was impressed by the fact that this concept was such an "instinctive" belief, found the world over.[140] He also struggled over the conflict that arose between the hope that humans would continue to evolve into a more perfect form and the grim realization that one day the sun would surely die out. The thought that all life was "doomed to complete annihilation" Darwin found "intolerable."[141] "To those who fully admit," he observed, "the immortality of the human soul, the destruction of our world will not appear so dreadful."[142] But Darwin's convictions on this matter were far from affirmative. He had told Lyell just a few years before that far too many people, Lyell included, "make themselves quite easy about immortality and the existence of a personal God, by intuition."[143] "I suppose," he explained, "that I must differ from such persons, for I do not feel any innate conviction on any such points."[144]

Beyond illusory oceanic feelings and vague ideas about immortality, Darwin found that another line of argument for belief had "much more weight."[145] This was the reasoned view that "follows from the extreme difficulty or rather impossibility of conceiving this immense & wonderful universe, including man with his capacity of looking far backwards & far into futurity, as the result of blind chance or necessity."[146] This belief that we are not simply the playthings of chance likewise went back to Darwin's Brazilian rainforest experiences. "I well remember," he recalled, "my conviction that there is more in man than the mere breath of his body."[147] Open to the possibility of a "First Cause having an intelligent mind," Darwin placed himself in the category of a "Theist."[148] Such a conviction, he wrote, served to undergird his *Origin of Species*. Admitting that this belief had gradually faded, Darwin bore in mind that there was a time when his own brand of theism took him to places where biblical literalism or natural theology dare not go. He recognized that he had contributed in a positive way to the theological debates of his day. The trouble was that the *Origin of Species* was not embraced in that spirit.

Despite these more progressive theological leanings, Darwin could not escape his "doubt." Why trust a brain born of ape-like ancestors when it "draws such grand conclusions"?[149] He ended up being equally skeptical of religion and irreligion. Unfurling Huxley's banner of agnosticism, Darwin concluded, "The mystery of the beginning of all things is insoluble by us; & I for one must be content to remain Agnostic."[150] Although he was something of a theist when writing the *Origin of Species*, Darwin by that point was well along the path toward the agnosticism of his later years. He retold the story of how before his marriage to Emma, his father had counseled him to hide his religious doubts from his fiancée, fearing the painful rift that would inevitably ensue for him.[151] His father had warned that doubts about a spouse's salvation during times of ill-health only ensured domestic distress. Better to keep silent and thereby keep peace in the family. While his father could only number a few skeptical women among his acquaintances, Darwin had come to know many women "who believe very little more than their husbands."[152] In fact, by the late 1870s, Darwin marveled at "the spread of scepticism or rationalism during the latter half of my life."[153] His thinking on religion fit in very well with the views of the skeptical social activists, liberal Christians, and the scientific agnostics of the day. He was hardly alone in his doubts about traditional faith or in his desire to look at religion in new ways.

Despite this skepticism, he could nonetheless play "devil's advocate" on behalf of theology.[154] When George Romanes sent Darwin his anonymously published *Candid Examination of Theism* (1878), demolishing the classic arguments for God's existence, Darwin took up the book with "very great interest."[155] But he challenged his colleague and friend by arguing that God could have impressed on matter the potentiality to evolve complex and beautiful forms. To claim that matter acted as a creative force by sheer necessity without a Creator's stamp seemed to Darwin merely to beg the question. "Please observe," adds Darwin, "it is not I, but a theologian who has thus addressed you, but I could not answer him." In his reply, Romanes tried to distinguish between science as a set of explanatory assumptions and science as an ultimate cosmological fact. He confessed, echoing sentiments he had recently heard from Darwin's own lips, that establishing ultimate philosophic facts was like "trying to illuminate the midnight sky with a candle."[156] Throwing up his hands in consternation, Romanes held the issue in abeyance, invoking an unnamed poet who said, "Believe it not, regret it not, but wait it out, O Man."

While Darwin wrestled valiantly with theological questions throughout his life, from the point of view of the aging man of science it looked as if this drift from orthodoxy to agnosticism was a gradual process: "Thus disbelief crept over me at a very slow rate, but was at last complete."[157] He added, "The rate was so slow that I felt no distress."[158] Unlike many of his contemporaries who were wrenched by the overturning of the Bible, the man at the eye of the storm experienced an inner peace in his skepticism. Having made the shift, he says that he "never since doubted even for a single second that my conclusion was correct."[159] Darwin's journey away from traditional religion to skepticism was a less troubled version of the lapse recounted by Winwood Reade's *The Outcast* (1875). Reade, a sometime correspondent with Darwin about African matters, depicted in his novel the travails of a young priest, Edward Mordaunt, who read Lyell's *Principles of Geology* and abandoned both his Bible and his fiancée. Though they did eventually marry, Edward's meager income brought rejection from his father and spelled ruin for his family as his wife succumbed to illness in their poverty. When he emerged from this nightmare through the kindness of an old clergy colleague and the support of a secular man of science, this lapsed priest, who blamed the biblical God for killing his wife, turned instead to a belief in "God the Incomprehensible," a being who spurred him to do battle with Nature's evils and seek to improve mankind. Reade's protagonist successfully learned to navigate the challenges posed by Malthus and Darwin—writings dubbed the Book of Doubt and the Book of Despair—by embracing a "Religion of Unselfishness," improving the here-and-now with little thought for the afterlife or "celestial rewards." By this point in his life, Darwin's own God was at best Reade's "God the Incomprehensible." This ambiguity may have been stamped by Mordaunt's kind of despair, for Darwin too had known tragedy in the Easter season death of his daughter Annie in 1851.[160] While one suspects her death affected negatively Darwin's religious convictions, we have no unambiguous evidence to this effect. The fact of the matter is that Darwin continued reading and researching the religion question long after her death. Yet it is hard not to wonder about the effect of his loss. In any event, despite their long correspondence, it is not known whether Darwin ever read Reade's novel. Nonetheless, what remained was for Darwin, like Reade's protagonist, to point the way to a new ethic. Despite the New Testament offering a "Beautiful . . . morality," he held that even these teachings rested "on the interpretation which we now put on metaphors & allegories."[161] Rather than resort to ancient texts for guidance, Darwin looked to the process of evolution itself for his guide. In his view, a person could have a life ethic without resorting to a personal God or clinging to a belief in a heavenly afterlife with its rewards and punishments. An evolutionary ethic was governed by learning "to follow those impulses & instincts which are the strongest or which seem . . . the best ones."[162] Highest of all were the social instincts. To gain the "approbation of his fellow men," said Darwin, "is the highest pleasure on this earth."[163] Such approbation came in the fall of 1877 when Darwin was awarded an honorary degree at Cambridge before a "gallery crammed to overflowing with undergraduates, and the floor crammed too with undergraduates climbing on the statues and standing up in the windows."[164] A monkey dangled from the ceiling was greeted with "shouts and jokes about our ancestors." But the numerous handshakes afterward signaled that the heretic of 1859 had returned home in triumph as the grand old man of science. Recognition of that service took an unusual form a year later when Anthony Rich bequeathed all his property to the Darwin family to honor the work Darwin had done "for the benefit of mankind."[165] Darwin's only regret in life? Not any "great sin" but simply his failure, due to ill-health, at not having done "more direct good to my fellow-creatures."[166] In the end, a life lived in the service of others constituted the highest human calling according to Darwin. Following this pole star of human conduct meant not indulging one's "sensuous passions," leading to inner conflict, but learning to follow one's "innermost guide or conscience."[167]

Darwin followed up his "Recollections" with another essay that again took stock of the religion question, this time in the form of biographical reflections on his grandfather Erasmus Darwin. The sketch, written in May–June 1879, was intended to serve as a "preface" to Ernst Krause's German essay on Erasmus. However, Darwin's so-called preface ran much longer than Krause's piece![168] Although Erasmus might have been written off as an atheistic freethinking evolutionist in some circles, Charles's reflections sought to temper this appraisal, turning his grandfather into "a theist in the ordinary acceptation of the term."[169] Darwin refused to believe that his grandfather was a callous skeptic devoid of conscience—a caricature promoted by Anna Seward who wrote an unflattering biography of his grandfather. Against Seward, he portrayed Erasmus as an imaginative thinker who appreciated the wonder of creation as revealed by science. While acknowledging the man's youthful skepticism, he is depicted as a figure who extolled the Creator's power as revealed in natural laws impressed on matter by the Deity.[170] Charles quotes an ode that Erasmus crafted that asks, "Dull atheist, could a giddy dance/Of atoms lawless hurl'd/Construct so wonderful, so wise,/So harmonised a world?"[171] For Charles Darwin, his grandfather was a theist who discounted revelation.[172] In his own mind, it would seem that both grandfather and grandson walked a narrow path between atheism and Christian theism, seeking to veer toward neither extreme. Although admitting his grandfather was "unorthodox," Charles excused the harsh accusations against him as the fruit of the "Christian feeling" of the time.[173] "We may at least hope," he opines, "that nothing of this kind now prevails."

It was perhaps wishful thinking. In any event, this essay on Erasmus Darwin strongly suggests that the theistic question was not entirely settled for Darwin even at this late date.

A growing hostility?

Two years after Darwin's death, as she reflected back on her dining room conversations with her uncle, Julia Wedgwood wrote to his son Frank about her impressions of Darwin's view of religion.[174] While she found him remarkably neutral in public, she knew privately of his "growing hostility" toward religion. As reflected in her own articles on religion and science, Julia said she was repelled by her uncle's talk of alternatives to belief in divine creation. Yet in these conversations at his home in the days before he published his *Origin of Species*, she also found he had "a certain sympathy" toward religion, inasmuch as he admitted, much to her "extreme surprise," that he shared in that "belief that *we are all naturally inclined to*, of a first cause." He, too, held this belief, but he told her that he was reluctant to trust that his animal mind was correct about this nagging suspicion concerning the origins of the universe. In this regard, she discovered that he "had no hostility towards Religion, as a view of the ultimate origin of things."

Yet his "growing hostility" helps us to understand Darwin's reluctance to accept the Archbishop of Canterbury's invitation to attend a "Private Conference" on science and religion that was slated to be held at Lambeth Palace in January, 1881.[175] The gathering was intended to counter "intelligent modern Infidelity" which set modern science in opposition to both natural and revealed religion.[176] Would Darwin consent to attend? Making excuses for health reasons, Darwin said that although he would be honored to meet "so many distinguished men," he had to decline attending because his lack of strength was not the only thing that kept him away. Frankly, he said, "I can see no prospect of any benefit arising from the proposed conference."[177] As if tone deaf, the Archbishop's representative wrote back asking Darwin to comment on the viability of such a conference.[178] To make his position clear, Darwin responded that people have to work out these matters for themselves. To be told that "a considerable number of men can reconcile the results of science with revealed or natural religion" mattered for naught when other equally eminent thinkers "cannot do so."[179] The "weight" of "authority" so cherished by the Archbishop carried little weight if they were in fact wrong about the religion question.[180]

Darwin's "certain sympathy" for belief, however, does help explain one final episode in Darwin's lifelong tussle over religion and its evolution. During the last year of his life a book came to his attention and caught his imagination.

William Graham's *Creed of Science* dared to reconstruct religious belief on the strong foundations of Darwin's own system.[181] Graham, originally educated at Trinity College in Dublin, was at the time a lecturer in mathematics at St Bartholemew's Hospital in London.[182] Science, according to Graham, had been a game changer for religion. The outmoded myth of the "Great Architect" had been replaced by the "startling series of tales issued by science during the past century."[183] Among these tales were the nebular origins of the solar system, the evolutionary development of plants and animals, and the rise of man from apes. The Darwinian view, however, was troubling for theology. With Darwin, "the marvel ceases."[184] Whether "a series of fortunate accidents" or "a series of fortunate events," the course of life's development was completely unforeseen: "Nature neither knew, nor cared, nor directed."[185] On the evolutionary view, nature had "no special aims whatever in view."[186] Darwin solved the problem of evil by insisting that "evil lies in the nature of things."[187] Regarding immortality, Darwin put to rest the afterlife question. In death, thought ceases as the brain dies. We return to the "borrowed" energies of Nature.[188] Graham held out the hope that our consciousness might resurrect elsewhere, but whatever our fate, the outcome would be dictated by a law-governed universe.[189] Such findings offered a challenge to traditional theology. Graham nonetheless wondered if there might not be a place for God in the evolutionary scheme. Certainly the old anthropomorphic Creator needed to go. A modern theology could only speak of a non-personal God. When it came to man, theologians would need to embrace Darwin's "total revolution" which derived humans from primordial animal roots.[190] Modern science's discovery that inside man an "animal sleeps at the bottom of his being" forces theology to adopt a scientific view of human nature, looking to physiology, psychology, sociology, and anthropology for theological understanding.[191] Likewise, theology had to look to Darwinism for ethical insight. While the myth of the Fall of Man in Genesis no longer served as a credible guide, the modern evolutionary view enables us to see how self-interest—man's "original selfish root"—is yielding to a pursuit of the common good by way of our emergent "unselfish sentiments".[192] As traditional religious beliefs faded before strides in scientific knowledge, Graham envisioned the rise of a revitalized Pantheism. This theology would be informed by the scientific view that the world encountered through our senses is a world beyond those senses—a world whose essence we do not know.[193] Behind the world of appearances there is a "Something" that moves all matter and thought.[194] This hidden "purpose" has birthed humans with their "immortal longings for a divine something."[195] Like Darwin, Graham refused to believe that a "mindless universe" gave rise to such an awareness.[196] This "Power" behind evolution would continue to evolve our world long after humans have disappeared.[197] If theology could only embrace "the advance of knowledge and the wider vision of truth," then science would "infuse fresh life into the old religious doctrines."[198]

Graham's vision was music to Darwin's ears. Darwin's response to Graham's book was nothing short of ecstatic. "It is a very long time since any other book has interested me so much," he wrote just eight months before his death.[199] We find him recommending this work to colleagues like Hooker and Romanes. There was much that Darwin agreed with but he couldn't help raising questions. He took issue with Graham's view that "the existence of so-called natural law implies purpose." He confessed to Graham his "inward conviction . . . that the universe is not the result of chance." Yet he also admitted that still the old "horrid doubt . . . arises whether the convictions of man's mind, which has been developed from the mind of the lower animals, are of any value or at all trustworthy." He added, "Would any one trust in the convictions of a monkey's mind?" He also challenged Graham on the high view Graham took of "our greatest men." He told Graham that in his research he learned to trust the findings of "2nd, 3rd and 4th rate men." Finally, he said he could "show fight on natural selection having done and doing more for the progress of civilization than you seem inclined to admit." Past "risks" have given way to the ridiculousness of continued conflict in the "hollow struggle for existence." He urged Graham to look at how Europe had outstripped the Turks in this regard. Despite such considerations, Darwin found "excitement" in Graham's effort to rethink religion and philosophy in light of his own theories.

Conclusion

In writing to Francis Darwin about this correspondence after Darwin's death, Graham suggested that while Darwin was agnostic, he was not a "true Agnostic" inasmuch as he held such an "inward conviction" about the universe—convictions the agnostic would not share in the least.[200] Indeed, Darwin kept puzzling over the religion question to the end of his life. This is not to say he experienced some sort of deathbed conversion to Christianity, a fraudulent legend promoted by Lady Elizabeth Hope (Elizabeth Reid Cotton).[201] He had long ago abandoned traditional biblical beliefs. It simply meant that Darwin's lively mind remained intrigued and puzzled by the religion question to the last.

Darwin's burial in Westminster Abbey on 26 April 1882, was a sign of his "approbation" by his colleagues—secular as well as religious—who came to recognize the good he had done in handing us the key to the "mystery of mysteries" through his theory of Natural Selection.[202] The Rev Frederic William Farrar encouraged Huxley to apply to the Dean of Westminster to have Darwin buried at the Abbey. When Huxley expressed his doubts about the Dean granting approval for such a burial, Farrar told Huxley with a smile, "we clergy were not all so bigoted as he supposed."[203] Farrar preached a funeral sermon for Darwin the following Sunday evening. "I would rather take my chance in the future life with such a man as Charles Darwin," Farrar proclaimed, "than with the many thousands who, saying, 'Lord, Lord,' and wearing the broadest of phylacteries, show very faint conceptions of honour, kindness, or the love of truth."[204] He went on to extol Darwin's integrity and modesty, reminding those gathered of the words of a friend who credited Darwin with "an intense and passionate honesty, by which all his thoughts and actions were irradiated as by a central fire."[205]

The Rev Harvey Goodwin, Lord Bishop of Carlisle, who also preached that day, embraced Darwin's intellect as a "gift of God."[206] Admiring Darwin's singular "devotion" to nature, Goodwin decried those who would needlessly place science and religion in conflict. "Mr. Darwin" he says, "has been the means of producing greater change in the current of thought on certain subjects than any other man."[207] He added, "there will be, and must be for a long time to come, connected with his name, not merely the thought of a remarkable scientific epoch, but also the thought of an intense emphasis given to the question, What is the relation in which natural science stands to religious faith?"[208] Goodwin insisted, there was no need to think "that having got the works of Darwin I may burn my Bible."[209]

Having attended Darwin's funeral, George John Romanes saw in the Abbey burial a meeting place for faith and science.[210] In his *Charles Darwin: A Memorial Poem*, Romanes discerned in Darwin the new point of departure for future reflection on God, suffering, and our place in the universe:

For he was one of that small band,
Who in the waves of History
Stand up, as rocks in ocean stand,
Above the wide and level sea;
And time shall come when men shall gaze
That wide and level sea along,
To mark through dim and distant haze
One rock that rises sheer and strong:
And they will say — Behold the place
Where true was steered the course of Thought;
For there it was the human race
First found the bearings that they sought.[211]

It is over 150 years since the publication of the *Origin of Species* and more than 200 years since Darwin's birth. The laudatory words are beginning to ring true. Charles Darwin was the unlikely herald of a new way of looking at the workings of Nature. But Darwin's theory of Natural Selection, important as it is, is only half of the story. His early doubts about the Bible and his global experiences became a springboard for a new understanding of human religiosity. He struggled after his voyage to find an adequate theory to explain the rise and function of religion. After the *Origin of Species* was published, he recognized that his work would not be complete until he made public his views on human evolution, especially the evolution of religion and morality. This contribution, unfortunately overshadowed by the so-called creation-evolution debates in our day, can now be seen as a major advance in our thinking about religion and ethics. While his ideas have raised qualms in certain circles, yet for those unafraid to explore, Darwin's theories about Nature and the evolution of religion remain a constructive meeting place between a critical faith and a rigorous science. As theologian John Haught writes, "A religiously adequate understanding of God not only tolerates but requires the adventurous extension of the cosmic frontiers that are implied in evolutionary science."[212] Darwin's claim that religion evolves is a profound insight. To Darwin, we are indebted for placing this insight at the heart of the religious quest.

We leave the final word on this matter to T. H. Huxley's article in *Nature*, written on the occasion of Darwin's passing.[213] Huxley captured Darwin's sagacity well when he observed, "One could not converse with Darwin without being reminded of Socrates. There was the same desire to find some one wiser than himself; the same belief in the sovereignty of reason; the same ready humour; the same sympathetic interest in all the ways and works of men." Likening him to a great Greek philosopher, Huxley credited Darwin with attacking and unlocking problems that others found intractable. "Once more the image of Socrates rises unbidden," says Huxley, "and the noble peroration of the 'Apology' rings in our ears as if it were Charles Darwin's farewell:—'The hour of departure has arrived, and we go our ways—I to die and you to live. Which is the better God only knows.'"

Conclusion: Reflecting on Darwin Today

"You have given articulation to a thousand things lying dumb within me," wrote James Shaw to Darwin in 1865.[1] For the Scottish schoolmaster, Darwin had ushered in a world in which "Truth is indeed stranger than Fiction."[2] Shaw confessed that he never dreamt that the day would come in his lifetime when "the deepest truth" of existence would be as plainly spelled out as Darwin had done. He adds rather poetically, "Newton's ocean of wonder on whose shore he gathered shells seems no longer a dark unnavigable sea crested with howling breakers." The wisdom in Darwin's vision left Shaw spellbound. In this conclusion, I want to offer some personal reflections concerning how we might apply Darwin's compelling insights to the seemingly intractable science and religion debate in our day.

We are over 150 years on since the publication of the *Origin of Species* and it is distressing to see that Darwin evokes more wrangling than wonder in certain quarters. A professor from Germany visiting my undergraduate class on the Genesis debates stayed on many days longer than he intended out of shock at learning that many Americans feel that conservative religious belief trumps modern science. "How," he asked in amazement, "can the most advanced scientific society in the world act as if the truths of science are subject to popular whim?" When I queried him about his own educational system he replied, "No matter who sponsors the school, whether church or state, we all teach the same science!" The continued conflict over creationism does not speak well for the effectiveness of the teaching of evolution in America. Nor does the adamant rejection of evolution in certain religious quarters bode well for religion in the public square. Perhaps Darwin's search for a deeper truth about religion—and his discovery that religion evolves—can serve as a corrective to the needless polarizations that surround the current creation-evolution debate.[3]

Intellectually fulfilled atheists?

While fundamentalist creationists today attack Darwin as a misguided atheist whose deranged ideas paved the way for Hitler, atheist apologists such as Richard Dawkins use Darwin as a sledgehammer to beat religion.[4] This sort of verbal fisticuffs may have its precursor in the writings of T. H. Huxley and his campaign for "agnosticism," but Darwin shunned this approach as counterproductive.[5] Darwin may have been happy to have his colleagues get in their digs at the religious conservatives, but when it came to the people he respected, such as Asa Gray and Charles Lyell, we find him quite able and willing to tackle religious questions and to agree to disagree. Even as he shunned mindless Biblicism, Darwin thought seriously about religion. At all stages of his career, we find Darwin reading works on theology and religion that informed his thinking about religious questions.[6] We have seen that early on Darwin was reading the more conservative works of Paley, Sumner, and Pearson. After his return from his voyage, he continued his investigation of natural theology (John Ray, William Buckland, Peter Mark Roget, Charles Bell, William Kirby, Hugh Miller, John MacCullough) and read a somewhat conservative work on the genuineness of the Gospels by the American Unitarian Andrews Norton. He turned in mid-career to more liberal theological works in which progressive, Transcendentalist, and Unitarian influences made their mark (Samuel Taylor Coleridge, Harriet Martineau, Joseph Priestley, Francis Newman, Frederick Temple, and James Allanson Picton).[7] Indeed, Newman's *Phases of Faith,* chronicling the author's journey from evangelicalism to Unitarianism to religious skepticism, was deemed by Darwin as "excellent" and was on his reading list the month before his daughter Annie died in 1851. When writing his *Descent of Man,* works on the anthropology of religion caught his attention. At the end of his days, we have seen how Graham's work filled the growing gap he sensed between his own scientific work and the lagging theological world. Far from discounting religious ideals and virtues, Darwin sought far and wide for new perspectives on religion. There is something to be gained from appreciating this aspect of Darwin's life-long interest in religion.

Thus, while it is certainly true that Darwin makes it possible to be an intellectually fulfilled atheist as Richard Dawkins claims, it is also the case that Darwin makes it possible to be an intellectually fulfilled *theist.* When a skeptical philosopher such as Michael Ruse can make a place for religious believers at Darwin's table, when biologists such as Kenneth Miller and Francisco Ayala can make room for theological reflection in the biological sciences, when Francis Collins, former head of the Human Genome Project, can find God speaking in the creative fabric of the human genome, when particle-physicist-turned-priest John Polkinghorne can construct a fruitful dialogue between science and modern theology, and when theologian John Haught can welcome Darwin as a friend of religion, we are justified in thinking that a productive conversation regarding the relation between religion and science is possible—on Darwinian terms.[8] Secular biologists are fond of quoting geneticist Theodosius Dobzhansky's dictum that "Nothing in biology makes sense except in the light of evolution." Would that they also quoted his words from the same article where he argues, "It is wrong to hold creation and evolution as mutually exclusive alternatives. I am a creationist *and* an evolutionist. Evolution is God's, or Nature's method of creation. Creation is not an event that happened in 4004 BC; it is a process that began some 10 billion years ago and is still under way."[9] In his book *The Biology of Ultimate Concern,* Dobzhansky exhibits a subtlety of theological and philosophic analysis sorely lacking in the writings of Richard Dawkins and the other so-called New Atheists. Dobzhansky works carefully with Paul Tillich's philosophy of "ultimate concern" and the programmatic evolutionary theology of Teilhard de Chardin, thinkers never engaged by Dawkins's *God Delusion.* This gap in Dawkins's work is regrettable. The same could be said of his overlooking David Lack's *Evolutionary Theory and Christian Belief,* a sensible appraisal of the relation between neo-Darwinism and modern theology written by a preeminent evolutionary biologist whose work *Darwin's Finches* is a landmark in the field. Likewise, since Dawkins considers Ronald Fisher the "greatest biologist since Darwin," a response to Fisher's *Creative Aspects of Natural Law* would seem appropriate.[10] The contrast between the approaches of Dobzhansky and Dawkins could not be more telling. The failure to engage serious theological reflections offered by his own peers and other modern theologians weakens Dawkins's case considerably. For Dobzhansky, on the other hand, the emergent evolution of self-awareness, death-awareness, and religious belief become points of departure in his quest for meaning in a Darwinian world.

Given Darwin's complex views on religious questions, it makes sense to suggest that both postures—atheist and theist—capture a truth about Darwin's ideas. The fact of the matter is that he embraced neither atheism in the strictest sense nor theism in its biblical variation. At one point in his autobiographical reflections, written late in his life, he says that when it came to ultimate origins he labeled himself both a "Theist" as well as an "Agnostic."[11] In a letter from roughly the same time period, as we have seen, he made it clear that he was not an "Atheist in the sense of denying the existence of God."[12] In his refusal to be pigeonholed, we must see a sincere desire to uncover new truths about religion. For one side or the other to try to seize Darwin's mantle is to distort the historical record. Darwin's thinking about religion was more sophisticated. He moved away from traditional faith toward a refined understanding of the rise, development, and function of religion. And he did so in a way that opened to him a path for making further progress on these questions through a healthy combination of skepticism and curiosity about religion. The skeptical side of Darwin is the side that refused to use the Bible as a substitute for good scientific work. The days of writing a history of religion or of life's biology from the Bible alone were over. Darwin's religious side, if we may use such an expression, is the side that remained curious about matters of religion even as he sought to develop a modern and critical take on the Bible and religion's evolution. That both a Kingsley and a Huxley could celebrate the *Origin of Species* does not reflect the weakness of Darwin's insights about religion, but shows us the richness of his contribution. The point is that neither atheists nor theists can hope to fashion a modern view of religion while ignoring or caricaturing Darwin. In any event, Darwin did not wish to be thought of as the next Voltaire. That was not his style. He took religion more seriously than that. His views on the evolution of religion deserve greater attention by all the parties in the current creation-evolution debate.

The benefits and drawbacks of religion

Beyond restoring to the conversation Darwin's contribution to the study of religion, his view of the relation between religion and altruism deserves particular attention. Unlike those today who use an evolutionary ideology to negate religion, Darwin recognized the good that religion can perform when it focuses on acts of charity to serve those in need. He assisted the Rev Brodie Innes as treasurer in administering his village's "Coal and Clothing Club" as they sought to insure against the inevitable economic struggles of the poorer residents of the parish.[13] Together with Innes, he founded the "Down Friendly Society," serving also as its treasurer. Friendly Societies were popular in the nineteenth century. These were voluntary associations that on a modest scale represented a kind of cross between a savings bank, an investment firm, a health insurance company, a pension fund, and a men's social drinking club.[14] The Down Friendly Society operated out of the village public house, the George Inn, under rules laid down by Darwin's mentor John Stevens Henslow, guidelines which, as Desmond and Moore explain, attempted to curtail swearing, drunkenness, fighting, and gambling on the part of the association's members.[15] Such organizations provided a much-needed safety net for those who suffered from physical illness or simply making ends meet. At one critical meeting, as Desmond and Moore recount, Darwin had to badger those assembled with "a long harangue" to goad them into keeping the Friendly Society alive rather than shortsightedly fold it to meet a temporary but very real farming financial crisis.[16] The next day he reported to Innes that the diatribe "acted like a bomb-shell for all the members seem to have quarrelled for the next two hours." Proud of his triumph, he felt certain the organization would not disband and said that he "had much satisfaction in reading aloud the penal clause."[17] By which he meant that the officers of the organization would end up in prison if they foolishly disbanded the group. At that point in 1877, after having served as treasurer of the society for twenty-seven years, he was not about to let their joint efforts fail. Darwin, unlike today's New Atheists, was unafraid to promote a positive role for the Church in society.

Another case in point is his support for the evangelist James Fegan's efforts at social reform. Fegan was instrumental in helping destitute boys find jobs and places to live. In early 1881, Darwin wrote to Fegan, "Your services have done more for the village in a few months than all our efforts for many years."[18] He explained, "We have never been able to reclaim a drunkard, but through your services I do not know that there is a drunkard left in the village." Darwin was quite willing to turn over the local Reading Room to Fegan's spiritual campaign. His servants Joseph Parslow and Mrs. Sales appear to have been converts to Fegan's mission.[19] Regarding "Old M.," whom Henrietta identified as "a notable old drunkard in the village of Down," Emma Darwin could only praise Fegan's success. "Hurrah for Mr Fegan!," she exclaims and then tells her daughter that "Mrs Evans attended a prayer meeting in which old M. made 'as nice a prayer as ever you heard in your life.'"[20] Fegan was deeply impressed by the Darwin family's willingness to alter their dinner hour to allow their servants to attend his services.[21] He was likewise impressed with Darwin's chivalry and benevolence which led him—despite his agnosticism—to support Fegan's own social works. That benevolence, as we have seen, also caused Darwin to support the South American Missionary Society's work in Patagonia.[22]

Today's New Atheists, such as Richard Dawkins, Daniel Dennett, and Sam Harris, could learn from Darwin on this point.[23] There is a marked tendency among those in this camp to use Darwin as a whip to scourge religion when it comes to such perplexities as the suffering of the innocent, the problem of evil, political violence, and the social welfare crisis. The promise of Dawkin's *The God Delusion,* in particular, appears to be that if we were to banish religion, all would be well. As if by getting rid of religion, we would get rid of war, slip out of the philosophic knot of the problem of evil, and solve all society's ills. If Charles Darwin is right, however, our aggressive tendencies long preceded the advent of religion and would still be present or possibly even magnified in the absence of the religious call to altruism.[24] The traits of violence and aggression were prompted as our ancestors competed for resources in primordial times and these tendencies, which served them so well, were passed down as part of the evolutionary process. As such, these factors do not owe their origins to religion as a latecomer on the scene. Evolution, likewise, gave us altruism. Religion, following its own course of evolution, has a choice to make whether to reinforce human violence or to build on the deep evolutionary roots of the Golden Rule. By understanding that religion has evolved as part of the human psyche, we can encourage those symbols, myths, and rituals that advance the human quest while dismantling those that do not. Foundational works in the evolution of religious psychology by Atran, Barrett, and Boyer, offer valuable insights to students of religion and theology, without the needless diatribes of the New Atheists.[25] In particular, as the evolutionary psychologist Justin Barrett, formerly of Oxford's Centre for Anthropology and Mind, states in his *Why Would Anyone Believe in God?*, "I do not regard belief in God as strange, loony, or irrational." He adds, "Indeed, once examined from a scientific perspective, both believers and nonbelievers should appreciate how very natural and almost inevitable widespread religious belief is."[26] Regardless of what each individual makes of the anthropological and psychological research on religion in relation to the truth claims of specific traditions, there is great value in looking carefully at the evolution of the religious and moral sense as charted by Darwin and his modern counterparts.

Darwin was more sophisticated about religion and morality than his secular handlers admit and his conservative critics care to embrace. Yet religion is neither the sole problem nor the single solution. Religion can indeed exacerbate our worst animalistic aggressions, but it can also induce noble acts of compassion. Darwin, it seems, understood and valued the difference. Knowing that religion has evolved enables us to be clear about its drawbacks when linked to our aggressions as well as to appreciate religion's benefits when nurturing our altruistic side. Darwin's understanding of the deep evolutionary roots of the "Golden Rule" remains instructive when thinking about the relation between theology, ethics, and science.[27] Secularists need not dismiss theology out of hand nor should religionists reject Darwinism. Darwin models for us the progress to be made by reading deeply in theology and yet remaining committed to the scientific enterprise.

A final word

In his book *Pale Blue Dot*, Carl Sagan called conservative religion to task for closing its eyes to scientific advance while clinging to an outmoded view of God.[28] He goes on to suggest that science has ushered in new levels of wonder that could become the foundation for a deeper belief system. "Sooner or later," he said, "such a religion will emerge."[29] The war between science and religion in America, however, has left us in an undesirable place. Religion has been exiled from the curriculum out of fear that creationists will want to hog the science lectern. A variety of legal decisions concerning the teaching of evolution have had the unfortunate effect of stifling serious reflection on the philosophic and religious implications of Darwin's work, perspectives that were integral to his life project. Darwin's lifelong argument was, after all, an argument about both science and religion. Building a firewall between these spheres is not conducive to civil discourse on these pressing issues. The creationist attempt to demonize Darwin and the secularist need to defend Darwin at all costs have served to remove the man and his own writings from a place of sober discussion. Instead of critical reflection, we have the fuming of the fundamentalists and the posturing of the New Atheists.[30] This is an unfortunate state of affairs because it means that the full range of Darwin's ideas about religion and ethics will remain unexplored. In particular, the positive aspects of his view of the evolution of religion and morality will go unappreciated by the combatants. A more informed Darwinian discourse would go a long way toward putting us back in the business of seeking answers in a universe that sparks in us deep questions about science, religion, and morality. Somehow, we need to find our way into the relationship Darwin had with the Rev John Innes, Vicar of Down, who believed that the scientific and religious communities would be better off if they could only get along as well as these two friends and colleagues did. "Dear me!," he wrote Darwin, "if some of your naturalist, and my ritualist friends were to hear us two saying civil things to each other, they would say the weather was going to change, or Paris to be relieved [of war], both of which I wish might happen."[31] Civility is a virtue not always practiced in the places where science and religion meet. "How nicely things would go on," he told Darwin on another occasion, "if other folk were like Darwin and Brodie Innes!"[32]

The truth about religion, as Darwin came to understand, was greater than the half-truths of the past. Like many of his generation, Darwin left the world of traditional religion behind. Yet rather than simply "lose his faith," Darwin paved the way for a new view of religion's rise, development, and function. As his longtime friend and colleague Charles Lyell said of Darwin's theory in an update to his *Principles of Geology*, "even where it failed to make proselytes, it gave a shock to old and time-honoured opinions from which they have never since recovered."[33] That is all to the good for those who seek a deeper understanding of the relation between religion and science. Darwin's lifelong curiosity about religion and his discovery that religion evolves point the way.

Notes

Preface

1 Nash, "Reassessing the 'Crisis of Faith' in the Victorian Age," suggests that neither the worn out Victorian "crisis of faith" paradigm nor the supposed reconversion from secularism pattern ("individuals who lost their doubt") capture the "fluid" character of the Victorian search for moral truth (with or without religion). He argues instead that those whose search straddled the secular/sacred divide should be labeled "seekers." While he does not discuss Darwin in this connection, I would argue that Nash's revised religious and philosophical seeker construct can illuminate Darwin's journey as religious skeptic, theory maker, and finally evolution's moral sage. At all points, both religion and materialism stamp his quest.

Chapter 1

1 Letter from Caroline Darwin, 22 March 1826. DAR.204.2; CCD 1: 36.
2 Letter to Caroline Darwin, 8 April 1826. DAR.154; CCD 1: 39.
3 CUL-DAR.26.25.
4 Ibid.
5 See Desmond and Moore, *Darwin*, 48–9.
6 Darwin, *Autobiography*, 58. It is unfortunate that W. W. Norton elected to issue a new version of the *Autobiography* under the same ISBN number and with the same cover, making it impossible to distinguish the two editions in this way. The newer version, however, has a modernized typeface and a radically different pagination. All references here are to the original edition.
7 CUL-DAR.26.26. All quotations are taken from Darwin's "Recollections of the development of my mind and character" and are quoted with permission.
8 Darwin, *Autobiography*, 62–3, 69–70.
9 For a complete list of books taken aboard the *Beagle*, see CCD 1: 553–66. Sharon Turner's, *The Sacred History of the World*, evoked a skeptical comment from Darwin about its defense of divine benevolence in creation (CCD 1: 320–21). The only other work of theological import known from Darwin's collection aboard the Beagle was Richard Whately's *A View of the Scripture Revelations Concerning a Future State*, which was sent to Darwin by his sister Caroline (DAR.204.6.1; CCD 1: 346) as a

reminder that "we often used to find we liked the same kind of books." Valuable overviews of the development of Darwin's personal ideas about religion can be found in Brown, *The Evolution of Darwin's Religious Views* and Moore, "Darwin of Down." For background on Darwin's early life and education, see most recently Thomson, *The Young Charles Darwin*. For Darwin's exposure to Lamarckian developmentalist ideas at Edinburgh, see also Secord, "Edinburgh Lamarckians." On the Cambridge educational context, see Fyfe, "The Reception of William Paley's *Natural Theology* in the University of Cambridge," and Garland's *Cambridge Before Darwin*. On Henslow's liberal Christian influence, see Walters and Stow, *Darwin's Mentor*, ch. 9. Among the more important works for situating the development of Darwin's thinking contextually against the backdrop of the breakup of the "common context" of natural theology in England is Young's *Darwin's Metaphor*. See also Ospovat, *The Development of Darwin's Theory*, for a textured reading of the growth of Darwin's view of adaptation. While, in the end, Darwin rejects natural theology, both Young and Ospovat show that he was also reinventing these categories and resetting the boundaries between religion and science, not simply rejecting religion. We should also observe that it would be wrong to think that there was one brand of "natural theology" in Darwin's day since practitioners varied as to how they integrated religion and science as well as regarding where to draw the line between these spheres. Indeed, the eight Bridgewater Treatises (1833–1836) demonstrate quite well something of this diversity. On the Bridgewater Treatises, see Topham, "Beyond the 'Common Context'," Brock, "The Selection of the Authors of the Bridgewater Treatises," and Robson, "The Fiat and Finger of God." In many ways, Darwin was deepening the natural theology discussion even as he undermined its conclusions. For an incisive treatment of Darwin's historical context as well as the history of the current debates over Darwin, see Peter Bowler, *Monkey Trials and Gorilla Sermons: Evolution and Christianity from Darwin to Intelligent Design*. See also, Ruse, *The Darwinian Revolution*, especially ch. 3. Numbers, "Science and Religion," provides a nuanced discussion of the history of the science vs. religion "battle" metaphor in the American setting. The essential overview of the history of the creationist controversy remains Numbers, *The Creationists*. While the biographies of Browne as well as of Desmond and Moore remain foundational, a fine abbreviated overview of Darwin's life is provided by Berra, *Charles Darwin*.

10 Keynes, Diary, 13; Darwin, Autobiography, 85.

11 The book is on display at Down House in Kent.

12 Darwin, *Voyage*, 267.

13 Ibid.

14 Ibid.

15 Darwin, *Voyage*, 267. While Darwin's England exhibited a marked anti-Catholic streak, with debates over the rights of Catholics being a key topic

of conversation, Darwin himself never seems to display these tendencies. In the *Descent of Man* (I, 178–9), he does argue that priestly celibacy ruined Europe as the Inquisition imprisoned or did away with "those who doubted and questioned." Despite this "incalculable" evil, he says, Europe still progressed. As Darwin reminded his readers, "without doubting there can be no progress. In any event, his writings and correspondence do not display any marked degree of anti-Catholic bigotry.

16 Chacellor and van Whye, 383, 386.

17 See Moore's article "Of love and death: Why Darwin 'gave up Christianity'" in Greene, *History, Humanity and Evolution*; Keynes, *Darwin, His Daughter, and Human Evolution*. For the Edinburgh context, see Thomson, *The Young Charles Darwin,* 32–83. For an alternative view see Van Whye and Pallen, "The Annie Hypothesis."

18 See Desmond and Moore, *Darwin*, especially ch. 25. In his review of Desmond and Moore, Michael Ruse complains, "I am just not convinced . . . that Darwin was all that tormented." See Ruse, "Will the Real Charles Darwin Please Stand Up?," 229.

19 Browne, *Voyaging,* 326; a fact noted by Spencer, *God and Darwin,* 31.

20 See Browne, *Voyaging,* 272–3, 322–3, 334. In fact, she suggests that Darwin's clerical career died a "natural death" (p. 322).

21 Desmond and Moore, *Darwin*, mention in passing Darwin's curiosity about the origins of the Fuegians (146–7) and do not take up the question of the evolution of religion.

22 Here I will refer to the first edition (1839) as the *Journal of Researches* and the updated edition (1845) as the *Voyage of the Beagle*.

23 Darwin, Voyage, 211.

24 Darwin, *Voyage*, 212–3; For their names, see FitzRoy, *Narrative*, vol. 2, 135. Their phrenological descriptions are given on pages 148–9.

25 FitzRoy, *Narrative,* vol. 2, 12.

26 FitzRoy, *Narrative,* Appendix to vol. 2, 147–8; Hazlewood, *Savage,* 87–9.

27 Letter to J. S. Henslow, 11 April 1833. Royal Botanic Gardens, Kew Catalogue Reference DAR/1/1/17, quoted with permission; CCD 1: 306.

28 Keynes, *Diary,* 122–5.

29 Darwin, *Voyage,* 209. The precise roots of Darwin's own thinking about the "savage" in relation to "civilization" are difficult to ascertain. Certainly Darwin's reading of Humboldt's *Personal Narrative* during his last year at Cambridge will have offered some contextualization of the term for him (see Darwin, *Autobiography,* 67–8). For a study of Humboldt's influence on Darwin, see Leask, "Darwin's 'Second Sun.'" General background for these ideas (and prejudices) during this time period is offered by Stocking, *Victorian Anthropology*, Chs. 1–4. Tracing the function of the "savage" in Darwin's works, see Schmitt, "Darwin's Savage Mnemonics." See also, Day, "Godless Savages and Superstitious Dogs," who proposes that Darwin linked civilized and savage peoples in terms of bodily form (to preserve monogenism) but separated them in terms of their religious

variations (or the absence of religion). The problem became, says Day, one of sorting out the gradations that would unfold an evolutionary lineage, allowing nonreligious proto-humans to become religious (and moral) humans of one sort or another. For additional contextualization of the anthropological discussion of the concept of the savage, see Bowler, "From 'savage' to 'primitive.'"

30 Letter [manuscript]: Valparaiso, Charles Darwin to Charles Whitley, College, Durham, 23 July 1834, National Library of Australia, MS 4260. Quoted by permission of the National Library of Australia, NLAref69584. This letter can be found online at nla.gov.au/mla.ms-ms4260. See CCD 1: 397. On Darwin's relationship to Whitley, see Browne, *Voyaging*, 104–7.

31 Letter to Caroline Darwin, 30 March–12 April 1833. DAR.233; CCD 1: 303.

32 As Schmitt, "Darwin's Savage Mnemonics," explains, Darwin's indelible memory of his initial shock at seeing the savage Fuegians became for him the crucial evolutionary link between animals and civilized humans. Yet, for Darwin, the horror of that memory also served to distance the Fuegians from "civilized" man, a view not shared by FitzRoy or Captain King, commander during the *Beagle*'s first voyage, both of whom came to view the Fuegians as fully human. In Schmitt's judgment (p. 67), by contrast, the Fuegians remained for Darwin inferior relics of the past, an "earlier incarnation of humanity" and "stand-ins for prehistoric forms of life." Duncan, "Darwin and the Savages," is particularly instructive regarding Darwin's difficulty navigating the tension between the human character of the savage and the need to define primitives as other than civilized.

33 Letter to Charles Kingsley, 6 February 1862. Cleveland Health Sciences Library, Robert M. Stecher Collection; CCD 10: 71.

34 Darwin, *Voyage*, 506–7.

35 Darwin, *Voyage*, 507.

36 Ibid.

37 Ibid.

38 Darwin, *Voyage*, 210–1. One should bear in mind that E. Lucas Bridges, *Uttermost Part of the Earth,* Ch. 1, takes issue with Darwin's portrait of the Fuegians, especially any talk of cannibalism. Bridges, son of a missionary to the region, lived among the Fuegians for many decades and has argued that the natives either misunderstood the foreigners' questions or were pulling their legs. In our study of the *Beagle* voyage, what was decisive for Darwin's theorizing was his impression of the Fuegians and not the anthropological accuracy of his observations.

39 Darwin, *Voyage*, 210.

40 Ibid., 213.

41 See Browne, *Voyaging*, 239–53.

42 Letter to Caroline Darwin, 30 March–12 April 1833. DAR.233; CCD 1: 303.

43 Darwin, *Voyage*, 231.

44 Ibid.
45 Ibid.
46 Ibid.
47 Darwin, *Voyage*, 408.
48 Ibid.
49 Darwin, *Voyage*, 413.
50 Ibid.
51 Darwin, *Voyage*, 412.
52 Ibid.
53 Darwin, *Voyage*, 414.
54 Darwin, *Voyage*, 423.
55 Ibid.
56 See Browne, *Voyaging*, 310.
57 Darwin, *Voyage*, 434.
58 Ibid., 437.
59 Darwin, *Voyage*, 438.
60 Ibid.
61 Ibid.
62 Ibid.
63 Darwin, *Voyage*, 454.
64 Ibid.
65 Ibid.
66 Ibid.
67 Ibid.
68 Darwin, *Voyage*, 506.
69 Ibid., 54.
70 Darwin, *Voyage*, 75.
71 Ibid.
72 Ibid.
73 Darwin, *Voyage*, 220.
74 Ibid.
75 Ibid.
76 Ibid.
77 Darwin, *Voyage*, 219.
78 Ibid.
79 Ibid.
80 Darwin, *Voyage*, 219–20.
81 Darwin, *Voyage*, 292.
82 Ibid.
83 Ibid.
84 Darwin, *Voyage*, 371–3.
85 Darwin, *Voyage*, 415.
86 Ibid.
87 Ibid.
88 Ibid.

89   Keynes, *Diary*, 373.
90   Darwin, *Voyage*, 433.
91   Ibid.
92   Ibid.
93   Ibid.
94   Ibid.
95   Ibid.
96   Ibid.
97   Ibid.
98   Darwin, *Voyage*, 462.
99   Ibid.
100 Darwin, *Voyage*, 48.
101 Ibid., 487.
102 Darwin, *Voyage*, 50.
103 Ibid.
104 Darwin, *Voyage*, 345.
105 Ibid.
106 Ibid.
107 Darwin, *Voyage*, 347.
108 Ibid., 366.
109 Ibid., 367.
110 Darwin, *Voyage*, 267.
111 Ibid.
112 Ibid.
113 Keynes, *Diary*, 114.
114 Darwin, *Voyage*, 282–3.
115 Ibid., 283.
116 Ibid., 281–2.
117 Darwin, *Voyage*, 370.
118 Ibid.
119 Darwin, *Voyage*, 12.
120 Ibid., 13.
121 Darwin, *Voyage*, 149.
122 Ibid.
123 Darwin, *Voyage*, 305.
124 Ibid., 311.
125 Ibid., 312.
126 Darwin, *Voyage*, 309.
127 Ibid.
128 Ibid.
129 Darwin, *Voyage*, 306
130 Darwin, *Voyage*, 310.
131 Ibid.
132 Darwin, *Voyage*, 311.
133 Keynes, *Diary*, 299.

134 Darwin, *Voyage*, 311.
135 Ibid., 312.
136 CUL-DAR.26.62.
137 Darwin, *Voyage*, 313; see T. D. Kendrick, *The Lisbon Earthquake* (Philadelphia: J. B. Lippincott, N.D.).
138 Darwin, *Voyage*, 312.
139 Ibid.
140 Darwin, *Voyage*, 314.
141 Ibid., 356–7.
142 Darwin, *Voyage*, 44.
143 Ibid.
144 Ibid.
145 Ibid.
146 Darwin, *Origin of Species*, 202; CCD 8: 224.
147 Darwin, *Voyage*, 445.
148 Keynes, *Diary*, 402.
149 Ibid.
150 Ibid.
151 Ibid.
152 Keynes, *Diary*, 403.
153 Ibid.
154 Ibid.
155 Ibid.
156 See Desmond and Moore, *Darwin's Sacred Cause*.
157 Darwin, Voyage, 74, 78.
158 Darwin, *Voyage*, 108.
159 Ibid.
160 Darwin, *Voyage*, 109.
161 Ibid., 110.
162 Ibid., 149.
163 Ibid., 110.
164 Darwin, *Voyage*, 126.
165 Ibid.
166 Keynes, *Diary*, 179.
167 Ibid.
168 Keynes, *Diary*, 180.
169 Ibid.
170 Darwin, *Voyage*, 371.
171 Ibid.
172 Darwin, *Voyage*, 305.
173 Darwin, *Voyage*, 133.
174 Ibid.
175 Ibid.
176 Darwin, *Voyage*, 74.
177 Ibid., 78.

178 Ibid., 79.
179 Darwin, *Voyage*, 108.
180 Ibid.
181 Darwin, *Voyage*, 116.
182 Ibid., 111.
183 Darwin, *Voyage*, 299.
184 Ibid.
185 Ibid.
186 Darwin, *Voyage*, 304.
187 Darwin, *Voyage*, 284.
188 Ibid.
189 Ibid.
190 Ibid.
191 Ibid.
192 Darwin, *Voyage*, 286.
193 Ibid., 423.
194 Darwin, *Voyage*, 424.
195 Ibid.
196 Ibid.
197 Keynes, *Diary*, 180.
198 Ibid., 181.
199 Spencer, *God and Darwin*, 23.
200 Darwin, *Voyage*, 303.
201 Ibid.
202 Ibid.
203 Keynes, *Diary*, 289.
204 Ibid.
205 See Barrett, ed., *The Collected Papers of Charles Darwin*, Vol.1, 19–38; Browne, *Voyaging*, 330. For background on this surprising common cause between FitzRoy and Darwin, see Browne, "Missionaries and the Human Mind."
206 Darwin, *Voyage*, 414.
207 Ibid.
208 Ibid.
209 Darwin, *Voyage*, 415.
210 Ibid.
211 Darwin, *Voyage*, 416.
212 Ibid., 415.
213 Ibid., 416.
214 Darwin, *Voyage*, 417; Darwin is referring to Frederick William Beechey, *Narrative of a voyage to the Pacific and Beering Strait., 1825, 1826, 1827, 1828* (London 1831) and Otto von Kotzebue, *A voyage of discovery, into the South Sea and Beering Straits*, translated by H. E. Lloyd. 2 vols. (London 1821). See CCD 1: 558, 561. Browne, *Voyaging*, 306, indicates that it was Kotzebue's *A New Voyage Round the World* (1830) that goaded FitzRoy and

Darwin with its scathing critique of the missionaries operating in Tahiti. To be fair to Kotzebue, however, we should note that he did credit the English missionaries with having had a positive effect on the Tahitians regarding theft, sex, and alcohol. What he decried were the bloody wars undertaken by King Tajo whose conversion to Christianity led to its violent imposition on the islanders. In addition, he judged the religion of the missionaries not to be true Christianity but an ignorant and bigoted enterprise. He was further troubled by the inordinate political influence the missionaries exerted over the young child King and his missionary appointed Guardian.

215 Darwin, *Voyage*, 417.
216 Ibid.
217 Ibid.
218 Darwin, *Voyage*, 418.
219 Ibid.
220 Ibid.
221 Ibid.
222 Keynes, *Diary*, 376.
223 Browne, *Voyaging*, 309.
224 Keynes, *Diary*, 376.
225 Darwin, *Voyage*, 419.
226 Ibid.
227 Ibid.
228 Darwin, *Voyage*, 422.
229 Ibid., 428.
230 Darwin, *Voyage*, 429.
231 Ibid.
232 Darwin, *Voyage*, 430.
233 Ibid.
234 Ibid.
235 Ibid.
236 Ibid.
237 Ibid.
238 Ibid.
239 Darwin, *Voyage*, 432.
240 Ibid.
241 Darwin, *Voyage*, 423.
242 CUL-DAR.139.12.5.
243 Ibid.
244 On this faith, see Sulivan, *Life and Letters*, ix.
245 Hazlewood, *Savage*, 342–4.
246 Indeed, the disastrous nature of this misadventure was compounded in subsequent years after the Patagonian Missionary Society began enticing small groups of Fuegians to live and work at their missionary station in the region. Deteriorating relations eventually led to a massacre of several missionaries and fellow crew members. Jemmy Button narrowly

escaped being held accountable for these killings. The Society changed its name to the South American Missionary Society to distance itself from this debacle. After Jemmy died, his son "Threeboys" became one of four Fuegians brought to England by the Society. Threeboys met FitzRoy during that visit. See Hazlewood, *Savage*.

247 Keynes, *Diary*, 133.
248 These failed efforts among the Fuegians are chronicled by Hazlewood, *Savage*.
249 Letter to Caroline Darwin, 27 December 1835. DAR.233; CCD 1: 472.
250 Darwin, *Voyage*, 35.
251 Ibid., 506.
252 Keynes, *Diary*, 59.
253 Darwin, *Autobiography*, 52.
254 Chancellor and van Whye, *Charles Darwin's Notebooks*, 45; noted by Spencer, *Darwin and God*, 121, though without a clear indication of the source of this quote.
255 Darwin, *Voyage*, 506.
256 Ibid.
257 Letter to Caroline Darwin, 30 March–12 April 1833; CCD 1: 303.
258 Keynes, *Diary*, 111.
259 Ibid.
260 CUL-DAR.26.61.
261 Keynes, *Diary*, 111, which notes Milton, *Paradise Lost*, Book 4, line 800.
262 Burton-Christie, "Darwin's Contemplative Vision," 91.
263 Darwin, *Voyage*, 47, 38, 507.
264 Ibid., 163.
265 Ibid., 286.
266 Ibid., 258.
267 Ibid., 285.
268 Ibid., 326.
269 Ibid., 421.
270 Darwin, *Voyage*, 507.
271 Ibid.
272 CUL-DAR.26.71.
273 Darwin, *Voyage*, 292, 294.
274 Ibid., 509.

Chapter 2

1 CUL-DAR.26.49.
2 CUL-DAR.26.53.
3 CUL-DAR.26.61.
4 Letter from Caroline Darwin 12 [–18] September 1832. DAR.204.6.1; CCD 1: 271.

5 Letter to Caroline Darwin, 25–6 April, [1832]. DAR.223; CCD 1 :227.
6 Letter from Caroline Darwin, 28 October 1833. DAR.204.6.1; CCD 1: 346.
7 Letter from Caroline Darwin, 28 October 1833. DAR.204.6.1; CCD 1: 346.
8 Letter from Charlotte Wedgwood, 22 September 1831. DAR.204.5; CCD 1: 165.
9 Letter from Charlotte Wedgwood, 22 September 1831. DAR.204.5; CCD 1: 165.
10 Letter from Charlotte Wedgwood, 22 September 1831. DAR.204.5; CCD 1: 165.
11 White, *Thomas Huxley: Making the "Man of Science,"* 15.
12 White, *Thomas Huxley*, 15.
13 Letter from Catherine Darwin, 25 July [–3 August] 1832. DAR.204.6.1; CCD 1: 254.
14 Letter from Catherine Darwin, 25 July [–3 August] 1832. DAR.204.6.1; CCD 1: 254.
15 Letter from Catherine Darwin, 25 July [–3 August] 1832. DAR.204.6.1; CCD 1: 254.
16 Letter from Catherine Darwin, 25 July [–3 August] 1832. DAR.204.6.1; CCD 1: 254.
17 Letter from Catherine Darwin, 25 July [–3 August] 1832. DAR.204.6.1; CCD 1: 254.
18 Letter from Catherine Darwin, 25 July [–3 August] 1832. DAR.204.6.1; CCD 1: 254.
19 Letter from Charlotte Wedgwood, 12 January–1 February 1832; DAR.204.6.2; CCD 1: 197.
20 Letter from Charlotte Wedgwood, 12 January–1 February 1832; DAR.204.6.2; CCD 1: 197.
21 Letter from Charlotte Wedgwood, 12 January–1 February 1832; DAR.204.6.2; CCD 1: 197.
22 Letter from Charlotte Wedgwood, 12 January–1 February 1832; DAR.204.6.2; CCD 1: 197.
23 Letter from Charlotte Wedgwood, 12 January–1 February 1832; DAR.204.6.2; CCD 1: 197.
24 Letter from Charlotte Wedgwood, 12 January–1 February 1832; DAR.204.6.2; CCD 1: 197.
25 Letter to Caroline Darwin, 2–6 April 1832; DAR.223; CCD 1: 220.
26 Letter from Fanny Biddulph [c. 21 October 1833]. DAR.204.4; CCD 1: 341.
27 Eliot, *Scenes of Clerical Life.*
28 Eliot, *Scenes of Clerical Life*, 71, 68.
29 Kepple, "The Country Parson," 319.
30 Kepple, "The Country Parson," 321.
31 Letter from Catherine Darwin, 27 September 1833. DAR.204.6.1; CCD 1: 333.
32 F. Darwin, *Life and Letters*, vol. 1, 147.

33 Letter to W. D. Fox, 5 November 1830. Christ's College Library, Cambridge University (Fox 34); CCD 1: 110.
34 Browne, *Voyaging*, 326.
35 Letter to W. D. Fox [9-12 August] 1835. Christ's College Library, Cambridge University (Fox 47a); CCD 1: 460.
36 Letter to W. D. Fox [9-12 August] 1835. Christ's College Library, Cambridge University (Fox 47a); CCD 1: 460.
37 Letter to W. D. Fox [9-12 August] 1835. Christ's College Library, Cambridge University (Fox 47a); CCD 1: 460.
38 Letter to W. D. Fox [11 December 1837]. Christ's College Library, Cambridge University (Fox 53); CCD 2: 64.
39 CCD 1: 258.
40 Letter from E. A. Darwin, 18 August 1832. DAR.204.6.1; CCD 1: 259.
41 Letter from E. A. Darwin, 18 August 1832. DAR.204.6.1; CCD 1: 259.
42 Letter from Susan Darwin, 12 February 1836. DAR.97 (ser. 2): 30-1; CCD 1: 488-89.
43 Letter from Susan Darwin, 12 February 1836. DAR.97 (ser. 2): 30-1; CCD 1: 489.
44 See Browne, *Voyaging*, 380.
45 On Macaw, see Litchfield, *Emma Darwin*, vol. 2, 18. The church is noted in vol. 2, 26.
46 Litchfield, *Emma Darwin*, vol. 2, 12.
47 Letter to Emma Wedgwood [20 January 1839]. DAR.210.19; CCD 2: 166.
48 Letter to Emma Wedgwood [20 January 1839]. DAR.210.19; CCD 2: 166.
49 Browne, *Voyaging*, 400.
50 This work began life in 1839 as volume III of Robert FitzRoy's edited set on the voyage but was also issued separately that same year. A second revised edition appeared in 1845. For a full accounting of editions, see Freeman, *The Works of Charles Darwin*, 31-54. Here we shall distinguish the editions by referring to the 1839 work as *Journal of Researches* and the 1845 edition as *Voyage of the Beagle*.
51 Litchfield, *Emma Darwin*, vol. 2, 50.
52 Browne, *Voyaging*, 424-425, 430. Litchfield, *Emma Darwin*, vol. 2, 54.
53 Darwin's Notes on Marriage. DAR.210.10; CCD 2: 444.
54 Darwin's Notes on Marriage. DAR.210.10; CCD 2: 443.
55 Darwin's Notes on Marriage. DAR.210.10; CCD 2: 445.
56 Darwin's Notes on Marriage. DAR.210.10; CCD 2: 444.
57 Darwin's Notes on Marriage. DAR.210.10; CCD 2: 444.
58 Darwin's Notes on Marriage. DAR.210.10; CCD 2: 444.
59 Darwin's Notes on Marriage. DAR.210.10; CCD 2: 444.
60 Darwin's Notes on Marriage. DAR.210.10; CCD 2: 444.
61 Darwin's Notes on Marriage. DAR.210.10; CCD 2: 445.
62 Darwin's Notes on Marriage. DAR.210.10; CCD 2: 444.
63 Darwin, *Autobiography*, 95.
64 Browne, *Voyaging*, 396.

65 Litchfield, *Emma Darwin*, vol. 2, 173.
66 Litchfield, *Emma Darwin*, vol. 2, 173.
67 F. Darwin, *Springtime*, 52-53.
68 F. Darwin, *Springtime*, 52. The village was later named Downe.
69 F. Darwin, *Springtime*, 52.
70 Litchfield, *Emma Darwin*, vol. 2, 201.
71 F. Darwin, *Springtime*, 53.
72 Litchfield, *Emma Darwin*, vol. 2, 175.
73 Litchfield, *Emma Darwin*, vol. 2, 178-179.
74 Letter from Emma Wedgwood, 21-2 November 1838. DAR.204.13; CCD 2: 123.
75 Letter from Emma Wedgwood, 21-2 November 1838. DAR.204.13; CCD 2: 123.
76 Letter from Emma Wedgwood, 21-2 November 1838. DAR.204.13; CCD 2: 123.
77 Letter from Emma Wedgwood, 21-2 November 1838. DAR.204.13; CCD 2: 123.
78 Letter from Emma Wedgwood, 21-2 November 1838. DAR.204.13; CCD 2: 123.
79 Letter from Emma Wedgwood, 21–2 November 1838. DAR.204.13; CCD 2: 123.
80 Letter from Emma Wedgwood, 21-2 November 1838. DAR.204.13; CCD 2: 123.
81 Letter from Emma Wedgwood, 21-2 November 1838. DAR.204.13; CCD 2: 123.
82 Letter from Emma Wedgwood, 25-6 November 1838. DAR.204.13; CCD 2: 126.
83 Quoted in CCD 2: 173.
84 Letter from Emma Darwin, c. February 1839. DAR.210.10; CCD 2: 172.
85 Letter from Emma Darwin, c. February 1839. DAR.210.10; CCD 2: 172.
86 Letter from Emma Darwin, c. February 1839. DAR.210.10; CCD 2: 172.
87 Letter from Emma Darwin, c. February 1839. DAR.210.10; CCD 2: 172.
88 Healey, *Emma Darwin,* 130-133.
89 Letter from Emma Darwin, c. February 1839. DAR.210.10; CCD 2: 172.
90 Letter from Emma Darwin, c. February 1839. DAR.210.10; CCD 2: 172.
91 Letter from Emma Wedgwood [23 January 1839]. DAR 204.13.CCD 2: 169.
92 Wedgwood and Wedgwood, *The Wedgwood Circle*, 240-241. In later years, Henrietta would have her own struggles over religion, expressing in her private journal some of the same doubts as her father. See CCD 19: 802-804.
93 Litchfield, *Emma Darwin*, vol. 2, 32, 38, 69, 154, 156, 163, 166, 187, 221.
94 Litchfield, *Emma Darwin*, vol. 2, 48.
95 Litchfield, *Emma Darwin*, vol. 2, 51.
96 Letter to Susan Darwin, 26 April 1838. DAR.92.5-6; CCD 2: 82.

 97 Letter to W. D. Fox, 23 August 1841. Christ's College Library, Cambridge (Fox 61); CCD 2: 303.
 98 Letter to W. D. Fox, 23 August 1841. Christ's College Library, Cambridge (Fox 61); CCD 2: 303.
 99 Pleins, *When the Great Abyss Opened*, 75-94.
100 Letter to Caroline Wedgwood, 27 October 1839. DAR.154; CCD 2: 236.
101 Fitz Roy, *Narrative*, 682.
102 Fitz Roy, *Narrative*, 657.
103 Fitz Roy, *Narrative*, 657.
104 Fitz Roy, *Narrative*, 682, 663.
105 Fitz Roy, *Narrative*, 660-61.
106 Fitz Roy, *Narrative*, 666-68.
107 Fitz Roy, *Narrative*, 670.
108 Fitz Roy, *Narrative*, 670.
109 Fitz Roy, *Narrative*, 670.
110 Fitz Roy, *Narrative*, 671.
111 Fitz Roy, *Narrative*, 680.
112 Fitz Roy, *Narrative*, 680.
113 Fitz Roy, *Narrative*, 680.
114 Fitz Roy, *Narrative*, 682.
115 Letter to Caroline Wedgwood, 27 October 1839. DAR.154; CCD 2: 236.
116 Letter from Charles Lyell, 13 February 1837. Kinnordy House, Kirriemuir, Angus, Scotland, quoted with the permission of Lord Lyell; CCD 2: 4-5.
117 Letter to Caroline Wedgwood, 27 October 1839. DAR.154; CCD 2: 236.
118 Letter from Caroline Darwin, 21 1837. DAR.204.11; CCD 2: 7.
119 Cannon, "The Impact of Uniformitarianism," 308.
120 Letter to Caroline Darwin, 27 February 1837; CCD 2: 8.

Chapter 3

 1 Wedgwood, *The Moral Ideal*, 455.
 2 Wilkin, *Sir Thomas Browne's Works*, vol. 2, 23; Paul H. Barrett et al, eds, *Charles Darwin's Notebooks, 1836-1844: Geology, Transmutation of Species, Metaphysical Enquiries* (Ithaca: Cornell University Press, 1987), 350.
 3 Wilkin, *Sir Thomas Browne's Works*, vol. 2, 26.
 4 Ibid., 6.
 5 Ibid., 13.
 6 CUL-DAR.26.59.
 7 The conventions used in transcribing Darwin's notebooks are as follows: <<>> indicates an insertion by Darwin, usually above the line; <> indicates material Darwin struck out. The notebooks referenced here are as follows in the Cambridge University Library Darwin Archive: B = CUL-DAR.121.-; C = CUL-DAR.122.-; E = CUL-DAR.124.-;

M = CUL-DAR.125.-; N = CUL-DAR.126.-; OUN = CUL-DAR.91.-.
All quotations are taken from the 1987 edition of Barrett, *Charles
Darwin's Notebooks,* with the permission of David Kohn. I have in the
process checked all the quotations against the handwritten materials. One
important revision will be noted later in this chapter.

8 CUL-DAR.26.60.

9 Sandra Herbert's essays on "The Place of Man in the Development of
Darwin's Theory of Transmutation" seeks to carefully delineate the subject
of man in relation to eight key notebooks penned in 1836–1839. Herbert's
scheme correctly suggests that Darwin's work on geology (notebook A)
and transmutation (notebooks B, C, D, and E) run parallel. On Herbert's
view, the subject of man, morals, and expression forms a significant
branching off of his work on transmutation (notebooks M and N).
However, this scheme does not give enough weight to the fact that from
January to September of 1837 Darwin was at work on man and culture as
he revised his voyage *Diary* into his *Journal of Researches.* Herbert tends
to overlook the topics of creation and religion in the notebooks which
would suggest that M and N build on Darwin's experience of religion as
recounted in his *Journal of Researches;* see Herbert, Part I, 233. Restoring
the writing on the voyage to its proper place in time makes it clear that
notebooks M and N are not simply an offshoot of his transmutation
work but have deep roots in Darwin's writing on his travels. In a valuable
essay "Charles Darwin in London," which explores the tensions between
Darwin's public involvement in the Geological Society of London at the
time he was privately sorting out the species question, Rudwick suggests
that Darwin's editing of his *Journal* may have served as the "immediate
occasion for his first transformist conjectures in the spring of 1837."
However, like Herbert, Rudwick does not see that this *Journal* editing also
provides the essential *context* for Darwin's work on man. The *Journal* offers
initial thoughts on geology, organic forms, and human culture. In that
sense, Notebooks M and N on man and morals are a logical outgrowth of
Darwin's *Journal* efforts, not an isolated or tertiary development. Similarly,
Gruber, *Darwin on Man,* is right to say that the notebooks reveal "that
Darwin, *from his very first musings on evolution onward,* viewed man as
part of the web of evolutionary change" (p. 20), but he overlooks the fact
that this insight was sparked much earlier during Darwin's travels. While
the creation idea garners Gruber's attention, certainly an appropriate
focus, he gives little attention to Darwin's search for a theory of the
evolution of the religious and moral sense (p. 208), preferring instead
to tackle the topics of mind and instinct. While Richards, *Darwin and
the Emergence of Evolutionary Theories of Mind and Behavior,* 110–111,
recognizes that Darwin observed moral facts during his voyage, his book
does not characterize the content of these facts nor tie the editing of the
voyage volume to Darwin's further work on man in the notebooks. The
work of Herbert, Rudwick, Gruber, and Richards are pathbreaking and

essential, so what I am suggesting here is a matter of nuance and not a general critique of this important body of research. For a concise overview of the notebooks and their place in Darwin's thought, see Eldredge, *Darwin: Discovering the Tree of Life*, esp. Ch. 3.

10 B18. Barrett, *Notebooks*, 213.
11 B169. Barrett, *Notebooks*, 213.
12 C77. Barrett, *Notebooks*, 213.
13 Ibid., 263.
14 C79. Barrett, *Notebooks*, 264.
15 Darwin's Journal. DAR.158; CCD 2: 432.
16 Barrett, *Notebooks*, 180.
17 Brooke, "Darwin's Science and his Religion," 47.
18 M84e. Barrett, *Notebooks*, 539–40.
19 Barrett, *Notebooks*, 374–6.
20 M81. Barrett, *Notebooks*, 539. While it is true that Harriet Martineau, a friend of Darwin's brother Erasmus, issued a translation of Comte, this publication appeared much later and does not bear on Darwin's encounters with Comte's work.
21 M69. Barrett, *Notebooks*, 535.
22 M135. Barrett, *Notebooks*, 553.
23 M69. Barrett, *Notebooks*, 535.
24 Ibid.
25 Ibid.
26 Ibid.
27 Ibid.
28 Barrett, *Notebooks*, 568, n. 19-1; Lyell 1827:475.
29 N19e. Barrett, *Notebooks*, 568.
30 M135–6. Barrett, *Notebooks*, 553.
31 M137. Barrett, *Notebooks*, 553.
32 M136. Barrett, *Notebooks*, 553.
33 Ibid.
34 Desmond and Moore, *Darwin*, 269.
35 OUN12. Barrett, *Notebooks*, 603.
36 Staunton, *Embassy*, vol. 2, 406.
37 OUN12. Barrett, *Notebooks*, 603.
38 See Hume, *The Natural History of Religion* in Hume, *Writings on Religion*, 107–82.
39 N101. Barrett, *Notebooks*, 592.
40 Hume, "Natural History of Religion," in *Philosophic Works*, vol. 4, 443.
41 Darwin's reading notebooks date his reading of Hume's *Dialogues Concerning Natural Religion* and *The Natural History of Religion* to September, 1839, the year after his reading of Comte (CCD 4: 458).
42 Hume, *Writings on Religion*, 110.
43 Ibid., 109–110.
44 Ibid., 114–7.

45 OUN18. Barrett, *Notebooks*, 604.
46 OUN19ᵛ. Barrett, *Notebooks*, 605.
47 Ibid.
48 Ibid.
49 Barrett, *Notebooks*, 604.
50 C244. Barrett, *Notebooks*, 316.
51 Ibid.
52 Ibid.
53 Ibid.
54 Ibid.
55 OUN18. Barrett, *Notebooks*, 604.
56 Ibid.
57 OUN19ᵛ. Barrett, *Notebooks*, 605.
58 N59. Barrett, *Notebooks*, 579.
59 M74. Barrett, *Notebooks*, 536.
60 Barrett, *Notebooks*, 536.
61 C166. Barrett, *Notebooks*, 291.
62 Ibid.
63 Barrett, *Notebooks*, 613, note 36-3.
64 Barrett, *Notebooks*, 613; See Kirby, *On the Power, Wisdom, and Goodness of God*, vol. I, xxviii.
65 OUN36. Barrett, *Notebooks*, 613.
66 Ibid.
67 Ibid.
68 C166. Barrett, *Notebooks*, 291.
69 M19. Barrett, *Notebooks*, 524.
70 OUN37. Barrett, *Notebooks*, 614.
71 Ibid.
72 Ibid.
73 Ibid.
74 E49. Barrett, *Notebooks*, 409.
75 B49. Barrett, *Notebooks*, 182.
76 Litchfield, *Emma Darwin*, vol. 2, 53.
77 On the development of Darwin's views on ethics, see Richards, *Darwin and the Emergence of Evolutionary Theories of Mind and Behavior,* Chs. 2, which emphasizes the debate over instinct. Also, Dixon, *The Invention of Altruism*, Ch. 4, offers useful contextual considerations regarding Darwin's work on ethics, but unfortunately does not trace the threads of his notebook speculations apart from spare comments about Comte.
78 For this background, see Richards, *Darwin and the Emergence of Evolutionary Theories of Mind and Behavior* Chs. 2–3. Richards shows that not all natural theologians separated animal instinct from human intelligence. Elsewhere in the notebooks, Darwin also engaged the natural theology of Babbage, Buckland, Ray, and Whewell.
79 M26-7. Barrett, *Notebooks*, 525–6.

80 M30. Barrett, *Notebooks*, 526.
81 Barrett, *Notebooks*, 526.
82 M31. Barrett, *Notebooks*, 527.
83 M72, 73. Barrett, *Notebooks*, 536.
84 M73. Barrett, *Notebooks*, 536.
85 M74. Barrett, *Notebooks*, 536.
86 M132e. Barrett, *Notebooks*, 552.
87 M118. Barrett, *Notebooks*, 549.
88 M120. Barrett, *Notebooks*, 549.
89 M118. Barrett, *Notebooks*, 549.
90 M119. Barrett, *Notebooks*, 549.
91 M119-20. Barrett, *Notebooks*, 549.
92 M118. Barrett, *Notebooks*, 549.
93 M121. Barrett, *Notebooks*, 549.
94 Ibid.
95 M122. Barrett, *Notebooks*, 549.
96 M121. Barrett, *Notebooks*, 549.
97 M123. Barrett, *Notebooks*, 549.
98 Ibid., 550.
99 Ibid., 550.
100 M124. Barrett, *Notebooks*, 550.
101 Ibid.
102 M124, 125. Barrett, *Notebooks*, 550.
103 OUN28. Barrett, *Notebooks*, 608.
104 OUN26. The word "wicked" here is transcribed by others as "wrecked" (see Barrett, *Notebooks*, 608), but a comparison with how Darwin writes "wickedness" in the same passage clearly indicates that the correct reading is 'wicked." I am thankful to David Kohn for confirming this revised reading (private correspondence).
105 OUN26. Barrett, *Notebooks*, 608.
106 N4. Barrett, *Notebooks*, 564.
107 N5. Barrett, *Notebooks*, 564.
108 OUN37. Barrett, *Notebooks*, 614.
109 OUN52. Barrett, *Notebooks*, 625.
110 Ibid.
111 OUN52. Barrett, *Notebooks*, 626.
112 Ibid.
113 OUN43-4. Barrett, *Notebooks*, 619-20.
114 OUN42-3. Barrett, *Notebooks*, 619.
115 OUN45, 46. Barrett, *Notebooks*, 620.
116 OUN46. Barrett, *Notebooks*, 620.
117 OUN45. Barrett, *Notebooks*, 620.
118 E49. Barrett, *Notebooks*, 49.
119 N46-7. Barrett, *Notebooks*, 576.
120 OUN54, 53. Barrett, *Notebooks*, 628.

121 M75. Barrett, *Notebooks*, 537.

122 Quoted in Barrett, *Notebooks*, 537, n. 75-2.

123 M76, 77. Barrett, *Notebooks*, 537.

124 M142. Barrett, *Notebooks*, 555.

125 See the incident recounted in Barrett, *Notebooks*, 555. As noted in Chapter 1, the missionary's son E. Lucas Bridges, *Uttermost Part of the Earth*, Ch. 1, who had extensive experience among the Fuegians, argued that they either misunderstood the questions asked of them or were pulling the leg of the *Beagle*'s crew.

126 Richards, *Darwin and the Emergence of Evolutionary Theories of Mind and Behavior,* Appendix 2 offers a spirited defense of a contemporary evolutionary ethic.

Chapter 4

1 CUL-DAR.26.105.

2 Darwin, *Origin of Species*, 1st edition, 488.

3 CUL-DAR.26.105.

4 Letter to Fritz Müller, 22 February 1867. F. Darwin, *Life and Letters*, 2: 293. Erroneously dated by Francis Darwin to 1869. See CCD 15: 93.

5 See Harvey, *Almost a Man of Genius*, Ch. 4.

6 Letter to Asa Gray, 10–20 June 1862. Gray Herbarium, Harvard University (66). Quoted with the permission of the Archives of the Gray Herbarium, Harvard University, Cambridge, Massachusetts, USA. See also, CCD 10: 241.

7 Letter to Asa Gray, 10--20 June 1862. Gray Herbarium, Harvard University (66). Quoted with the permission of the Archives of the Gray Herbarium, Harvard University, Cambridge, Massachusetts, USA. See also CCD 10: 241.

8 As an anonymous reviewer of this manuscript has pointed out to me.

9 Quoted in Richards, *Darwin and the Emergence of Evolutionary Theories of Mind and Behavior*, 219. While agreeing that the human body may have evolved (though not necessarily through natural selection), the anonymous reviewer (W. Boyd Dawkins according to *The Wellesley Index to Victorian Periodicals*) proceeded to deny in the strongest possible terms that morality and religion had evolved from animalistic roots, treating Darwin''s theories as scientifically ludicrous, religiously deficient, and politically dangerous.

10 Litchfield, *Emma Darwin*, vol. 2, 196.

11 CCD 18: 192.

12 Quoted in Desmond and Moore, *Darwin*, 573. See CCD 18: 25.

13 Darwin, *Descent*, vol. 1, 31.

14 Ibid., 12.

15 Ibid., 16.

16 Ibid., 17.

17 Ibid., 20.

18 Ibid., 22.

19 Ibid., 31.

20 Darwin, *Descent*, vol. 1, 32.

21 Ibid.

22 Ibid.

23 On this context, see Richards, *Darwin and the Emergence of Evolutionary Theories of Mind and Behavior*, Chs. 4–5. Unfortunately, Richards" cursory treatment of the religious dimension in connection with Darwin (198–9) and his reluctance to pursue Darwin"s reading of anthropological literature at the time (192, 200) tends to skew somewhat the contextualization of Darwin"s work on the *Descent of Man*.

24 Darwin, Descent, vol. 1, 44.

25 Ibid., 46.

26 Ibid., 49.

27 Ibid., 54.

28 Ibid., 65.

29 Ibid., 68.

30 For essential background, see Stocking, *Victorian Anthropology*, Chs. 5–7. Oddly, Harrison's centenary essay ("The Influence of Darwinism on the Study of Religions") failed to assess the impact of Darwin"s *Descent of Man,* despite acknowledging that since Darwin the question of the evolution of religion had become more acute. Ritter, *Charles Darwin and the Golden Rule,* recognizes that Darwin treated religion and ethics as natural evolutionary developments but he argues that Darwin's theory of religion's evolution was terribly inadequate. He then proceeds to give an account of religion as a natural though often deceptive phenomenon. In this regard Ritter fails to appreciate Darwin's use of anthropological research to undergird his theory in the *Descent of Man*.

31 Farrar, *Men I Have Known*, 140–149.

32 Farrar, "On the Universality of Belief in God and in a Future State." On the polygenist politics of the Anthropological Society of London, which Darwin would not have shared, see Rainger, "Race, Politics, and Science."

33 The key figures in Darwin's anthropology, namely Tylor, McLennan, and Lubbock, are the focus of Stocking, *Victorian Anthropology,* Ch. 5, who contextualizes their evolutionary approaches. On the contrasts between these figures regarding primitive religion, see Stocking, *Victorian Anthropology,* 188–97.

34 Darwin, *Descent*, vol. 1, 66. For background on McLennan, see Stocking, *Victorian Anthropology,* 164–68.

35 Ferguson, "The Worship of Animals and Plants," *Fortnightly Review* 4 (1869): 415.

36 Ibid.: 422.

37 Darwin, *Descent,* vol.1, 65.

38 Ibid., 66.

39 Tylor, *Early History of Mankind,* 6. Tylor's major work, *Primitive Culture,* appeared in 1871 and was not available to Darwin for his *Descent of Man.* When Darwin read the work subsequent to the publication of his book, he praised the volume to Tylor and regretted he was not able to make use of it when writing his book. In particular, he endorsed Tylor's views on the evolution of religion. He also thought Tylor's work dealt a serious blow to Argyll's claims. Darwin told Tylor, "The Duke of Argyll ought never to hold up his head again." See CCD 19: 347, 597–8, 604, 611–12.

40 Darwin, *Descent of Man,* I, 66.

41 Spencer, "The Origin of Animal Worship," 309.

42 Ibid., 329.

43 Darwin, *Descent,* vol. 1, 66.

44 After Darwin's death, Huxley wrote "The Evolution of Theology: An Anthropological Study," an anthropological history of religion that ties the theology of ancient Israel to religious practices found in Polynesia and elsewhere. For Huxley, religion ultimately arose out of primitive ghost worship and then developed more formally into the totemism and ancestor worship found in the Bible and other cultures. While this essay was obviously dated in its historical reconstruction of early Israel, Huxley's piece shows what a Darwinian could contribute to the study of religion by attending carefully to anthropological data, the biblical text, and the history of theology, rather than simply using the idea of evolution merely to bludgeon religion. In fact, Huxley found the ethical teachings of the biblical prophets to be a "great reformation" worthy of note.

45 On the role of debates in psychology as context for Darwin's work, see Young, *Darwin's Metaphor,* Ch. 3.

46 Darwin, *Descent,* vol. 1, 68.

47 Pike, "The Psychical Elements of Religion," lxii.

48 Pike, "The Psychical Elements of Religion," lxiii.

49 Ibid.

50 Ibid.

51 Pike acknowledged that a few in each tradition, such as Buddha or Pyrrho, approached religious questions with an intellectual rather than an emotional orientation, as did Atheists, but he argued that these intellects were deceived by language into thinking that their projections of abstractions, such as the Infinite or the Absolute, were external realities they could know by reason apart from their senses. The philosopher was no more in touch with the Infinite than a religious devotee was in touch with the goddess Dawn.

52 Pike, "The Psychical Elements of Religion," lxii

53 Ibid., lxiv.

54 Ibid., lxi.
55 Darwin, *Descent,* vol. 1, 68.
56 Ibid.
57 Among laborers, Lubbock was hailed as the founder of "St. Lubbock's Days," a series of four bank holidays he helped create in 1871.
58 Timothy L. Alborn, "Lubbock, John." *Oxford Dictionary of National Biography.*Online. Available: http://0-www.oxforddnb.com.sculib.scu.edu/view/article/34618, accessed 9 March 2009.
59 Alborn, "Lubbock."
60 Darwin, *Descent,* vol. 1, 66.
61 Letter to John Lubbock, 21 July 1870. CCD 18: 218.
62 Lubbock, *Origin of Civilization,* 121.
63 Ibid., 123.
64 Ibid., 139.
65 Lubbock, *Origin of Civilization,* 160.
66 Ibid.
67 Lubbock, *Origin of Civilization,* 182.
68 Ibid., 188.
69 Ibid., 192.
70 Lubbock, *Origin of Civilization,* 245.
71 Ibid.
72 Lubbock, *Origin of Civilization,* 157, 191, 237, 243.
73 Ibid., 208.
74 Ibid., 209–210, 166, 148.
75 Lubbock, *Origin of Civilization,* 256.
76 Ibid.
77 Darwin, *Descent,* vol. 1, 68.
78 After Darwin's death, Huxley would add his own ideas about the "Evolution of Theology" by developing a natural history of Christian belief as well as arguing in his essay on "Agnosticism" that Jesus was merely yet another orthodox Jewish teacher. Huxley's dream of writing a thirty-four chapter book on the "Natural History of Christianity" was never realized. See Desmond, *Huxley,* 547.
79 Gillespie, "The Duke of Argyll," 1977.
80 CCD 10: 411, 514.
81 Browne, *Power of Place,* 194–5; CCD 10: 537; Campbell, "Supernatural," 394–5.
82 Letter to Asa Gray, 23 November 1862. Gray Herbarium, Harvard University (49). Quoted with the permission of the Archives of the Gray Herbarium, Harvard University, Cambridge, Massachusetts, USA. See also CCD 10: 546; cf. CCD 10: 253, 537.
83 Letter from J. D. Hooker, 29 December 1862; DAR.101.85; CCD 10: 637.
84 Campbell, *Primeval Man,* 65.
85 Ibid., 27–8.

86   Ibid., 127.

87   Ibid., 131.

88   Campbell, *Primeval Man*, 173. Later, the philologist F. Max Müller,
     "The Savage," would take issue with Darwin's assumption that modern day
     savages such as the Fuegians were relics of primeval man. Müller criticized
     Darwin not so much for his accuracy in reporting what he witnessed on
     his voyage but for seeing the Fuegians "with Darwinian eyes." Citing the
     fact that the Fuegian language was known to have at least 30,000 words,
     Müller suggested that this group represented a devolution as "retrogressive
     savages" descending from the great archaic civilizations of South America,
     not the starting point of human cultural evolution. Müller goaded
     Darwin by saying that he "must have either been very unlucky in the
     Fuegians whom he met, or he cannot have kept himself quite free from
     prejudice."

89   Darwin, *Descent*, vol. 1, 104.

90   Darwin, *Descent*, vol. 1, 70. Stocking, *Victorian Anthropology*, 163–4, notes
     that the final nail in the coffin against Argyll for Darwin came in the form
     of E. B. Tylor's *Primitive Culture*, which he took up late in 1871 after the
     publication of the *Descent of Man*. Stocking recounts that "after having
     Primitive Culture read aloud to him by his wife, and finding it "most
     profound", Darwin himself wrote to Tylor that 'the Duke of Argyll ought
     never to hold up his head again."

91   Darwin, *Descent*, vol. 1, 71.

92   Ibid., 76.

93   Ibid., 77.

94   That Darwin's treatment of "sympathy" stood apart from the Comtean
     stream of "altruism" is documented by Dixon, *The Invention of Altruism*,
     Ch. 4.

95   Darwin, Descent, vol. 1, 80.

96   Ibid., 81, n.17.

97   Smith, *Theory of Moral Sentiments*, 47.

98   Darwin, *Descent*, vol. 1, 82.

99   Ibid., 85.

100 Ibid., 84.

101 Ibid., 97.

102 Ibid., 98.

103 Ibid., 106.

104 Darwin, *Descent*, vol. 1, 106. The particular formulation used by Darwin is
     a quote from Luke 6:31 as found in the Authorized (King James) Version
     of the Bible, or nearly so. The text of the King James Bible inserts "also"
     in the latter clause to read "do ye also to them likewise." Perhaps this was
     an accidental omission on Darwin's part or serves to indicate that he
     copied this phrasing from some other source. If so, one wonders where he
     found his version. This formulation can be found both in theological and

secular works of the time. As an example of a theological work, see Jorgen Jorgenson's *The Religion of Christ is the Religion of Nature* (1827), pp. 288, 291, a work that offers a defense of Christianity in the face of Atheism. But the phrase is also found in news reports from 1848 regarding the Constitution of the French Republic—Rights of Man, Article 1: « The duties of man in society are summed up in respect for the constitution, in obedience to the laws, in the defence of the country, in the accomplishment of his family duties, and in the practice of that fraternal maxim: 'As ye would that men should do to you, do ye to them likewise." See, e.g., *The Newspaper,* Saturday, 24 June 24, 1848, 202. In any event, Darwin does not speak of the "Golden Rule" in a general fashion which might have a varieties of formulations but he uses a specific phrasing which has its own peculiar history. Unfortunately, Darwin did not indicate the source of his quote.

105 Darwin, *Descent*, vol. 1, 165.
106 Ibid., 165–6.
107 Ibid., 394.
108 Ibid., 173.
109 Ibid., 172.
110 Ibid., 87.
111 Ibid., 88.
112 Ibid., 89.
113 Ibid., 92.
114 Ibid., 96.
115 Darwin, *Descent*, vol. 1, 99.
116 Ibid.
117 Darwin, *Descent*, vol. 1, 104.
118 Darwin, *Descent of Man*, vol. 1, 184.
119 Darwin, *Descent of Man,* vol. 2, 395. See Picton, *New Theories and the Old Faith,* 37–8, 48–55, 65, 84, 193–5.
120 Darwin, *Descent of Man,* vol. 2, 394–5.

Chapter 5

1 On the popular reception of *Descent of Man*, see Ellegård, *Darwin and the General Reader,* ch. 14. See also Richards, *Darwin and the Emergence of Evolutionary Theories of Mind and Behavior,* 219–230.
2 For comprehensive background on Mivart, see Gruber, *A Conscience in Conflict.*
3 Mivart, *Genesis*, 3.
4 St George Mivart, *On the Genesis of Species* (London: Macmillan, 1871).
5 Mivart, *Genesis,* 189.
6 Ibid., 191, 195, 196.

7 Ibid., 199.

8 Ibid., 204.

9 Ibid., 255, 261.

10 Quoted in Mivart, *Genesis*, 255.

11 Mivart, *Genesis*, 256–7.

12 Ibid., 258.

13 Mivart, *Genesis*, 280; quoting Wallace, *Contributions*, 368.

14 Wallace, "Review of Descent of Man," 183; Mivart, *Genesis*, 276.

15 Quoted in Desmond and Moore, *Darwin*, 578.

16 Mivart, *Descent*, 87.

17 Ibid., 90.

18 For the reaction among the Darwinians, see Gruber, *A Conscience in Conflict*, ch. 6.

19 CUL-DAR.26.99.

20 Darwin, *Origin of Species*, 219.

21 Huxley, *Darwiniana*, 125.

22 Letter from T. H. Huxley and H. A. Huxley, 20 September 1871. DAR.99: 39–42; CCD 19: 586.

23 Huxley, *Darwiniana*, 138.

24 Ibid., 146.

25 Ibid., 149.

26 Ibid., 150.

27 Mivart, *Essays and Criticisms*, vol. 2, 60.

28 Mivart, *Genesis*, 252.

29 While Mivart on occasion sought to rekindle ties with Huxley, their relationship remained cool for the next decade despite encounters at the gatherings of the Metaphysical Society. See Mivart, "Some Reminiscences of Thomas Henry Huxley," 996–7. Later insults to Darwin's son George only served to harden the battle lines.

30 Letter to T. H. Huxley, 30 September 1871. Quoted with the permission of Imperial College London, Huxley 5: 283; CCD 19: 605; Gruber, *A Conscience in Conflict*, 89.

31 Letter from T. H. Huxley and H. A. Huxley, 20 September 1871. DAR.99: 39–42; CCD 19: 586.

32 Letter from T. H. Huxley, 28 September 1871. DAR.99: 39–42; CCD 19: 602.

33 See Gruber, *A Conscience in Conflict*, 98–114; Desmond and Moore, *Darwin*, 610–3.

34 Gruber, *A Conscience in Conflict*, ch. 11.

35 CCD 19: 49–50.

36 Letter to John Murray 19 February 1871. DAR.143:280; CCD 19: 78.

37 Cobbe, *Darwinism in Morals*, 11.

38 Ibid., 14.

39 Letter from Emma Darwin to F. P. Cobbe, 14 April 1871. Quoted with the permission of the Huntington Library, San Marino; CCD 19: 282.

40 Letter to F. E. E. Wedgwood, 19 December 1871. Quoted with the permission of the Huntington Library, San Marino; CCD 19: 726–7 and n. 2.

41 Darwin, *Descent of Man,* 2nd ed., 113.

42 Cobbe, *Darwinism in Morals,* 30.

43 Letter from "A Child of God" [after 24 February 1871]. DAR.201.1; CCD 19: 103.

44 Letter from James Grant, 6 March 1878. CUL-DAR.165:89.

45 Ibid.

46 The letter appeared in the *The British Weekly; A Journal of Social and Christian Progress* 4 (3 August 1888): 233. See also Warfield, "Charles Darwin's Religious Life," 601.

47 Crawford, *The Women's Suffrage Movement in Great Britain and Ireland,* 70, 77. Fordyce moved to Belfast in 1883 and published his treatment of skepticism at that time with an extensive discussion of Darwin. He later emigrated to Australia.

48 Fordyce, *Aspects of Scepticism,* 190.

49 Letter to John Fordyce, 7 May 1879. CUL-DAR.270 & 139.12:12.

50 Letter from Charles Kingsley, 8 November 1867. DAR.169:37; CCD 15: 423.

51 Ibid.

52 Kingsley, *Westminster Sermons,* vii.

53 Ibid., vii–ix.

54 Ibid., *Westminster Sermons,* xxiii.

55 Letter to T. H. Huxley, 28 December 1862. Quoted with the permission of Imperial College London, Huxley 5:189, 19:209–12; CCD 10: 634.

56 Kingsley, *Water Babies,* 270–3. On the importance of the natural theology dimension of *Water Babies,* unfortunately shorn from later editions, see Beatty and Hale, "*Water Babies*: an evolutionary parable."

57 Letter to T. H. Huxley, 28 December 1862. Quoted with the permission of Imperial College London, Huxley 5:189, 19:209–12; CCD 10: 633.

58 Litchfield, *Emma Darwin,* vol. 2, 211.

59 Conway, *Idols and Ideals,* 86. Regarding the sermon and visit with Darwin see Conway, *Autobiography,* 348–65.

60 Conway, *Idols and Ideals,* 86.

61 Conway, *Idols and Ideals,* 87.

62 Ibid.

63 Conway, *Idols and Ideals,* 84, 88, 90.

64 Ibid., 100.

65 Ibid., 91.

66 Ibid., 89.

67 Ibid., 89, 94.

68 Conway, *Idols and Ideals,* 98.

69 Ibid.

70 Conway, *Autobiography,* 358.

71 Darwin, *Life and Letters,* vol. 1, 277.
72 Häckel, *Die Naturanschauung,* 60.
73 Häckel, *Naturanschauung,* 47–9, 60–64.
74 Desmond and Moore, *Darwin,* 634–5.
75 Letter from F. E. Abbot, 20 August 1871. DAR.159:2; CCD 19: 541.
76 Abbot, Francis Ellingwood. Papers of Francis Ellingwood Abbot. Letter from Charles Darwin to Abbot, 6 September 1871. HUG 1101, Box 44. Harvard University Archives. Courtesy of the Harvard University Archives. Permission to use this material has also been granted by Betsey Farber, great-granddaughter of Francis Ellingwood Abbot. See CCD 19: 551.
77 Abbot, Francis Ellingwood. Papers of Francis Ellingwood Abbot. Letter from Charles Darwin to Abbot, 6 September 1871. HUG 1101, Box 44. Harvard University Archives. Courtesy of the Harvard University Archives. Permission to use this material has also been granted by Betsey Farber, great-granddaughter of Francis Ellingwood Abbot. See CCD 19: 551. See CCD 19:551.
78 Darwin, *Life and Letters,* vol. 1, 276.
79 Himmelfarb, *Darwin and the Darwinian Revolution,* 383.
80 CUL-DAR.162:201. On Doedes, see van der Heide, "Darwin's Young Admirers."
81 Letter to N. D Doedes, 23 March 1873. CUL-DAR.139.12:11.
82 Ibid.
83 Ibid.
84 Ibid.
85 Ibid.
86 Ibid.
87 Ibid.
88 Ibid.
89 Ibid.
90 Letter to George Darwin, 21 October 1873. CUL-DAR.210.1:14.
91 Ibid.
92 Feuer, "Is the 'Darwin-Marx Correspondence' Authentic?," 3.
93 Aveling, *The Religious Views of Charles Darwin,* 5. See the account in Desmond and Moore, *Darwin,* 656–8.
94 Tyndall, *Address,* 1874.
95 Ibid., 41.
96 Tyndall, *Fragments of Science,* especially volume two.
97 Tyndall, *Address,* 36, 42.
98 Ibid, 60.
99 Tyndall, *Address,* 58.
100 Ibid.
101 Tyndall, *Address,* 61.
102 Ibid., 60.

103 CUL-DAR.26.1–121; Litchfield, *Emma Darwin*, vol. 2, 223.
104 CUL-DAR.26.62.
105 Ibid.
106 Ibid.
107 CUL-DAR.26.63.
108 Darwin's "Reading Notebooks." DAR.119:21a; CCD 4: 476.
109 CUL-DAR.26.64.
110 Ibid.
111 CUL-DAR.26.65.
112 CUL-DAR.26.65, 64.
113 Darwin, *Autobiography*, 87, n. 1.
114 Ibid.
115 CUL-DAR.26.65.
116 Ibid.
117 Ibid.
118 CUL-DAR.26.66.
119 Ibid.
120 Ibid.
121 CUL-AR.26.67.
122 Ibid.
123 CUL-DAR.26.68.
124 CUL-DAR.26.69.
125 Ibid.
126 Ibid.
127 CUL-DAR.26.69–70.
128 CUL-DAR.26.63.
129 CUL-DAR.26.72–3.
130 CUL-DAR.26.73.
131 Quoted in Brooke, *Science and Religion*, 281.
132 CUL-DAR.26.70–71.
133 CUL-DAR.26.70.
134 Ibid.
135 Ibid.
136 CUL-DAR.26.71.
137 Ibid.
138 Ibid.
139 Ibid.
140 CUL-DAR.26.71A.
141 Ibid.
142 Ibid.
143 F. Darwin, *More Letters*, vol. II, 237.
144 Ibid.
145 CUL-DAR.26.72.
146 Ibid.
147 CUL-DAR.26.71.

148 CUL-DAR.26.72.
149 Ibid.
150 CUL-DAR.26.73.
151 Darwin, *Autobiography*, 95.
152 CUL-DAR.26.73C.
153 CUL-DAR.26.73B.
154 Schwartz, "George John Romanes's Defense of Darwinism," 308. On Romanes and his relation to Darwin, see Turner, *Between Science and Religion*, ch. 6, and Richards, *Darwin and the Emergence of Evolutionary Theories of Mind and Behavior*, ch. 8.
155 Schwartz, *Darwin's Disciple*, 223.
156 Ibid., 225.
157 CUL-DAR.26.64.
158 Ibid.
159 Ibid.
160 See Keynes, *Darwin, His Daughter, and Human Evolution*.
161 CUL-DAR.26.63–4.
162 CUL-DAR.26.73A.
163 Ibid.
164 Litchfield, *Emma Darwin*, vol. 2, 230.
165 Ibid., 234, 258–9.
166 CUL-DAR.26.73B.
167 Ibid.
168 King-Hele, *Life of Erasmus Darwin*, xvii–xviii.
169 Ibid., 63.
170 Ibid., 22, 32.
171 Ibid., 62.
172 Ibid., 63.
173 Ibid., 89.
174 Letter from Julia Wedgwood to Francis Darwin, 3 October 1884; CUL-DAR.139.12.17.
175 Letter from the Archbishop of Canturbury, 16 December 1880; CUL-DAR.202:17.
176 Ibid.
177 Letter to the Archbishop of Canturbury, 18 December 1880; CUL-DAR.249:131.
178 Letter from the Archbishop of Canturbury, 21 December 1880; CUL-DAR.202:18.
179 Letter to the Archbishop of Canturbury, 14 December 1880; CUL-DAR.249:132.
180 Letter to the Archbishop of Canturbury, 16 December 1880; CUL-DAR.202:17.
181 For background on the debate over Graham and the kind of synthesis he presented, see MacLeod, "The 'Bankruptcy of Science' Debate."
182 Rae, "Graham."

183 Graham, *Creed of Science*, 7.
184 Ibid., 24.
185 Ibid., 26, 31.
186 Ibid., 36.
187 Ibid., 38.
188 Ibid., 148–57.
189 Ibid., 166–96.
190 Ibid., 56.
191 Ibid., 84, 88.
192 Ibid., 62, 96, 373.
193 Ibid., 357, 307–8.
194 Ibid., 304.
195 Ibid., 336–7.
196 Ibid., 337.
197 Ibid., 349.
198 Ibid., 357.
199 F. Darwin, *Autobiography*, 68–9.
200 Letter from William Graham to Francis Darwin, undated. CUL-DAR.139.12.9.
201 Moore, *The Darwin Legend*, 1994.
202 Browne, *Power of Place*, 496.
203 Farrar, *Men I Have Known*, 148.
204 Farrar, *Life of Frederic William Farrar*, 109.
205 Ibid., 110.
206 Goodwin, *Walks*, 299.
207 Ibid., 302.
208 Ibid., 307.
209 Ibid., 308.
210 For background on Romanes, see Richards, *Darwin and the Emergence of Evolutionary Theories of Mind and Behavior*, 331–53; and Turner, *Between Science and Religion*, 134–63.
211 Romanes, *Charles Darwin: A Memorial Poem (Typescript)*; the poem also appears in Romanes, *Selection*, 4–5.Quoted with the kind permission of Mrs Joan Westmacott, granddaughter of George John Romanes.
212 Haught, *God After Darwin*, x.
213 Huxley, "The Funeral of Charles Darwin," *The Times* (27 April 1882), p. 5.

Conclusion

1 Letter from James Shaw, 20 November 1865. DAR.177:149; CCD 13: 311–2. Great
2 Letter from James Shaw, 20 November 1865. DAR.177:149; CCD 13: 311.

3 Carrie Sager's publication *Voices for Evolution* and other resources offered through the National Center for Science Education in Oakland, California provide a much-needed corrective to the view that all religionists reject evolution.

4 For a typical fundamentalist diatribe, see Comfort, "Special Introduction." The volume by Dawkins referred to here is Dawkins, *God Delusion.* By contrast, Hinde, *Why Gods Persist,* vii, calls for an end to the "sledgehammer" approach in favor of "a scientific understanding of religion's extraordinary resilience."

5 Huxley, *Science and Christian Tradition* (New York: Appleton, 1896), Ch. 7–9. Also, *Christianity and Agnosticism: A Controversy* (New York: Appleton, 1890). To be fair to Huxley, his sometimes strident tone did not prevent his participation in the Metaphysical Society, a gentlemanly gathering of scientists, theologians, philosophers, and writers who reasonably but vigorously debated matters of religion and science from all manner of positions. Huxley presented papers to the society on immortality, resurrection, and the soul. See Brown, *The Metaphysical Society,* 89, who indicates that when Huxley was chair of this society (1875–1877), he "unquestionably kept the discussions of the papers at a high level of discursive analysis and witty repartee, even if not always of disinterested logical and philosophical objectivity."

6 On the importance of Darwin's broad humanistic reading, see Stevens, "Darwin's Humane Reading."

7 For a discussion of the transitions and continuities of Unitarianism represented in some of this reading, see Webb, "The Faith of Nineteenth-Century Unitarians: A Curious Incident."

8 Ruse, *Can a Darwinian be a Christian?: The Relationship Between Science and Religion*; Miller, *Finding Darwin's God: A Scientist's Search for Common Ground Between God and Evolution*; Ayala, *Darwin's Gift to Science and Religion*; Polkinghorne, *Science and Religion in Quest of Truth*; Collins, *The Language of God: A Scientist Presents Evidence for Belief*; and Haught, *Deeper than Darwin.* See also Ruse, *The Darwinian Revolution* and his *Darwin and Design.* Pointing in the same direction is Bowler's suggestive defense of a new "Middle Way," built around human freedom and the reality of suffering in the universe, as a meeting point for liberal Christianity and the neo-Darwinian synthesis. See Bowler, *Monkey Trials and Gorilla Sermons,* 217–28.

9 Dobzhansky, "Nothing in Biology Makes Sense Except in the Light of Evolution," 127. For Dobzhansky's religious background, see Van der Meer, "Theodosius Dobzhansky."

10 See Dawkins' comment on Fisher at http://edge.org/conversation/who-is-the-greatest-biologist-of-all-time). On Fisher, see Moore, "R. A. Fisher: A Faith Fit for Eugenics."

11 CUL-DAR 26.72–3.

12 Darwin, F. *Life and Letters,* vol. 1, 274.

13 CCD 4: 138.

14 On Friendly Societies see, Gosden, *Self-Help.*

15 CCD 4: 264–5, 5: 222–3. On Darwin's involvement in such efforts, see Desmond and Moore, *Darwin,* 332, 398, 525, 600, 619, 625.

16 Desmond and Moore, *Darwin,* 625. For Darwin's letter castigating the members of the Down Friendly Club, see CUL-DAR 138.5.1.

17 Stecher, "The Darwin-Innes Letters," 242.

18 Fullerton, *J. W. C. Fegan: A Tribute,* 30.

19 Moore, *Darwin Legend,* 155, 157.

20 Litchfield, *Emma Darwin,* vol. 2, 244.

21 Moore, *Darwin Legend,* 155, 162.

22 Moore, *Darwin Legend,* 156, 157, 162. To be sure, Darwin does add secular motivations for acts of altruism that counter the process of Natural Selection. See Darwin, *Descent,* vol. 1, 168–9.

23 For a general response and critique, see Haught, *God and the New Atheism.* For a spirited rebuttal to Dawkins, see Robertson, *The Dawkins Letters.*

24 Harris, *Letter to a Christian Nation,* 40–41, tries to skirt this issue by labeling Hitler, Stalin, Mao, Pol Pot, and Kim Il Sung "quasi-religious" when we could just as easily say they were quasi-atheistic, quasi-secular, or quasi-nationalistic. He wants Christians to own their sordid past but resists taking responsibility for secularism's killing fields (to which I would add the existence and use of the atomic bomb, which one half expects Harris to blame on Jesus). For Harris, only religion sparks the great atrocities of human history. Likewise, the late Christopher Hitchens, *god is not Great,* Ch. 17, blamed the religious crowd for the secularist, nationalist, and Marxist atrocities of the twentieth century. His attempt to treat totalitarian states as theocracies hardly rings true to the political reality. The millions killed under Stalin are passed over rather quickly—comments interlarded with further religious invective—and one searches in vain for the apology Hitchens claims humanism can make for its own crimes (pp. 244–50). Harris only grudgingly admits religion's altruistic force. Echoing Hitchens, Mother Teresa is his target here (pp. 35–6). While it is quite true, as he contends, that one need not be religious to be altruistic, the horrific cases of totalitarianism that he himself is forced to acknowledge demonstrate that being unreligious or irreligious is no guarantor of altruism either. More people were killed in the name of the ideologies of the five dictators he names (and in the wars fought against them) than in all the Christian centuries put together. One need simply do the math. (See Guinness, *Unspeakable,* 40–44; Ward, *Is Religion Dangerous?,* ch. 3.) Their reigns of terror hardly instill great confidence in secular ideologies or in secular moral systems. Finally, Harris and Hitchens fail to develop a philosophic case as to why one might be *obligated* to be altruistic from a nonreligious point of view, rather than merely as a "rational" matter of personal taste. For Harris and Hitchens, religion is always the problem

rather than any sort of solution. As Haught observes in *God and the New Atheism,* "If a hammer is your only tool, then everything looks like a nail" (p. 83). What Harris's and Hitchens's writings demonstrate, however, is nothing more than the fact that religious fundamentalism is an easy target. Modern science beats Iron Age religion. If contemporary religious thinkers constantly railed against alchemy, we would hardly take this seriously as an engagement of science. Yet Harris and Hitchens are content to fight against straw figures and caricatures. Their failure to explore modern theology or biblical criticism is in some sense understandable. Clearly, such an engagement would seriously inconvenience their arguments. In writing off religious liberalism, religious tolerance, and religious moderation as much too dangerous, Harris opts for the simplistic divide of his brand of atheism vs. conservative Christians (pp. 3–5). For all these and other reasons, the writings of the New Atheists can hardly be taken as serious intellectual resources for students of modern theology or contemporary religious philosophy. Contrast the more scientifically productive, religiously insightful, and less intellectually combative approaches to the evolution of religion question outlined by Boyer and Bergstrom, "Evolutionary Perspectives on Religion." My hope is that my own book will be seen to offer constructive historical perspectives that bear on the discussion of the relation between religion and science today.

25 See, e.g., Atran, *In Gods We Trust;* Boyer, *Religion Explained;* and Barrett, *Why Would Anyone Believe in God?* For one typical example of a needless diatribe, consider Dennett's dismantling of divination (*Breaking the Spell,* pp. 132–5). For Dennett, the ancient practice of divination is merely a comical "passing the buck to an external decision-making gadget." With Wikipedia as his source for examples and talk of "Dumbo's magic feather" and "crutches for the soul" guiding the discussion, he scoffs that "divination provides relief and makes them feel good—like tobacco." As if this sort of approach penetrates the ancient and time-honored practice. Now, one need not be a believer in divination (I'm not) to realize that this treatment hardly grapples with the phenomenon in question. One glance at Ivan Starr's *The Rituals of the Diviner* (Malibu: Undena, 1983) tells a serious scholar of religion that there is much more to divination than Dennett's simplistic dismissals. If we are going to "break the spell," we should at least try to understand the nature of that spell. Divination is, after all, a rational, evidence-based, proto-science. In Dennett's case, as is common in the writings of the New Atheists, the antitheist agenda overrides making the effort to grapple with the subject matter in a nuanced way. One appreciates Hinde's candor in this regard (*Why Gods Persist,* ch. 18). To be fair to Boyer, his *Fracture of an Illusion* makes plain that he regards "religion" as an illusion, arguing instead that cognitive science can only explore religious thoughts and behaviors. Nonetheless, he admits that Dawkins engages in a type of "advocacy" (p. 90) that does

not offer rigorous insight regarding how religion works as a psychological phenomenon. Barrett's *Cognitive Science, Religion, and Theology*, by contrast, demonstrates how cognitive science can indeed be a resource to theology, suggesting that the science does not automatically substantiate the negative theological claims made by Dawkins, Dennett, or even Boyer.

26 Barrett, *Why Would Anyone Believe in God?*, vii.

27 The numerous works of primatologist Frans de Waal on primate reconciliation, peacemaking, and altruism are foundational to such a discussion.

28 Sagan, *Pale Blue Dot*, 52. These perspectives are worked out more fully in his Gifford Lectures, see Sagan, *The Varieties of Scientific Experience*.

29 Sagan, Pale Blue Dot, 52.

30 Dawkins, *God Delusion*, 125, is merely bemused by religiously minded scientists like Polkinghorne and Collins, yet never actually addresses their arguments.

31 Letter from J. B. Innes, 21 January 1871. DAR.167:28; CCD 19: 29.

32 Letter from John Innes, 1 December 1878. CUL-DAR.167.34.

33 Appleman, *Darwin*, 287. Lyell apparently picked up this sentiment from Queen Victoria's eldest daughter. See CCD 13: 23, 25 n. 14. Even the Queen was worried that Darwin had corroded her daughter's religious beliefs.

Bibliography

Alborn, Timothy L. "Lubbock, John." *Oxford Dictionary of National Biography.* Online source: http://0-www.oxforddnb.com.sculib.scu.edu/view/article/34618, accessed 9 March 2009.

Appleman, Philip (2001). *Darwin: Texts, Commentary.* 3rd ed. New York: W.W. Norton.

Atkinson, Henry George and Harriet Martineau (2009). *Letters on the Laws of Man's Nature and Development, 1851.* Cambridge: Cambridge University Press.

Atran, Scott (2002). *In Gods We Trust: The Evolutionary Landscape of Religion.* New York: Oxford University Press.

Aveling, Edward B. (1883). *The Religious Views of Charles Darwin.* London: Freethought Publishing Company.

Ayala, Francisco J. (2007). *Darwin's Gift to Science and Religion.* Washington, D.C.: Joseph Henry Press.

Barlow, Nora, ed. (1969). *Charles Darwin's Diary of the Voyage of H. M. S. "Beagle."* Cambridge: Cambridge University Press, 1933. Reprint, New York: Kraus.

Barrett, Justin (2004) *Why Would Anyone Believe in God?* Walnut Creek: AltaMira Press.

— (2011). *Cognitive Science, Religion, and Theology: From Human Minds to Divine Minds.* West Conshohocken, NY: Templeton Press.

Barrett, Paul H., ed. (1977). *The Collected Papers of Charles Darwin,* 2 vols. Chicago, IL: University of Chicago.

Barrett, Paul H., Peter J. Gautrey, Sandra Herbert, David Kohn, and Sydney Smith, eds (1987). *Charles Darwin's Notebooks, 1836-1844: Geology, Transmutation of Species, Metaphysical Enquiries.* Ithaca, NY: Cornell University Press.

Beatty, John and Piers J. Hale (2008). "*Water Babies*: An Evolutionary Parable." *Endeavor* 32/4: 141–6.

Behe, Michael J. (1996). *Darwin's Black Box: The Biochemical Challenge to Evolution.* New York: Touchstone/Simon and Schuster.

Bell, Charles (2004). *The Hand: Its Mechanism and Vital Endowments as Evincing Design.* London: William Pickering, 1833. Reprint, Adamant Media Corporation.

Berra, Tim M. (2009). *Charles Darwin: The Concise Story of an Extraordinary Man.* Baltimore, MD: Johns Hopkins University Press.

Bowler, Peter J. (1992). "From 'savage' to 'primitive': Victorian evolutionism and the interpretation of marginalized peoples." *Antiquity* 66/252: 721–9.

— (2007). *Monkey Trials and Gorilla Sermons: Evolution and Christianity from Darwin to Intelligent Design.* Cambridge: Harvard University Press.

Boyer, Pascal (2001). *Religion Explained: The Evolutionary Origins of Religious Thought*. New York: Basic Books.

— (2010). *The Fracture of an Illusion: Science and the Dissolution of Religion*. Gottingen: Vandenhoeck and Ruprecht.

Boyer, Pascal and Brian Bergstrom (2008). "Evolutionary Perspectives on Religion." *Annual Review of Anthropology* 37: 111–30.

Brewster, David (1838). "Cours de Philosophie Positive. Par M. Auguste Comte." *Edinburgh Review* 136: 271–309.

Bridges, Esteban Lucas (2007). *Uttermost Part of the Earth: A History of Tierra del Fuego and the Fuegians. New Introduction and Epilogue by R. Natalie P. Goodall*. New York: Overlook/Rookery.

Brock, William Hodson (1966). "The Selection of the Authors of the Bridgewater Treatises." *Notes and Records of the Royal Society of London* 21: 162–79.

Brooke, John Hedley (1985). "The Relations between Darwin's Science and his Religion." In *Darwin and Divinity: Essays on Evolution and Religious Belief*. Edited by John Durant. Oxford: Basil Blackwell, pp. 40–75.

— (1991). *Science and Religion: Some Historical Perspectives*. Cambridge: Cambridge University Press.

— (2009a). "Darwin and Victorian Christianity." In *The Cambridge Companion to Darwin: Second Edition*. Edited by Jonathan Hodge and Gregory Radick. Cambridge: Cambridge University Press, pp. 197–218.

— (2009b). "Genesis and the Scientists: Dissonance among the Harmonizers." In *Reading Genesis after Darwin*. Edited by Stephen C. Barton and David Wilkinson. New York: Oxford University Press, pp. 93–109.

— (2009c). "'Laws impressed on matter by the Creator'?: The *Origin* and the Question of Religion." In *The Cambridge Companion to the "Origin of Species."* Edited by Michael Ruse and Robert J. Richards. Cambridge: Cambridge University Press, pp. 256–74.

Brougham, Henry Peter (1839). *Dissertations on Subjects of Science Connected With Natural Theology: Being the Concluding Volumes of the New Edition of Paley's Work*, 2 vols. London: C. Knight.

Brown, Alan Willard (1947). *The Metaphysical Society: Victorian Minds in Crisis, 1869-1880*. New York: Columbia University Press.

Brown, Frank Burch (1986). *The Evolution of Darwin's Religious Views*. Macon, GA: Mercer University Press.

Browne, Janet (1994). "Missionaries and the Human Mind: Charles Darwin and Robert Fitzroy." In *Darwin's Laboratory: Evolutionary Theory and Natural History in the Pacific*. Edited by Roy MacLeod and Philip F. Rehbock. Honolulu: University of Hawai'i Press, pp. 263–82.

— (1995). *Charles Darwin: Voyaging*. Princeton, NJ: Princeton University Press.

— (2002). *Charles Darwin: The Power of Place*. New York: Alfred A. Knopf.

Buckland, William (1820). *Vindiciae Geologicae; or the Connexion of Geology with Religion Explained*. Oxford: Oxford University Press.

— (1978). *Reliquiae Diluvianae or, Observations in the Organic Remains Contained in Caves, Fissures, and Diluvial Gravel and on Other Geological*

Phenomena Attesting to the Action of a Universal Deluge. London: John Murray, 1823. Reprint, New York: Arno.

— (2003). *Geology and Mineralogy Considered with Reference to Natural Theology*. 2 vols. London: William Pickering, 1837. Reprint, Adamant Media Corporation.

Burkhardt, Frederick and Sydney Smith, eds (1985). *A Calendar of the Correspondence of Charles Darwin, 1821-1882, with Supplement*. Cambridge: Cambridge University Press.

Burton-Christie, Douglas (2009). "Darwin's Contemplative Vision." Spiritus 9: 89–95.

Campbell, George Douglas (1862). "The Supernatural." *Edinburgh Review* 116: 378–97.

— (1867). *The Reign of Law*. London: Alexander Strahan.

— (1874). *Primeval Man: An Examination of Some Recent Speculations*. New York: George Routledge and Sons.

Cannon, Walter F. (1961). "The Impact of Uniformitarianism: Two Letters From John Herschel to Charles Lyell, 1836-1837." *Proceedings of the American Philosophical Society* 105/3: 301–14.

CCD = Burkhardt, Frederick et al, eds *The Correspondence of Charles Darwin*. Cambridge: Cambridge University Press, 1985-.

Chancellor, Gordon and John van Whye (2009). *Charles Darwin's Notebooks from the Voyage of the Beagle*. Forward by Richard Darwin Keynes. Cambridge: Cambridge University Press.

Christianity and Agnosticism: A Controversy. New York: Appleton, 1890.

Cobbe, Francis Power. *Darwinism in Morals and Other Essays*. London: Williams and Norgate, 1872. Reprint, Kessinger, n.d.

Collins, Francis S. (2006). *The Language of God: A Scientist Presents Evidence for Belief*. New York: Free Press.

Colp, Ralph (1980). "'I was born a naturalist': Charles Darwin's 1838 Notes about Himself." *Journal of the History of Medicine and Allied Sciences*. 35/1: 8–39.

— (1986). "'Confessing a Murder': Darwin's First Revelations about Transmutation." *Isis* 77/1: 9–32.

Comfort, Ray (2009). "Special Introduction." In Charles Darwin, *The Origin of Species: 150th Anniversary Edition*. Alachva, FL: Bridge Logos Foundation.

Conway, Moncure Daniel (1877). *Idols and Ideals with an Essay on Christianity*. London: Trübner and Co.

— (1904). *Autobiography, Memories and Experiences, in two volumes*. Boston, MA: Houghton Mifflin.

Crawford, Elizabeth (2006). *The Women's Suffrage Movement in Great Britain and Ireland: A Regional Survey*. London: Routledge.

CUL-DAR = Cambridge University Library Darwin Archive.

Cumming, D. A. (2004). "MacCulloch, John (1773-1835)." Oxford: *Oxford Dictionary of National Biography*. Online. Available: http://0-www. oxforddnb.com. sculib.scu.edu:80/view/article/17412. 2 April 2007.

DAR = Cambridge University Library Darwin Archive.

Darwin, Charles (1874). *The Descent of Man, and Selection in Relation to Sex*, 2nd ed. New York: A. L. Burt.

— (1937a). *The Origin of Species*. 6th ed. New York: P. F. Collier and Son.

— (1937b). *The Voyage of the Beagle*. 2nd ed. New York: P. F. Collier and Son.

— (1952). *Journal of Researches into the Geology and Natural History of the Various Countries Visited by the H. M. S. Beagle, Under the Command of Captain FitzRoy, R. N. from 1832 to 1836*. London: Henry Colburn, 1839. Reprint, New York: Hafner.

— (1958). *The Autobiography of Charles Darwin, 1807-1882, with Original Omissions Restored, Edited with Appendix and Notes by his Granddaughter Nora Barlow*. New York: W.W. Norton.

— (1959). *The Origin of Species, A Variorum Text*. Edited by Morris Peckham. Philadelphia: University of Pennsylvania Press.

— (1964). *On The Origin of Species by Charles Darwin: A Facsimile of the First Edition with an Introduction by Ernst Mayer*. Cambridge: Harvard University Press.

— (1981). *The Descent of Man, and Selection in Relation to Sex*, 2 vols. London: John Murray, 1871. Reprinted with an introduction by John Tyler Bonner and Robert M. May. Princeton, NJ: Princeton University Press.

— (1998). *The Variation of Animals and Plants under Domestication*, with a new foreword by Harriet Ritvo, 2 vols. Baltimore, MD: Johns Hopkins University Press.

Darwin, Charles and Alfred Russel Wallace (1858). "On the Tendency of Species to Form Varieties; and on the Perpetuation of Varieties and Species by Natural Means of Selection." *Journal of the Proceedings of the Linnean Society of London (Zoology)* 3: 46–50.

Darwin, Emma (1915). *A Century of Family Letters, 1792-1896*. Edited by Henrietta Lichfield. 2 vols. New York: D. Appleton.

Darwin, Erasmus (1803). *The Temple of Nature; or the Origin of Society: A Poem, with Philosophical Notes*. London: J. Johnson.

Darwin, Francis, ed. (1903). *More Letters of Charles Darwin: A Record of his Work in a Series of Hitherto Unpublished Letters*. 2 vols. New York: D. Appleton.

— (1959). *The Life and Letters of Charles Darwin: Including an Autobiographical Chapter*. 2 vols. New York: Basic Books.

Dawkins, Richard (1995). *River Out of Eden: A Darwinian View of Life*. New York: Basic Books.

— (1996). *The Blind Watchmaker: Why the Evidence of Evolution Reveals a Universe without Design. With a New Introduction*. New York. W. W. Norton.

— (2006). *The God Delusion*. Boston, MA: Houghton Mifflin.

Day, Matthew (2008). "Godless Savages and Superstitious Dogs: Charles Darwin, Imperial Ethnography, and the Problem of Human Uniqueness." *Journal of the History of Ideas* 69/1: 49–70.

DCP = Darwin Correspondence Project (http://darwinproject.ac.uk).

Dembski, William (2009). *The End of Christianity*. Nashville, TN: B&H Publishing Group.

Dennett, Daniel (2006). *Breaking the Spell: Religion as a Natural Phenomenon*. New York: Penguin.

"*The Descent of Man and Selection in Relation to Sex*. By Charles Darwin." *Edinburgh Review* 134 (1871): 195–235.

Desmond, Adrian (1994/1997). *Huxley: From Devil's Disciple to Evolution's High Priest*. Reading, MA: Helix/Perseus.

Desmond, Adrian and James Moore (1991). *Darwin: The Life of a Tormented Evolutionist*. New York: Warner.

— (2009). *Darwin's Sacred Cause: How a Hatred of Slavery Shaped Darwin's Views on Human Evolution*. New York: Houghton Mifflin Harcourt.

Dixon, Thomas (2008). *The Invention of Altruism: Making Moral Meanings in Victorian Britain*. Oxford: Oxford University Press.

Dobzhansky, Theodosius (1969). *The Biology of Ultimate Concern*. New York: Meridian Books.

— (1973)."Nothing in Biology Makes Sense Except in the Light of Evolution." *The American Biology Teacher* 35: 125–9.

Duncan, Ian (1990–1). "Darwin and the Savages." *Yale Journal of Criticism* 4: 13–45.

Eldredge, Niles (2005). *Darwin: Discovering the Tree of Life*. New York: W. W. Norton.

Eliot, George (2000). *Scenes of Clerical Life*. Amherst, New York: Prometheus Books.

Ellegård, Alvar (1990). *Darwin and the General Reader: The Reception of Darwin's Theory of Evolution in the British Periodical Press, 1859-1872, with a New foreward by David L. Hull*. Chicago, IL: The University of Chicago Press.

Engel-Ledeboer, Maria Sara Johanna and Hendrik Engel (1964). *Carolus Linnaeus Systema Naturae 1735 Facsimile of the First Edition, with an Introduction and a First English Translation of the "Observationes"*. Nieuwkoop: B. De Graaf.

Farrar, Frederic W. (1864). "On the Universality of Belief in God, and in a Future State." *Journal of the Anthropological Society* 2: ccxvii–ccxxii.

— (1897). *Men I Have Known*. New York: Thomas Y. Crowell.

Farrar, Reginald (1904). *The Life of Frederic William Farrar, Sometime Dean of Canturbury*. London: James Nisbit.

Feuer, Lewis S. (1975). "Is the 'Darwin-Marx Correspondence' Authentic?" *Annals of Science* 32: 1–12.

Fisher, Ronald Aylmer (1950). *Creative Aspects of Natural Law*. Cambridge: Cambridge University Press.

FitzRoy, Robert J. (1966). *Narrative of the Surveying Voyages of His Majesty's Ships Adventure and Beagle between the Years 1826 and 1836, Describing their Examination of the Southern Shores of South America and the Beagle's*

Circumnavigation of the Globe, 3 vols. London: Henry Colburn, 1839. Reprint, AMS Press.

Fordyce, John (1883). *Aspects of Scepticism: with Special Reference to the Present Time.* London: Elliot Stock.

Freeman, Richard Broke (1977). *The Works of Charles Darwin: An Annotated Bibliographical Handlist.* 2nd ed., Revised and Enlarged. Folkestone, Kent, England: Dawson.

— (1978). *Charles Darwin: A Companion.* Folkestone, Kent, England: Dawson.

Fullerton, William Young (1931). *J. W. C. Fegan: A Tribute.* London: Marshall, Morgan, and Scott.

Fyfe, Aileen (1997). "The reception of William Paley's *Natural Theology* in the University of Cambridge," *The British Journal for the History of Science* 30: 321–35.

Garland, Martha McMackin (1980). *Cambridge Before Darwin: The Ideal of a Liberal Education 1800-1860.* Cambridge: Cambridge University Press.

Gillespie, Neal C. (1977). "The Duke of Argyll, Evolutionary Anthropology, and the Art of Scientific Controversy." *Isis* 68: 40–54.

Goodwin, Harvey (1883). *Walks in the Regions of Science and Faith: A Series of Essays.* London: John Murray.

Graham, William (1884). *The Creed of Science: Religious, Moral, and Social.* 2nd ed. Revised. London: C. Kegan Paul, Trench, and Co.

Gruber, Howard E. and Paul H. Barrett (1974). *Darwin on Man: A Psychological Study of Scientific Creativity.* New York: E. P. Dutton.

Gruber, Jacob W. (1980). *A Conscience in Conflict: The Life of St. George Jackson Mivart.* Westport: Greenwood Press.

Guinness, Os (2005). *Unspeakable: Facing Up to Evil in an Age of Genocide and Terror.* San Francisco: HarperSanFrancisco.

Häckel (Haeckel), Ernst (1882). *Die Naturanschauung von Darwin, Goethe und Lamarck.* Jena: Gustav Fischer.

Harris, Sam (2004). *The End of Faith: Religion, Terror, and the Future of Reason, with a New afterword.* New York: W. W. Norton.

— (2006/2008). *Letter to a Christian Nation.* New York: Vintage Books.

Harrison, Jane Ellen (1909). "The Influence of Darwinism on the Study of Religions." In *Darwin and Modern Science: Essays in Commemoration of the Centenary of the Birth of Charles Darwin and of the Fiftieth Anniversary of the Publication of The Origin of Species.* Edited by A. C. Seward, Cambridge: Cambridge University Press, pp. 494–511.

Harvey, Joy (1997). *"Almost a Man Of Genius":* Clémence *Royer, Feminism, and Nineteenth-Century Science.* New Brunswick, New Jersey: Rutgers University Press.

Haught, John F. (2003). *Deeper than Darwin: The Prospect for Religion in the Age of Evolution.* Boulder: Westview.

— (2008a). *God After Darwin: A Theology of Evolution.* 2nd ed. Boulder, CO: Westview.

— (2008b). *God and the New Atheism: A Critical Response to Dawkins, Harris, and Hitchens*. Louisville, KY: Westminster.

Hazlewood, Nick (2000). *Savage: The Life and Times of Jemmy Button*. London: Hodder and Stoughton.

Healey, Edna (2001). *Emma Darwin: The Inspirational Wife of a Genius*. London: Headline.

Henslow, John Stevens (1823). "On the Deluge," *The Annals of Philosophy*, new series, 6: 344–8.

Herbert, Sandra (1974). "The Place of Man in the Development of Darwin's Theory of Transmutation. Part I. To July 1837." *Journal of the History of Biology* 7/2: 217–58.

— (1977). "The Place of Man in the Development of Darwin's Theory of Transmutation. Part II." *Journal of the History of Biology* 10/2: 155–227.

Himmelfarb, Gertrude (1967). *Darwin and the Darwinian Revolution*. Gloucester, Mass.: Peter Smith.

Hinde, Robert A. (1999). *Why Gods Persist: A Scientific Approach to Religion*. 2nd ed. London: Routledge.

Hitchens, Christopher (2007/2009). *God is not Great: How Religion Poisons Everything*. New York: Reading Group Guide/Hachette.

Hodge, Jonathan and Gregory Radick, eds (2009). *The Cambridge Companion to Darwin: Second Edition*. Cambridge: Cambridge University Press.

Humboldt, Alexander von (1853). *Personal Narrative of Travels to the Equinoctial Regions of America During the Years 1799-1804*. Translated and edited by Thomasina Ross. 3 vols. London: Henry G. Rohn.

Hume, David (1826). *The Philosophical Works of David Hume*. 4 vols. Edinburgh: Adam Black and William Tait.

— (1992). *Writings on Religion*. Edited by Antony Flew. La Salle: Open Court.

Huntley, William B. (1972). "David Hume and Charles Darwin." *Journal of the History of Ideas* 33/3: 457–70.

Huxley, Thomas H. (1886). "The Evolution of Theology: An Anthropological Study," *The Nineteenth Century* 19: 346–65, 485–506.

— (1896a). *Darwiniana: Essays*. New York: D. Appleton.

— (1896b). *Science and Christian Tradition*. New York: Appleton.

— (1959). *Man's Place in Nature*. Ann Arbor: The University of Michigan.

— (1970). "Agnosticism." *Collected Essays (1893-1894), Vol. V, Science and Christian Tradition*. Hildesheim: Georg Olm Verlag, pp. 209–62.

Johnson, Phillip E. (1993). *Darwin on Trial*. 2nd ed. Downers Grove: Intervarsity Press.

Jorgenson, Jorgen (1827). *The Religion of Christ is the Religion of Nature*. London: Joseph Capes.

Kendrick, Thomas D. *The Lisbon Earthquake*. Philadelphia: J. B. Lippincott, n.d.

Kepple, T. E. (1887). "The Country Parson as He was, and as He is." *Blackwood's Edinburgh Magazine* 142: 317–28.

Keynes, Randal Darwin, ed. (1988). *Charles Darwin's Beagle Diary*. Cambridge: Cambridge University Press.

Bibliography

— (2001). *Darwin, His Daughter, and Human Evolution*. New York: Riverhead Books.

King-Hele, Desmond, ed. (2003). *Charles Darwin's The Life of Erasmus Darwin*. Cambridge: Cambridge University Press.

Kingsley, Charles (1874). *Westmister Sermons*. London: Macmillan.

— (1889). *The Water-Babies: A Fairy Tale for a Land-Baby*. London: Macmillan.

Kirby, William (2005). *On the Power, Wisdom, and Goodness of God as Manifested in the Creation of Animals and in Their History, Habits, and Instincts*. 2 vols. London: William Pickering, 1835. Reprint, Elibron Classics.

Kottler, Malcolm Jay (1974). "Alfred Russel Wallace, the Origin of Man, and Spiritualism." *Isis* 65/2: 145–92.

Kotzebue, Otto von (1830). *A New Voyage Round the World, in the Years 1823, 24, 25, and 26*. Vol. I. London: Henry Colburn and Richard Bentley.

Lack, David (1957). *Evolutionary Theory and Christian Belief: The Unresolved Controversy*. London: Methuen.

Lamarck, Jean-Baptiste (1984). *Zoological Philosophy: An Exposition with Regard to the Natural History of Animal*. Chicago, IL: University of Chicago.

Landauer, Walter and Tso Kan Chang (1949). "The Ancon or Otter Sheep: History and Genetics." *Journal of Heredity* 40: 105–112.

Leask, Nigel (2003). "Darwin's 'Second Sun': Alexander von Humboldt and the Genesis of *The Voyage of the Beagle*." In *Literature, Psychoanalysis, 1830-1970*. Edited by Helen Small and Trudi Tate. Oxford: Oxford University Press, pp. 13–36.

Lessl, Thomas M. (2012). *Rhetorical Darwinism: Religion, Evolution, and the Scientific Identity*. Waco: Baylor University Press.

Lightman, Bernard (2001). "Victorian Sciences and Religions: Discordant Harmonies." *Osiris*, 2nd Series, 16: 343–66.

Litchfield, Henrietta, ed. (1915). *Emma Darwin a Century of Family Letters, 1792-1896*, 2 vols. New York: D. Appleton.

Lubbock, John (1863). "The Antiquity of Man from Geological Evidences." *The Natural History Review* 3: 211–9.

— (1871). *The Origin of Civilization and the Primitive Condition of Man*. New York: D. Appleton.

Lyell, Charles (1868). *Principles of Geology or the Modern Changes of the Earth and its Inhabitants*, Tenth and Entirely Revised Edition. London: John Murray.

— (2006). *The Geological Evidences of the Antiquity of Man*. London: John Murray, 1863. Reprint, Elibron Classics.

MacCulloch, John (1837). *Proofs and Illustrations of the Attributes of God from the Facts and Laws of the Physical Universe, being the Foundation of Natural and Revealed Religion*, 3 vols. London: James Duncan.

Mackintosh, James (1872). *On the Progress of Ethical Philosophy: Chiefly During the XVIIth and XVIIIth Centuries*. 4th ed. Edinburgh: Adam and Charles Black.

MacLeod, Roy (1982). "The 'Bankruptcy of Science' Debate: The Creed of
Science and its Critics, 1885–1900." *Science, Technology, & Human Values.*
7/41: 2–15.

Malthus, Thomas (1798). *An Essay on the Principle of Population, As It Affects
the Future Improvement of Society, with Remarks On the Speculation of
Mr. Godwin, M. Condorcet, and Other Writers.* London: J. Johnson.

— (1986). *The Works of Thomas Robert Malthus, vols. 2–3, An Essay on the
Principle of Population: The Sixth Edition (1826) with Variant Readings
from the Second Edition (1803).* Edited by E. A. Wrigley and David Souden.
London: William Pickering.

Martineau, Harriett (1838). *How to Observe: Morals and Manners.* London:
Charles Knight.

Matthew, Henry Colin G. "Campbell, George Douglas," *Oxford Dictionary of
National Biography.* Online source: http://0-www.oxforddnb.com.sculib.scu.
edu/view/article/4500, accessed 8 March 2009.

McClennan, John Ferguson (1869). "The Worship of Animals and Plants."
Fortnightly Review 6: 407–27.

— (1870). "The Worship of Animals and Plants." *Fortnightly Review* 7: 194–216.

Miller, Hugh (1857). *The Testimony of the Rocks; Or, Geology in its Bearings on
the Two Theologies, Natural and Revealed.* Edinburgh: Thomas Constable.

— (1860). *The Footprints of the Creator: or, The Asterolepis of Stromness.* Boston,
MA: Gould and Lincoln.

Miller, Kenneth R. (1999). *Finding Darwin's God: A Scientist's Search for
Common Ground Between God and Evolution.* New York: HarperCollins.

Mivart, St. George (1871a). "The Descent of Man, and Selection in Relation to
Sex." *Quarterly Review* 131: 47–90.

— (1871b). *On the Genesis of Species.* London: Macmillan.

— (1892). *Essays and Criticisms,* 2 vols. London: James R. Osgood, McIlvaine,
and Co.

— (1897). "Some Reminiscences of Thomas Henry Huxley." *The Nineteenth
Century* 42: 985–98.

Moore, James R. (1979). *The Post-Darwinian Controversies: A Study of the
Protestant Struggle to Come to Terms with Darwin in Great Britain and
America 1870-1900.* Cambridge: Cambridge University Press.

— (1985). "Darwin of Down: The Evolutionist as Squarson-Naturalist."
The Darwinian Heritage. Edited by David Kohn. Princeton, NJ: Princeton
University Press, pp. 435–81.

— (1994). *The Darwin Legend.* Grand Rapids: Baker Books.

— (2007). "R. A. Fisher: A Faith Fit for Eugenics." *Studies in History and
Philosophy of Biological and Biomedical Sciences.* 38/1: 110–35.

Müller, F. Max (1885). "The Savage." *The Nineteenth Century* 17: 109–32.

Nash, David (2011). "Reassessing the 'Crisis of Faith' in the Victorian Age:
Eclecticism and the Spirit of Moral Inquiry." *Journal of Victorian Culture*
16/1: 65–82.

Newman, Francis (1849). *The Soul, Her Sorrows and Her Aspirations: An Essay Towards the Natural History of the Soul, as the True Basis of Theology*. London: John Chapman.

— (1970). *Phases of Faith*, with an introduction by U.C. Knoepflmacher. New York: Humanities Press.

Norton, Andrews (1846). *The Evidences of the Genuineness of the Gospels*, vol. 1, 2nd ed. Cambridge: John Owen.

Numbers, Ronald L. (1985). "Science and Religion." *Osiris*, 2nd series, 1: 59–80.

— (1993). *The Creationists: The Evolution of Scientific Creationism*. Berkeley, CA: University of California.

Ospovat, Dov (1981). *The Development of Darwin's Theory: Natural History, Natural Theology, and Natural Selection, 1838-1859*. Cambridge: Cambridge University Press.

Paley, William (1972). *Natural Theology: or, Evidences of the Existence and Attributes of the Deity, Collected from the Appearances of Nature*. Reprint, Houston, TX: St. Thomas Press.

— (2002). *The Principles of Moral and Political Philosophy*, foreword by D. L. Le Mahieu. Indianapolis, IN: Liberty Fund.

Pearson, John (1832). *An Exposition of the Creed with an Appendix, containing the Principle Greek and Latin Creeds*. London: J. F. Dove.

Phipps, William E. (2002). *Darwin's Religious Odyssey*. Harrisburg, PA: Trinity Press International.

Picton, J. Allanson (1870). *New Theories and the Old Faith*. London: Williams and Norgate.

Pleins, J. David (2003). *When the Great Abyss Opened: Classic and Contemporary Readings of Noah's Flood*. New York: Oxford University Press.

Polkinghorne, John (2011). *Science and Religion in Quest of Truth*. New Haven: Yale University Press.

Priestley, Joseph. *Letters to a Philosophical Unbeliever*, 2nd ed. Birmingham: Pearson and Rollason. 1787. Reprint, Kessinger Publishing, n.d.

Rae, John (2004). "Graham, William." Revised by C.A. Creffield. *Oxford Dictionary of National Biography*. Oxford: Oxford University Press. Online source: http://0-www.oxforddnb.com.sculib.scu.edu/view/article/33507, accessed 6 Aug 2009.

Rainger, Ronald (1978). "Race, Politics, and Science: The Anthropological Society of London in the 1860s." *Victorian Studies* 22/1: 51–70.

Reade, Winwood. *The Outcast*. New York: Peter Eckler, n.d.

Richards, Robert J. (1987). *Darwin and the Emergence of Evolutionary Theories of Mind and Behavior*. Chicago, IL: University of Chicago Press.

Ritter, William Emerson (1954). *Charles Darwin and the Golden Rule*. Edited by Edna Watson Bailey. Washington: Science Service.

Robertson, David (2007). *The Dawkins Letters: Revised Edition*. Geanies House: Christian Focus Publications.

Robson, John M. (1990). "The Fiat and Finger of God: The Bridgewater Treatises." In *Victorian Faith in Crisis: Essays on Continuity and Change in*

Nineteenth-Century Religious Belief. Edited by Richard J. Helmstadter and Bernard Lightman. Stanford, CA: Stanford University Press, pp. 71–125.

Roget, Peter Mark (1840). *Animal and Vegetable Physiology Considered with Reference to Natural Theology.* 2 vols. 3rd ed. London: William Pickering.

Romanes, George John (1896). *A Selection from the Poems of George John Romanes, with an Introduction by T. Herbert Warren.* London: Longmans, Green, and Co.

Rudwick, Martin J. S. (1982). "Charles Darwin in London: The Integration of Public and Private Science." *Isis* 73/2: 186–206.

Ruse, Michael (1993). "Will the Real Charles Darwin Please Stand Up?" *The Quarterly Review of Biology* 68/2: 225–31.

— (1999). *The Darwinian Revolution: Science Red in Tooth and Claw.* 2nd ed. Chicago, IL: University of Chicago.

— (2001a). *Can a Darwinian be a Christian?: The Relationship Between Science and Religion.* Cambridge: Cambridge University Press.

— (2001b). *The Evolution Wars: A Guide to the Debates.* New Brunswick, NJ: Rutgers University Press.

— (2003). *Darwin and Design: Does Evolution Have a Purpose?* Cambridge: Harvard University Press.

Ruse, Michael and Robert J. Richards, eds (2009). *The Cambridge Companion to the "Origin of Species".* Cambridge: Cambridge University Press.

Sagan, Carl (1994). *Pale Blue Dot: A Vision of the Human Future in Space.* New York: Random House.

— (2006). *The Varieties of Scientific Experience: A Personal View of the Search for God.* Edited by Ann Druyan. New York: Penguin.

Schmitt, Cannon (2004). "Darwin's Savage Mnemonics." *Representations* 88/1: 55–80.

Schofield, Robert E. "Priestley, Joseph." *Oxford Dictionary of National Biography.* Oxford: Oxford University Press. Online source: http://0-www.oxforddnb. com.sculib.scu.edu/view/article/22788, accessed 24 Aug 2009.

Schwartz, Joel S. (1995). "George John Romanes's Defense of Darwinism: The Correspondence of Charles Darwin and His Chief Disciple." *Journal of the History of Biology* 28/2: 281–316.

— (2010). *Darwin's Disciple: George John Romanes, a Life in Letters.* Philadelphia: American Philosophical Society.

Secord, James A. (1991). "Edinburgh Lamarckians: Robert Jameson and Robert E. Grant." *Journal of the History of Biology* 24: 1–18.

Sedgwick, Adam (1969). *A Discourse on the Studies of the University,* with an Introduction by Eric Ashby and Mary Anderson. New York: Humanities Press.

Shortland, M., ed. (1996). *Hugh Miller and the Controversies of Victorian Science.* Oxford: Clarendon Press.

Slotten, Ross A. (2004). *The Heretic in Darwin's Court: The Life of Alfred Russel Wallace.* New York: Columbia University Press.

Smith, Adam (1969). *The Theory of Moral Sentiments*, with an introduction by E.G. West. Indianapolis: Liberty Classics.

Spencer, Herbert (1891). "The Origin of Animal Worship." *Essays: Scientific, Political, and Speculative*, vol. 1. London. Williams and Norgate, pp. 308–30.

Spencer, Nick (2009). *Darwin and God*. London: SPCK.

Starr, Ivan (1983). *The Rituals of the Diviner*. Malibu: Undena.

Staunton, George (1797). *An Authentic Account of an Embassy from the King of Great Britain to the Emperor of China*, vol. II. London: W. Bulmer.

Stecher, Robert M. (1961). "The Darwin-Innes Letters: The Correspondence of an Evolutionist with His Vicar, 1848–1884," *Annals of Science* 17/4: 201–58.

Stevens, L. Robert (1982). "Darwin's Humane Reading: The Anaesthetic Man Reconsidered." *Victorian Studies* 26/1: 51–63.

Stocking, George W. (1987). *Victorian Anthropology*. New York: The Free Press.

Stoll, Mark (2009). "Edward Osborne Wilson." In *Eminent Lives in Twentieth-Century Science and Religion: Second Revised and Much Expanded Edition*. Edited by Nicolaas Rupke. Frankfurt am Main: Peter Lang, pp. 333–47.

Sulivan, Henry Norton, ed. (1896). *Life and Letters of the late Admiral Sir Bartholomew James Sulivan*, K.C.B., 1810–1890. London: John Murray.

Sumner, John Bird (1824). *The Evidence of Christianity, Derived from its Nature and Reception*. London: J. Hatchard and Son.

Thomson, Keith (2009). *The Young Charles Darwin*. New Haven: Yale University Press.

Topham, Jonathan R. (1998). "Beyond the 'Common Context': The Production and Reading of the Bridgewater Treatises." *Isis* 89: 233–62.

Turner, Frank Miller (1974). *Between Science and Religion: The Reaction to Scientific Naturalism in Late Victorian England*. New Haven: Yale University Press.

Tylor, Edward B. (1870). *Researches into the Early History of Mankind and the Development of Civilization*, 2nd ed. London: John Murray.

Tyndall, John (1874). *Address Delivered Before the British Association Assembled at Belfast, with Additions*. London: Longmans, Green, and Co.

— (1897). *Fragments of Science: A Series of Detached Essays, Addresses, and Reviews*. 2 vols. New York: D. Appleton.

Van der Heide, J. (2006). "Darwin's Young Admirers." *Endeavor* 30/3: 103–7.

Van der Meer, Jitse M. (2009). "Theodosius Dobzhansky." In *Eminent Lives in Twentieth-Century Science and Religion: Second Revised and Much Expanded Edition*. Edited by Nicolaas Rupke. Frankfurt am Main: Peter Lang, pp. 105–27.

Van Whye, John and Michael J. Pallen (2012). "The 'Annie Hypothesis': Did the Death of His Daughter Cause Darwin to 'Give up Christianity'?" *Centaurus* 54: 105–23.

Wallace, Alfred Russel (1871). *Contributions to the Theory of Natural Selection: A Series of Essays*. New York: Macmillan.

— (1925) *The Wonderful Century: The Age of New Ideas in Science and Invention, New Edition, Revised and Largely Re-written*. London: G. Allen and Unwin.

Walters, Stuart Max and Elizabeth Anne Stow (2001). *Darwin's Mentor: John Stevens Henslow, 1796-1861*. Cambridge: Cambridge University Press.

Ward, Keith (2007). *Is Religion Dangerous?* Grand Rapids: Eerdmans.

Warfield, Benjamin B. (1888). "Charles Darwin's Religious Life:—A Sketch in Spiritual Biography." *The Presbyterian Review* 9: 569–601.

Webb, Robert K. (1990). "The Faith of Nineteenth-Century Unitarians: A Curious Incident." In *Victorian Faith in Crisis: Essays on Continuity and Change in Nineteenth-Century Religious Belief*. Edited by Richard J. Helmstadter and Bernard Lightman. Stanford, CA: Stanford University Press, pp. 126–49.

Wedgwood, Barbara and Wedgwood, Hensleigh (1980). *The Wedgwood Circle, 1730-1897: Four Generations of a Family and Their Friends*. London: Studio Vista.

Wedgwood, Frances Julia (1860). "The Boundaries of Science: A Dialogue." *Macmillan's Magazine* 2: 134–8.

— (1861). "The Boundaries of Science: A Second Dialogue." *Macmillan's Magazine* 4: 237–47.

— (1882). "A Botanist on Evolution." *The Spectator* 55: 536–8.

— (1907). *The Moral Ideal: A Historic Study*. London: Kegan Paul, Trench, Trübner, and Co.

Whewell, William (1837). *Astronomy and General Physics Considered with Reference to Natural Theology*. London: William Pickering.

— (1853). *Of the Plurality of Worlds: An Essay*. London: John W. Parker.

White, Paul (2003). *Thomas Huxley: Making the "Man of Science"*. Cambridge: Cambridge University Press.

Wilkin, Simon, ed. *Sir Thomas Browne's Works, Including His Life and Correspondence*, vol. 2. London: William Pickering, 1835. Reprint, Kessinger Publishing, n.d.

Wilson, Edward O. (2006). *The Creation: An Appeal to Save Life on Earth*. New York: W. W. Norton.

Wilson, Leonard G., ed. (1970). *Sir Charles Lyell's Scientific Journals on the Species Question*. New Haven: Yale University Press.

Young, Robert M. (1985). *Darwin's Metaphor: Nature's Place in Victorian Culture*. Cambridge: Cambridge University Press.

Index

Abbot, Francis Ellingwood 91–2
Aborigines, Australian 8–9
afterlife 57–8, 74, 100, 103 *see also*
    immortality
agnostics/agnosticism
    from belief to 99–100
    Darwin as 90–3, 99, 104,
        109–10
altruism and religion 110–12
American education 112–13
ancestor worship 70, 73–4
animals 66–7, 77–8, 80–1
anthropology of religion,
    works on 108
anthropomorphism 69–70
Argyll, Duke of *see* Campbell,
    George Douglas
atheism/atheists
    and agnosticism 93
    on Darwin 92
    in Darwinism 84–5
    and evolution 88–9
    limitations of 109–10
    and materialism 54
    practical 72
    in primitive societies 68–9
attacks on Darwinism 83–8
Aveling, Edward 93
Ayala, Francisco 108

barbarians *see* savages
Barrett, Justin: *Why Would Anyone
    Believe in God* 112
Beagle, H. M. S., voyage of
    affecting religious views 2–5,
        29–31
    and Darwin's career choice
        34–7
    Fuegians on 5–7

geology data from 42–4
    path of 3–4
Beechey, Frederick William 23
belief, religious *see also* religion
    to agnosticism 99–100
    biology of 53–4
    critiqued 4–5
    and Darwin 98–9, 102–3
    natural selection of 49–50
    religion as 2–3
    and science 41, 106
    and transcendence 97–8
Bible, The
    creation myths in 76
    Darwin and 1–3, 17, 94–5, 100
    doubts about 4, 16, 42–4, 94–5,
        105–6
    reinterpreted 42–4
    as substitute for science
        90, 109–10
Biblicism 42–4, 65, 90–1
biological imperative *see* instincts
biology
    of belief 53–4
    in morality and ethics 54–61,
        75–81
    theological reflection
        in 108–10
British Association for the
    Advancement of Science
    (BAAS) 75, 93–4
Brooke, John Hedley 47–8
Brown, Frank Burch: *The Evolution
    of Darwin's Religious
    Views* 4
Browne, Janet: *Voyaging* 4, 23, 38
Browne, Thomas: *Religio Medici* 45
Büchner, Ludwig 93
Burton-Christie, Douglas 28

Button, Jemmy   5–6, 10
Button, Jemmy FitzRoy   26

Campbell, George Douglas, Duke
    of Argyll
    Primeval Man   75–6
    The Reign of Law   75
Candid Examination of Theism
    (Romanes)   99
Canterbury, Archbishop of   26, 102
career choices of Darwin   31–7
cathedral at Concepcion   14–16
Catholicism/Catholics
    on Darwinism   84–7
    Darwin on   2–3, 13–14,
        116–17n. 15
    and heretics   12–13
    and just wars   21–2
    missions and   22
Charles Darwin: A Memorial Poem
    (Romanes)   105–6
Chilotan religious practices   10
Christianity
    attacks on   92–3
    everlasting punishment in   95
    in just wars   18–22
    positive impact of   23–5
    as superstition   74
    traditional, rejected   91
civil discourse   112–13
civilization
    and missionaries   26–7
    natural selection in   104
    and religion   12
    and savages   5–8, 11
Coal and Clothing Club   110
Cobbe, Francis Power   87–8
Collins, Francis   108
Colonia del Sacramiento,
        Uruguay   14–15
Comte, Auguste   48
conscience   56–61, 80, 90
conversion of South
        Americans   22, 97

Conway, Moncure (Rev)   89–90
creation-evolution debate   106–10,
        112–13
Creative Aspects of Natural Law
        (Fisher)   109
Creator *see also* God
    atheists on   92
    Darwin's belief in   88, 91
    and evil   17–18
    laws of nature   48
Creed of Science (Graham)
        103–4
Cucao Indians   20

Dalton, John: *A New System of
        Chemical Philosophy*   54
Darwin, Annie (daughter of CD),
        death of   100
Darwin, Caroline (sister
        of CD)   1, 31–2, 44
Darwin, Catherine (sister
        of CD)   35
Darwin, Charles
    as an agnostic   90–3, 99, 104,
        109–10
    autobiographical reflections
        of   20, 94–101, 109
    career choices of   31–7
    death and burial of   104–6
    as a deist   92
    election of to the Royal
        Society   37
    honorary degree of   101
    religious doubts of   31,
        37–41, 99
    scholarship on   114–15n. 9
    as a theist   90–2, 98–9
Darwin, Emma (*née* Wedgwood)
    on Darwin's fame   90
    Darwin's marriage to   37–41
    on *The Descent of Man*   64
    on everlasting punishment   95
    and Francis Cobbe   87
    on social reforms   111

Darwin, Erasmus (brother
        of CD)   36, 40
Darwin, Erasmus (grandfather
        of CD)   1, 101–2
Darwin, Frank (son of CD)   39
Darwin, Henrietta (daughter
        of CD)   38–9
Darwin, Susan (sister of CD)   36–7
Darwin, William Erasmus
        (son of CD)   37
Darwin on Man (Gruber)
        129–30n. 9
Darwin's Religious Odyssey
        (Phipps)   4
*Darwin: The Life of a Tormented
        Evolutionist* (Moore)   3–4
Dawkins, Richard
        The God Delusion   109, 111
        use of Darwin by   107–8
deists/deism, Darwin as   92
Dennett, Daniel   147n. 25
"derivative" design *see* divine design
Descent of Man (Darwin)
        creator in   92
        debate with Argyll over   75–7
        morality and religion in   63–4
        religious criticism of   83–7
Desmond, Adrian: *Darwin: The
        Life of a Tormented
        Evolutionist*   3–4
*Dialogues Concerning Natural
        Religion* (Hume)   50
disasters, natural   14–16
diversity of belief   49–51
divination   147n. 25
divine design *see also* natural
        theology
        challenged by Nature   17–18
        and natural selection   47–8,
        84–5, 95–6
        orchids as proof of   75
Dobzhansky, Theodosius: *The
        Biology of Ultimate
        Concern*   108–9

Doedes, Nicholaas Dirk   92
doubts, religious
        about the Bible   4, 16, 42–4,
        94–5, 105–6
        Darwin's   31, 37–41, 99
Down Friendly Society   111
dreams   66–7, 69–70, 72

earthquakes   15–16
education and morality   78
Eliot, George: *Scenes of
        Clerical Life*   34
emotions
        as brain functions   54
        in evolution   66–7
        human   56–9
        in religious feelings   52–4
        and the sublime   70–1
Essay on the Origin of Language, An
        (Farrar)   68
*Essay on the Principle of Population,
        An* (Malthus)   47
ethics, evolutionary *see also* morality
        biology in   54–61, 75–81
        conscience in   56–9
        and instincts   54–9, 78–81,
        100–1
        Mivart on   84–5
        and modern theology   103
        pleasure/happiness in   56–7
        and religion   106
        rise of theory   46–7
        sympathy in   59–61, 80–1
European conquest   8–9, 21–2
Evidence of Christianity, The
        (Sumner)   1
*Evidence of the Genuineness of the
        Gospels, The* (Norton)   95
evil   16–18, 96–7, 103, 111–12
evolution
        and atheism   88–9
        and creationism   106–10,
        112–13
        and crime   58

emotions in   66–7
God in   103
homologies in   64–6
of human intellect   66–8, 70
physiology in   64–5
savages in   47, 118n. 32
and theism   81, 84–90
*Evolutionary Theory and Christian
      Belief* (Lack)   109
evolutionists, religious   88–90
*Evolution of Darwin's Religious Views,
      The* (Brown)   4
Exposition of the Creed, An
      (Pearson)   1
*Expression of the Emotions in
      Man and Animals*
      (Darwin)   66

faith, religious   2–5, 30,
      40–1 *see also* belief
Farrar, Frederic William (Rev)
      *An Essay on the Origin of
            Language*   68
      on Darwin's virtues   105
      "On the Universality of Belief
            in God, and in a Future
            State"   68
fear
      cosmic   70–1
      and religion   52–3, 66, 68
      as a universal emotion   72
Fegan, James   111
fetishism   70, 72
Fisher, Ronald: *Creative Aspects of
      Natural Law*   109
FitzRoy, Robert (Captain of the
      H. M. S. *Beagle*)   5–7, 23,
      42–4
Fordyce, John (Rev)   88–9
Fox, William Darwin   36, 42
freedom of thought and
      circumspection   92–3
free will   56, 58
Friendly Societies   111

Fuegians *see also* Tierra del Fuego
      cannibalism of   118n. 38
      captives returned   5–7, 10
      improved by missions   26
      language of   137n. 88
      as savages   47, 118n. 32
      superstitions of   52
fundamentalists and
      evolution   113

Galileo   49
Genesis, Book of   42, 76
Genesis of Species, On the
      (Mivart)   83–5
genome, human, God in   108
geology   15–16, 42–4, 129n. 9
ghost worship   135n. 44
God *see also* Creator
      evolutionary role of   103
      instinct to believe in   53–4
      metaphysics of   58–9
      in Nature   29
      and nature's evil   18, 96–7
      as a spatial concept   51
      and sublimity   98
God and Darwin (Spencer)   3
God Delusion (Dawkins)   109, 111
Golden Rule, The   78–9, 111–12
Goodwin, Harvey (Rev)   105
Gospels of the New Testament   95
Graham, William: *Creed of
      Science*   103–4
Grant, James   88
Gray, Asa   75, 84, 88–9
Gruber, Howard E.: *Darwin on
      Man*   129–30n. 9

Häckel, Ernst   91
Hammond, Robert   36
happiness   56–8, 96
Harris, Sam   111, 146–7n. 24
Haught, John   106, 108
Heathorn, Henrietta   32–3
Henslow, John Stevens   35–6, 110

Herbert, Sandra: "The Place of Man
    in the Development
    of Darwin's Theory of
    Transmutation" 129–30n. 9
heretics and Catholics 12–13
Herschel, Sir John 44
Hindu religious rites 12
Hitchens, Christopher 146–7n. 24
homologies in evolution 64–6
Hooker, Joseph Dalton 75
How to Observe (Martineau) 60
Human Genome Project 108
humans
    as animals 46–7, 53–4
    created by God 76
    cultural development of 7, 12,
        71–4
    origins of 57, 75–6
    purpose of 54–5
    souls of 53
Humboldt, Alexander von: *Personal
    Narrative* 117–18n. 29
Hume, David
    *Dialogues Concerning Natural
        Religion* 50
    *The Natural History of
        Religion* 50
Huxley, Thomas H.
    "Mr. Darwin's Critics" 85–7
    "The Evolution of
        Theology" 135n. 44
    "The Funeral of Charles
        Darwin" 106

Idolatry 73–4
immortality 74, 85, 98, 103
Innes, Brodie (Rev) 110
instincts
    and conscience 59–61
    and ethics 54–9, 79–81,
        100–1
    and happiness 57–8
    immortality belief as 98
    persistent 80

to religion 46–8, 51–4
    social 76–9, 100–1
intellect, human
    and conscience 57
    evolution of 66–8, 70
    God-given 75–6, 105

Journal of Researches (Darwin)
    on evil and nature 17–18
    evolution of religion in 4–5
    primitive religion in 5–12
    publication of 37
    South American
        genocide in 18–21
    sublimity of Nature in 27–9
just war theory 18–22

Keeling Islands 11
Kepple, T. E. 34–5
Kingsley, Charles (Rev): *Water
    Babies* 88–9
kinship bond 77–8
Kirby, William 53–4
Kotzebue, Otto von 23

Lack, David: *Evolutionary Theory and
    Christian Belief* 109
Lamarck, Jean Baptiste 53–4
Langton, Charles 33–4, 41
language 44, 67, 70, 95
Lemoy, Island of 14
Letter to a Christian Nation
    (Harris) 146–7n. 24
life ethic 100–1
Lima, Peru 19
Lion-Ant episode 17–18
Lubbock, John: *The Origin of
    Civilization and the Primitive
    Condition of Man* 71–5
Lyell, Charles 42–3, 49, 93

McDermott, Frederick A. 91
Mackintosh, James: *On the Progress of
    Ethical Philosophy* 60

McLennan, John F.: "The Worship of
        Animals and Plants" 69
Malay religion 11
Malthus, Thomas: *An Essay on the
        Principle of Population* 47
Maori Tribes 8
Marcus Aurelius, Emperor 78
marriage 33–4, 37–41
Martineau, Harriet: *How to
        Observe* 60
materialist explanations 48, 53–4
Matthews, Richard 5–7, 26
Mengden, Nicolai Alexandrovitch
        von 90–1
metaphysical abstraction 48–9
Metaphysical Society 145n. 5
Mill, John Stuart 78, 93
Miller, Kenneth 108
Milton, John: *Paradise Lost* 28
miracles 43, 47–8, 95
missions and missionaries 22–7, 97
Mivart, St. George Jackson
        attacks on Darwin by 83–7
        On the Genesis of Species 83–5
monarchy 73–4
monotheism 4, 9–10, 50–1, 68, 74
Moore, James: *Darwin: The
        Life of a Tormented
        Evolutionist* 3–4
morality
        animal roots of 47, 59–61,
                77–8
        biological development of 75–81
        Cobbe on 87–8
        and common good 60
        and instincts 54–9, 79–81,
                100–1
        and religion 78–9, 106
        and remorse 80
Mordaunt, Edward 100
mortification 57

Natural History of Religion, The
        (Hume) 50
natural order 9–10, 17–18, 104

natural selection
        in civilization 104
        and common good 60
        and divine design 47–8, 84–5,
                95–6
        and human purpose 55
        of religions 49
        and suffering 97
        and sympathy 77–8
natural theology
        see also divine design
        and evil 96–7
        and human purpose 55
        and morality 61, 75
        and natural selection 47–8,
                84–5, 95–6
Nature
        anthropomorphized 69–70
        and belief 97–8
        and divine design 17–18
        evil in 17–18, 96–7, 103
        and religion 15–16, 27–9,
                67–8
        worship 73
New Atheists 108, 111–13
Newman, Francis: *Phases of
        Faith* 95, 108
New System of Chemical Philosophy, A
        (Dalton) 54
New Theories and the Old Faith
        (Picton) 81
New Zealand and New
        Zealanders 8, 11, 21–2,
                24–5
Noah's flood 42–3
Norton, Andrews: *The Evidence of
        the Genuineness of the
        Gospels* 95
notebooks of Darwin
        (1837–1840) 45–8

original sin 58
*Origin of Civilization and the
        Primitive Condition of Man,
        The* (Lubbock) 71–5

Origin of Species (Darwin)
and human origins 63–4
Mivart on 84–5
modern controversy over 107
theism in 92, 98–9
Outcast, The (Reade) 100
Owen, Fanny 34

Pale Blue Dot (Sagan) 112
Paley, William (Rev) 2, 95–7
pantheism 69, 103–4
Paradise Lost (Milton) 28
Patagonian Missionary Society 26
see also South American
Missionary Society
Pearson, John: An *Exposition of the
Creed* 1
Personal Narrative
(Humboldt) 117–18n. 29
Peruvian religion 10–11
Phases of Faith (Newman) 95
Phipps, William E.: *Darwin's Religious
Odyssey* 4
phrenology 56
Picton, James A. (Rev): *New Theories
and the Old Faith* 81
Pike, Luke Owen: "On the
Psychical Elements of
Religion" 70–1
pleasure 56–7, 96
Polkinghorne, John 108
polytheism 50–1, 70
Pope, Alexander 45, 47
Primeval Man (Campbell) 75–6
Private Conference on science and
religion 102
Progress of Ethical Philosophy, On the
(Mackintosh) 60
psychology of religion 50–3, 68,
70–1, 112

Reade, Winwood: *The Outcast* 100
"Recollections of the Development
of my mind and character"
(Darwin) 20, 94–101, 109

Reign of Law (Campbell) 75
Religio Medici (Browne) 45
religion
and altruism 110–12
in American education 112–13
attacks on 92–3
benefits of 110–12
circumspection about 92–3
dark side of 18–22
and evolutionists 88–9
and fear 52–3, 66, 68
historical framework 48–51
hostility toward 102–4
instinct to 46–8, 51–4
and morality 78–9, 106
non-universality of 68–9, 72
primitive 5–12, 29, 68–9
psychology of 50–3, 68,
70–1, 112
of savages 67–9, 74–5
and science 49, 74, 90–2, 94,
103–4, 109–10
strata of 27
*Researches into the Early
History of Mankind*
(Tyler) 69–70
Rich, Anthony 101
Richards, Robert J.: *Darwin and the
Emergence of Evolutionary
Theories of Mind and
Behavior* 129–30n. 9
Rio de Janeiro field notebook 27
Rituals of the Diviner, The
(Starr) 147–8n. 25
Roman Catholic Relief Act
(1829) 13
Romanes, George John
*Candid Examination of
Theism* 99
*Charles Darwin: A Memorial
Poem* 105–6
Rosas, Juan Manuel de 18–20
Royer, Clémence 63
Rudwick, Martin J. S. 129–30n. 9
Ruse, Michael 108

Sagan, Carl: *Pale Blue Dot* 112
savages
  belief in spirits of 69–70, 97–8
  and Christians 18–27
  Darwin's encounters with 5–12
  in evolution 47, 118n. 32
  Lubbock on 72–4
  moral awareness of 80–1
  observations of 117n. 29
  and religion instinct 48–9
  religions of 67–9, 74–5
Scenes of Clerical Life (Eliot) 34
Schmitt, Cannon: "Darwin's Savage
    Mnemonics" 118n. 32
scholarship on religious
    evolution 4–5
science
  and belief 41, 106
  and marriage 37–8
  and morality 78–9
  and religion 49, 74, 90–2, 94,
    103–4, 109–10
  and superstition 16, 40
  and theology 88–90, 103–4
  in Victorian culture 32–3
secular atrocities 146–7n. 24
secularists on Darwin 92
Sedgwick, Adam 1, 17
selfishness and morality 78
Seward, Anna 101
Shamanism 73
Shaw, James 107
Shongi (New Zealand chief) 21–2
Sierra de las Animas 9–10
skepticism *see* doubts, religious
Smith, Adam: *Theory of Moral
    Sentiments* 77
sociability 77–8, 85
social ills 111–12
South America *see also* Tierra del
    Fuego
  conversion of natives of 22
  Darwin in 2–4, 12–14
  just war in 18–21

South American Missionary
    Society 26–7, 111
Spencer, Herbert: "The Origin of
    Animal Worship" 70
Spencer, Nick: *God and Darwin* 3
spirits 67–70, 72, 97–8
Starr, Ivan: *The Rituals of the
    Diviner* 147–8n. 25
Staunton, George 50
Suarez, Francisco (Friar) 85–6
sublime, the
  and belief 97–8
  and emotion 70–1
  in Nature 27–9
  in religious development 52–3
suffering 17, 96–7
Sulivan, B. J. 26
Sumner, John B.: *The Evidence of
    Christianity* 1
superstition
  Christianity as 74
  and morality 80
  in primitive cultures 10–12,
    49, 52
  and science 16, 40
sympathy 59–61, 77, 80–1

Tahitians 7, 11, 23–4
Tajo, King 122–3n. 214
tattooing 25
theists/theism
  Darwin and 90–1, 98–9
  and evolution 84–90
  limitations of 109–10
  Romanes on 99
  studying science 108–9
theology
  age of 48–9
  and biology 108–10
  and Darwin 1–2, 99
  and ethics 103
  and evolution 81
  and just wars 21
  and science 88–90, 103–4

Theory of Moral Sentiments (Smith) 77
Tierra del Fuego 5–7, 10, 26–7
  see also Fuegians
totemism 69, 73–4
transcendence and belief 97–8
transmutation 46–7, 129n. 9
Tyler, E. B.: *Researches into the Early History of Mankind* 69–70
Tyndall, John 93–4

Valdivia, Peru 19
Variation of Plants and Animals under Domestication (Darwin) 84
Voyage of the Beagle (Darwin) see *Journal of Researches*
Voyaging (Browne) 4, 23, 38

Wallace, Alfred Russel 68–9, 84–5
Walleechu 9–10

Water Babies (Kingsley) 89
Wedgwood, Caroline (née Darwin) 42
Wedgwood, Catherine (aunt of CD) 32–3
Wedgwood, Charlotte (cousin of CD) 33–4
Wedgwood, Emma *see* Darwin, Emma
Wedgwood, Fanny 33
Wedgwood, Julia (niece of CD) 45, 102
Westminster Abbey burial of Darwin 104–5
Whately, William (Rev): *A View of Scripture* 32
Whewell, William 17
White, Paul: *Thomas Huxley* 32–3
Why Would Anyone Believe in God (Barrett) 112

X-Club 93–4